An Evolutionary Psychology
of Sleep and Dreams

An Evolutionary Psychology of Sleep and Dreams

Patrick McNamara

PRAEGER

Westport, Connecticut
London

Library of Congress Cataloging-in-Publication Data

McNamara, Patrick, 1956–
    Evolutionary psychology of sleep and dreams / Patrick McNamara.
      p. cm.
    Includes bibliographical references and index.
    ISBN 0–275–97875–3 (alk. paper)
     1.   Rapid eye movement sleep. 2.   Dreams. I. Title.

QP425.M396   2004
154.6—dc22   2004017658

British Library Cataloguing in Publication Data is available.

Library of Congress Catalog Card Number: 2004017658
ISBN: 0–275–97875–3

First published in 2004

Praeger Publishers, 88 Post Road West, Westport, CT 06881
An imprint of Greenwood Publishing Group, Inc.
www.praeger.com

Printed in the United States of America

The paper used in the book complies with the
Permanent Paper Standard issued by the
National Information Standards Organization
(Z39.48–1984).

10 9 8 7 6 5 4 3 2

Copyright Acknowledgments

The author and publisher gratefully acknowledge permission for use of the
following material:

Excerpts from "REM Sleep, Early Experience, and the Development of
Reproductive Strategies" by McNamara, Dowdall and Auerbach. *Human Nature*,
13, 4 (2002): 405–435. Reprinted with permission.

Excerpts from "Counterfactual Cognitive Operations in Dreams" by
P. McNamara et al. *Dreaming*, *12*, 3 (2002): 121–133. Reprinted with permission.

For Jessica and Jena, Robbie, Rachel, and Jake, Heather, Stephanie, and Nick, Josh and Amanda.

Contents

Figures and Tables

Figures

Tables

Preface and Acknowledgments

The year 1953 was fateful and portentous in the history of the biological sciences as it was the year in which the molecular structure of the DNA molecule and the genetic code was worked out by Crick and Watson. It was also the year in which Aserinsky and Kleitman discovered REM sleep. While subsequent investigations of the DNA molecule and the genetic code have led to tremendous scientific, medical, technical, and industrial advances, subsequent investigations of REM have sometimes seemed only to deepen the mystery of REM's biology and functions. If REM's functions, including the potential functions of dreams, can be identified, I believe investigations of REM will lead to medical, technical, and industrial advances similar to those which followed the investigations of DNA structure and function.

The biology of REM sleep is a fascinating conglomeration of characteristics that have puzzled scientists ever since its initial description and discovery in 1953. The purpose of this book is to consider the psychobiology of rapid eye movement (REM) sleep in the light of evolutionary theory. I hope thereby to explore new approaches to potential functions of REM and REM-related dreaming. The functional biology of the other major mammalian sleep state, non-REM (NREM), will be explored only insofar as it sheds some light on REM.

I owe a special debt of gratitude to student interns in my laboratory for help in reviewing selected topics relevant to REM expression and issues discussed in this book. These students and I went over dozens of articles on multiple topics and in painstaking detail. It was fun and I think we all learned a lot! Among these students, Mary Klecan worked on pregnancy and sleep, as well as menstruation and sleep. Karima Hassan worked on mentation associated with stage NREM and slow wave sleep (SWS); Justin Gan worked on sleep and suicide and developed a fine master's thesis on the topic. Gillian Chapman worked on pregnancy and dreaming as well as the separate issue of perseveration and the frontal lobes. That work was later presented at the International Neuropsychologic Society meetings in 2004. Andrea Sparko worked on the psychology of deception as well as summarized data from experiments we ran on deception detection and production. Dana Smith and Deirdre McLaren worked on issues of REM versus NREM dream content and became very proficient in use of the Hall/Van de Castle dream scoring system. Deirdre McLaren also helped on tracking down references, collating data into tables and teaching me the basics of what the Hall/Van de Castle scoring categories mean.

Ariel Brown, my head research assistant, was involved in multiple aspects of research for this book. She directly supervised the work of the student interns and conducted meta-analytic studies on depression and dreams/ REM as well as dream recall among prosopagnosics (those data, however, are not reported in this book). The book would not have been possible without Ariel's expert help on all the things necessary in creating a monograph on a complex topic, from the mechanics of running experiments to discussions of relevant ideas.

I thank Bill Domhoff and Adam Schneider for answering our questions about the Hall/Van de Castle scoring categories; David Haig for answering questions on genomic imprinting; Charlie Nunn for detailed comments on my ideas concerning genetic conflict and sleep and discussions on phylogeny of sleep; Robert Barton for ongoing discussions on the phylogeny of sleep; Jay Belsky for incisive and constructive criticisms of my ideas on attachment and infant sleep; Thomas Anders and Melissa Burnham for helping me to correct mistaken notions about infant sleep, though they cannot be blamed for my own interpretations of the data on infant sleep; Sanford Auerback for discussions on all aspects of sleep; Raymon Durso for detailed and constructive feedback on my ideas concerning catecholaminergic contributions to cognition and affect and sleep; Robert Stickgold for discussions on REM versus NREM dreaming; Ernest Hartmann and Mike Zborowski for discussions on Freud and on theoretical approaches to dreams; Martin Albert, Loraine Obler, and Marlene Oscar-Berman for inspiration; and Betina Freidin, Al Gillis, Reema Khan, and Cynthia Merillat for listening patiently to (and providing incisive and constructive feedback on) some of the early versions of the ideas in this book.

An Evolutionary Psychology
of Sleep and Dreams

CHAPTER 1

REM Biology and Evolutionary Theory

REM Properties

Rapid eye movement (REM) sleep accounts for about 22% of total sleep time in humans. Although the cortex is activated in REM, arousal thresholds are higher in REM than in the waking state (or in slow-wave sleep [SWS] for that matter). The phasic aspects of REM, such as intermittent muscle twitching, autonomic nervous system (ANS) discharges, and rapid eye movements, occur in some mammals in association with bursts of pontine-geniculo-occipital (PGO) waves. Mammals (with the possible exception of humans) also exhibit a theta rhythm in the hippocampal formation during REM. REM is also associated with autonomic nervous system instabilities that become more extreme as duration of REM episodes increases across the night. Like non-REM (NREM) sleep deprivation, REM deprivation results in a rebound phenomenon indicating that a certain amount of REM is required and must be made up if lost. Interestingly, after total sleep deprivation, NREM sleep is made up before REM.

Thus, REM's tonic characteristics are a desynchronized electroencephalogram (EEG), penile erections, and atonia of the antigravity muscles. Its phasic characteristics include bursts of rapid eye movements under the closed eyelids, myoclonic twitches of the facial and limb muscle groups, increased variability in heart rate, respiration, and blood pressure, and autonomic nervous system discharges. Other correlates of REM include effects on release of selected hormones—especially growth factors. Virtually all mammals (with some crucial exceptions described later) exhibit both SWS and REM sleep.

The REM-NREM Cycle

In humans, sleep is composed of four "descending" stages with stages III and IV exhibiting SWS. The initiation of NREM sleep is gradual and is characterized by slowing of EEG frequency. This initial phase is termed stage 1. In stage 2, we see a further decrease in EEG frequency and the appearance of intermittent high-frequency spikes called sleep spindles. Sleep spindles decrease in stage 3 as the amplitude of slow waves increases. This mixed pattern gives way to very high-amplitude delta waves in the deepest sleep, stage 4 or SWS. Postural shifts precede and follow REM, with fewer shifts in NREM than REM. The REM/NREM phases alternate throughout the night at intervals of 90 minutes in adult humans. NREM stages dominate the first third of the night, while REM dominates the last third.

REM-On and REM-Off Cellular Networks

REM sleep onset is triggered by cholinergic neurons originating within the peribrachial regions of the brain, known as the laterodorsal tegmental (LDT) and pedunculopontine tegmental (PPT) nuclei (LDT/PPT). REM sleep may be inhibited by noradrenergic and serotonergic neurons in the locus coeruleus and dorsal raphe nucleus (LC/DRN), respectively. Activation of cholinergic REM (including phasic REM) is related to removal of inhibition exerted by these aminergic efferents on cholinergic cells in the LDT/PPT. When the aminergic neurons decrease their firing, cells of the LDT/PPT are released from inhibition and increase their firing. The release of acetylcholine from terminals of LDT/PPT cells triggers the onset of REM by activating brain regions that control various components of REM, including brain stem sites, hypothalamus, limbic, amygdala, and the basal forebrain. Cholinergic collaterals to the LC/DRN exert an indirect excitatory effect on aminergic cell groups in these nuclei. As REM proceeds, this excitatory effect on these aminergic cell groups eventually reaches a threshold at which point their activation results in a feedback inhibition on REM-on cells of the LDT/PPT, thus ending the REM period. The initiation of NREM sleep may be a GABA-ergic–mediated process characterized by loss of wake-related alpha waves and slowing of EEG frequency.

Selective Cerebral Activation in REM

Recently a number of positron emission tomography (PET) and functional magnetic resonance imaging (fMRI) studies of the sleeping brain have revealed that REM demonstrates high activation levels in pontine, midbrain tegmentum, anterior cingulate, limbic, and amygdaloid sites, and deactivation of prefrontal areas, parietal cortex, and posterior cingulate (Braun et al., 1997; Hobson, Stickgold, & Pace-Schott, 1998; Maquet & Franck, 1997; Maquet et al., 1996; Nofzinger et al., 1997). Crucially, these imaging studies have consistently revealed exceptionally high activation levels in the amygdala during REM.

Brain activation patterns are significantly different and even opposing for REM and NREM, demonstrating high activation levels in limbic/amygdaloid sites and deactivation of dorsolateral prefrontal cortex sites (Braun et al., 1997; Hobson et al., 1998; Maquet & Franck, 1997; Maquet et al., 1996; Nofzinger et al., 1997), while regional cerebral blood flow studies for NREM/SWS indicate deactivation of thalamic functions and activation in secondary association areas in the temporal and parietal lobes, including the language-related planum temporale and the inferior parietal lobule areas (Hofle et al., 1997).

REM Dream Content

When subjects are awakened from REM, they generally report a narrative involving the dreamer, with vivid visual detail, unpleasant emotions, and occasional bizarre and improbable events (Domhoff, 2003; Hobson & Pace-Schott, 2002; Nielsen, Kuiken, Hoffman, & Moffitt, 2001; Strauch & Meier, 1996). A more complete discussion of REM dream content is presented in chapter 8.

PGO Waves

PGO waves are associated with several of the phasic (or variable) events of REM, including rapid eye movements and ANS instabilities. PGO waves are generated in the pons and are propagated up through the lateral geniculate body (LGB) of the thalamus and then up to occipital and other cortical sites. Because the LGB and the occipital cortex are visual centers, it was originally thought that PGO waves could account for visual phenomena of dreams. It now appears that PGO waves are not confined to visual centers but may instead be quite prominent in the amygdala and in limbic and disparate cortical sites. PGO waves occur in bursts or spikes and thus are correlated with many phasic phenomena of REM. At the level of the pons, Datta (1999) has shown that PGO state-on cells in the caudolateral peri-brachial (C-PBL) region of the cat and the subcoeruleus region of the rat contain the triggering elements of PGO wave generation. During waking and NREM sleep, all of these cells are silent due to presynaptic inhibitory inputs from aminergic (5HT and noradrenergic) cells in the DRN, LC, and local C-PBL state-off cells. The local inhibitory cells may be GABA-ergic. When aminergic and local inhibitory inputs are removed from the state-on neurons of the C-PBL, they start discharging. PGO state-on cells activate LDT/PPT cells rostral to the peribrachial region and these, in turn, interact with triggering elements to generate PGO waves.

Morrison and colleagues (Morrison, 1979; Morrison, Sanford, & Ross, 1999) have suggested that PGO waves are comparable to the well-known orienting reflex (OR) that occurs after startle, interest, or fear during waking. If PGO waves are associated with orienting, startle, and fear reactions, then organisms experiencing PGO waves during REM are likely undergoing regular and repeated startle reactions, orienting reflexes, and stress-inducing mobilizations to defend against hallucinatory threats each time they go into REM.

Activation of the Amygdala in REM

As mentioned above, a number of PET and MRI studies of the sleeping brain have revealed that REM demonstrates high activation levels in pontine, midbrain tegmentum, anterior cingulate, limbic, and amygdaloid sites, as well as deactivation of prefrontal areas, parietal cortex, and posterior cingulate (Braun et al., 1997; Hobson et al., 1998; Maquet & Franck, 1997; Maquet et al., 1996; Nofzinger et al., 1997). These imaging studies have consistently revealed exceptionally high activation levels in the amygdala during REM, suggesting that the amygdala is key to REM physiology.

Maquet and Phillips (1999) point out that REM-related amygdaloid activation may contribute to the profile of forebrain sites that are activated and deactivated during REM. Specifically, activated cortical areas receive amygdaloid projections, while deactivated sites do not. Maquet and Philips also report significant positive interactions between amygdaloid blood flow and occurrence of REM in the temporal cortex.

The high activation levels of amygdaloid circuits during REM may carry negative health consequences for the organism because the central nucleus of the amygdala appears to be a regulatory center for neural circuits involved in fear, aggression, defense, the fight-or-flight response, and autonomic reactivity (Ledoux, 2000; Sah, Faber, Lopez de Armentia, & Power, 2003). The central nucleus is particularly important for mediation of fear responses. Fear-related responses are characterized by freezing, startle, release of stress hormones, rises in blood pressure and heart rate, respiratory distress, piloerection, and stereotypical threat displays. In humans, these autonomic responses are accompanied by a sense of dread, despair, anguish, anxiety, and intense distress. Activation of the central nucleus induces autonomic instabilities associated with these negative emotions. The medial portion of the central nucleus has substantial projections to the hypothalamus, bed nucleus of the stria terminalis, and several nuclei in the midbrain, pons, and medulla, associated with regulation of the ANS. Projections to the brain stem are to three main areas: (1) the periaqueductal gray matter, which mediates startle, analgesia, vocalizations in response to threat, and cardiovascular changes; (2) the parabrachial nucleus, which is involved in pain transmission; and (3) the nucleus of the solitary tract, which contributes to regulation of the vagal system. Thus, the neuroanatomy of the amygdala allows it to regulate fight-or-flight responses, cardiac and respiratory functions, and other fundamental ANS responses. REM-induced phasic discharges occurring in the central nucleus may help to explain REM-related cardiac, respiratory, and autonomic instabilities.

Animal studies have, in fact, linked amygdaloid activation to phasic signs of REM. Electrical stimulation of the central nucleus of the amygdala increases PGO wave frequency (Calvo, Badillo, Morales-Ramirez, & Palacios-Salas, 1987) and other signs of phasic REM. Carbachol injection within the same nucleus increases REM sleep duration and other REM indices (Calvo, Simon-Arceo, & Fernandez-Mas, 1996). Thus, activation of the amygdala during REM may be considered a phasic process of REM that is super-imposed on a more tonic activation of the limbic forebrain in general during REM. Interestingly, measures of both REM and amygdaloid activation are enhanced in depression (Whalen, Shin, Somerville, McLean, & Kim, 2002).

REM Sleep and Autonomic Nervous System Storms

Relative to the waking state, sympathetic activity rises during phasic portions of REM. As the duration of phasic REMs increases over the course of the night, so do the durations of sympathetic discharges giving rise to periodic REM-related sympathetic discharges or "storms." These sympathetic discharges, in turn, may be linked to a host of negative cardiopulmonary changes that occur during phasic REM.

REM Sleep and the Cardiovascular System

Cardiac output declines over the course of the night, reaching its lowest levels during the last REM period. During all REM periods, an acceleration of heart rate occurs at least 10 beats before EEG signs of phasic arousal, and then fluctuates dramatically during phasic REM. Systemic arterial blood pressure (BP), pulmonary BP, and intracranial arterial BP all exhibit increased variability relative to NREM and waking levels. There is marked vasodilation in all of the major vascular beds, including selected cerebral vascular systems. Because of the hemodynamic, ANS, and sympathetic alterations of REM, plaque rupture and coronary arterial spasm become more likely.

There is a well-documented increased risk for cardiac arrest during the late morning hours coincident with the final REM period (Asplund & Aberg, 1998; Peters, Zoble, & Brooks, 2002). As mentioned, cardiac output is lowest during this REM period. Persons with cardiopulmonary disease are more likely to die during this REM period than at any other time of the 24-hour day. Sei and Morita (1999) report that REM-related phasic increases in arterial BP are associated with hippocampal theta activity in rats. Similarly, Rowe et al. (1999) report that REM-related heart rate surges were associated with increased frequency of hippocampal theta and increased PGO waves in cats. Heart rate surges were dramatically reduced by administration of atenolol, indicating that the phenomenon is sympathetically mediated by beta-adrenergic synapses. Interestingly, Rodriguez et al. (2004) documented an association between mutations in the insulin-like growth factor 2-insulin-tyrosine hydroxylase gene cluster and risk for traits related to cardiovascular disease. Two of the genes in this cluster are known to be genomically imprinted (at least in developmental tissue; see chapter 5), and all three code for products that influence sleep. Similarly, Schins, Honig, Crijns, Baur, and Hamulyak (2003) discussed a range of data demonstrating a link between the 5HT2A receptor and the ability of platelets to aggregate and cardiovascular disease. 5HT2A is imprinted as well. I return to the issue of the role of imprinted genes in expression of sleep states in chapter 5.

REM-Related Respiratory Changes

Both REM and NREM show reductions in ventilation (alveolar hypoventilation), but the REM-related reduction is severe (see review in Douglas, 2000). During this REM period, oxygen desaturation levels are maximal and Cheyne-Stokes-like breathing patterns predominate. As a result of the fall in alveolar ventilation, there are changes in blood gas levels, with rises in CO_2 and decreases in oxygen saturation. During phasic REM, respiration becomes irregular, with a waxing and waning of tidal volume that resembles Cheyne-Stokes breathing. The natural response to lowered O_2 levels is to increase inspiratory breathing, but this response (the hypoxic ventilatory response) is decreased by over 50% of normal capacity during REM. The REM-related hypoxemia and abnormal breathing patterns may cause life-threatening complications in vulnerable persons, including infants with immature lung capacity and in adults with various respiratory ailments and disorders.

REM-Related Lapse in Thermoregulation

REM appears to involve a reversion to a poikilothermic state (Bach, Telliez, & Libert, 2002; Parmeggiani, 2000; Szymusiak, Alam, Steininger, & McGinty, 1998). Although brain temperature rises during REM, thermoregulatory responses such as sweating and panting do not occur in REM. However, they are not absent in NREM. Sleep onset in humans is associated with a reduction in body temperature of about 1 to 2 degrees centigrade. The reduction appears to depend on NREM SWS, as it does not occur if the organism is selectively deprived of SWS. If body temperature increases during waking hours, SWS increases during sleep. Thus, NREM SWS appears to serve a thermoregulatory function. Given that body temperature influences metabolic rates, NREM SWS may also be implicated in energy conservation functions. REM sleep, however, does not appear to serve clear thermoregulatory or energy conservation functions because it cannot mount an effective defense against thermal loads.

REM-Related Motor Paralysis

One of the most paradoxical features of REM is that phasic eye movements and muscle twitches occur upon a background of paralysis in the antigravity musculature, including the jaw, neck, and limbs. Two major pathways seem to be involved in REM-associated muscle atonia. The first includes the pontine cholinergic neurons that activate glutaminergic neurons in the medullary reticular formation. These in turn activate glycinergic neurons that inhibit motor neurons. In the second pathway, GABA-ergic neurons inhibit serotonin and noradrenergic neurons that "normally" maintain excitatory drive on motor neurons.

Penile Erections

Every REM period is associated with penile tumesecence. These REM-related erections apparently even occur in infants. They persist throughout the lifespan but are not reliably associated with erotic desire. There is some evidence that REM-related sexual activation may also occur in women as uterine contractions and pelvic thrusting, appearing with REM onset, but too few studies have been done on this topic to draw any firm conclusions. I review the literature on sexual activation in REM in chapter 2.

Muscle Twitching

During phasic REM, a number of muscle groups begin to twitch, including the middle ear muscles, legs, arms, and selected facial muscles. Occasionally the twitching in the legs becomes so prominent as to cause restless legs syndrome, whereby the patient experiences an uncontrollable urge to move the legs, and this keeps the patient awake all night.

REM Interactions with NREM in Control of Growth Hormone Release

Circulating levels of a number of growth-related factors appear to be influenced by REM-NREM interactions. Nighttime levels of these hormones typically exceed their daytime levels. Nocturnal growth hormone (GH) levels, for example, are at least four times the daytime level of GH in young men (Mueller, Locatelli, & Cocchi, 1999). SWS of NREM is associated with a major surge in GH release (Mueller et al., 1999; Van Cauter, Plat, & Copinschi, 1998). The surge in GH release in humans is particularly marked in males. GH-release hormone (GHRH) promotes NREM sleep, while somatostatin (SS) inhibits both GH and GHRH release. SS release appears to be partially dependent on REM activation, as SS levels rise with onset of REM. Stimulation of GH secretion and promotion of NREM sleep are dependent on activity of GHRH-ergic neurons of the anterior pituitary and the medial preoptic region. In addition to the regulatory control of SS, GH and insulin-like growth factor I feedback on GHRH to inhibit GH release and regulate GH levels.

Significant reductions in NREM sleep amounts are found in transgenic mice with GHRH deficiency and in mutant rats with a defect in the GHRH receptor signaling system (Hajdu, Obal, Fang, Krueger, & Rollo, 2002). In giant transgenic mice with excess GH (100-200 times the normal levels of GH), NREM sleep times were increased moderately, but REM sleep times were increased substantially during the light period (when rats typically sleep), suggesting a response by REM to increase SS levels in response to, and to take advantage of, rising GH levels. Consistent with a role for REM vis-à-vis GH levels, systemic injection of the powerful SS analog octreotide suppresses sleep in normal rats but not in transgenic mice with excess GH levels (Hajdu et al., 2002). Systemic administration of GH enhances REM, and phasic REM activation can modulate NREM and GH release. In sum, REM and NREM appear to interact with respect to one another's growth hormonal effects, with NREM enhancing levels of GH and REM-related SS release increasing or decreasing its activity in response to fluctuating GH levels. These levels in turn depend to some extent on the depth of NREM sleep and delta power. The situation, however, is complex, with multiple metabolic inputs and hormonal and neurotransmitter signaling systems contributing to GH release during sleep.

Rates and amounts of GH release influence sleep amounts, as evidenced by sleep rebound effects after sleep deprivation. SS release, for example, in the rat causes an accumulation of GHRH in the rat hypothalamus (Gardi, Szentirmai, Hajdu, Obal, & Krueger, 2001), suggesting perhaps that NREM rebound amounts after sleep deprivation involve the discharge of stores of GHRH/GH. Toppila et al. (1996; 1997) have reported that sleep deprivation in the rat increases both SS and GHRH mRNA (messenger RNA) levels in the hippocampus. Antisera to SS or to GHRH can block sleep rebound effects after sleep deprivation (Obal & Krueger, 2003). GHRH and GH are also known to indirectly stimulate action of gonadotropins and sex steroids.

Interim Summary: REM Properties as Injurious to Health

This brief review of major physiologic properties of REM, including REM-related PGO waves, activations of the amygdala, ANS storms, cardiovascular instabilities, respiratory impairment, thermoregulatory lapses, dynamic changes in GH release, and so on, suggests that REM is risky for one's health. These risky properties of REM appear to be primarily phasic processes, occurring in tandem with PGO waves and amygdaloid activation.

Even the tonic properties of REM (limbic forebrain activation with prefrontal deactivation, muscle twitching and muscle atonia, penile erections, etc.), however, may increase vulnerability to predators while not providing any apparent benefit. There can be little doubt, then, that REM or at least phasic processes of REM are energetically costly and can be injurious to health. As if to confirm this assessment of REM physiology, a number of reports have linked enhanced measures of REM to increased mortality rates. If standard features of REM are injurious to the health of the organism, then "too much" REM should be associated with increased mortality rates.

REM Sleep and Mortality

Increased REM sleep durations (relative to the population norm) and sleep complaints are significantly associated with increased risk for mortality, even after adjusting for age, gender, mental illness, and medical burden or physical health status (Brabbins et al., 1993; Dew et al., 2003; Kripke, 2003). Dew et al. (2003) were able to analyze measures of sleep architecture in relation to risk for mortality. They reported that three measures of sleep architecture best predicted mortality: (1) sleep latencies of greater than 30 minutes, (2) poor sleep efficiency, and (3) an unusually high or low percentage of REM sleep. Sleep latencies greater than 30 minutes, for example, more than doubled the risk of mortality in their cohort of initially healthy elders across an average of 13 years of follow-up. The authors noted that too much REM is often associated with disorders of mood such as depression that are independently associated with increased health and mortality risks. But it may be that REM itself or at least excessive amounts of REM directly contribute to ill health. After all, Dew et al.'s data show that the effect of REM on mortality rates was independent of symptoms of mental illness.

REM Properties and REM Functions

The above inventory of REM sleep properties and correlates demonstrates that REM is risky for the health of an organism. If a physiologic system demonstrates properties that are risky to the health of the organism, identifying potential adaptive functions of that system may seem misguided at best. Yet the preservation of REM in all terrestrial mammals studied to date suggests that its benefits outweigh its costs, although the benefits have not, as yet, been identified. In this book, I argue that serious consideration of the costs associated with REM might help us identify its benefits and therefore its adaptive functions.

Although many functions of REM have been proposed, harmful properties of REM have received very little theoretical attention. Parmeggiani's work is an exception, and in a review of sleep state biology he noted that in stark contrast to the stable homeostatic regulatory capacities of NREM, "REM sleep is characterized by the disintegration of a homeostatic physiological equilibrium" that brings about "effector responses of great instability that are primarily of central origin but secondarily complicated by local autoregulation" (Parmeggiani, 2000, p. 172). Importantly, these REM-induced physiologic instabilities affect every major physiologic system in mostly adverse ways and thus are theoretically puzzling and of potentially great clinical importance. After reviewing a large amount of evidence, which suggests that "functional changes in REM sleep depend essentially on the suppression of a highly integrated homeostatic regulation that is operative in NREM" (p. 173), Parmeggiani concluded that "sleep entails a physiological risk" (p. 175) independent of the risks normally associated with loss of sensory input and increased arousal thresholds.

The above inventory of the basic properties of REM tells us what needs to be explained in any theory of REM function. Approximately every 90 minutes while we sleep, access to external sensory information is blocked, the brain becomes highly activated, particularly networks supporting emotional functions, and the body is essentially paralyzed. As the night progresses, these REM periods become more and more violent, eliciting ANS storms and serious fluctuations in heart rate and respiratory functions. In addition, the dreamer finds himself a central participant in a series of hallucinatory dream-dramas that vary from the prosaic to the epic and bizarre. Sometimes banal and sometimes frightening, experience of these dreams is involuntary—we are compelled to participate whether we like it or not. Finally, to add a note of the absurd to the whole affair, the male experiences an erection, regardless of dream content, and the female may experience uterine contractions and even pelvic thrusting—again regardless of dream content.

If these nightly events had some clear functional logic, then they could perhaps be dismissed as an odd collection of absurd but necessary traits. Instead, these traits are manifestly injurious to the health of the organism. They are not mere curiosities. REM traits are at the very least "nonoptimal" or "risky" as Parmegianni (2000) put it. Add to the picture that an animal is vulnerable to predation while asleep, and the case for an adaptive function of REM seems lost. Indeed, some authorities have dubbed REM "superfluous" (Horne, 2000).

Given the apparently risky, injurious, costly, and paradoxical properties of REM, why would Nature produce such a system? There are several major possibilities. First, REM has a primary biologic function, not yet identified, that is so important for the mammalian organism that it overrides the negative consequences of REM's other risky traits. REM's risky traits, in themselves, have no function and instead are considered unfortunate side effects of REM's primary function. Alternatively, SWS of NREM has a primary biologic function, and REM evolved to facilitate NREM's actions. REM's role in facilitation of NREM's actions is so important as to outweigh the negative effects of REM's risky traits, which, once again, are considered to have no function themselves. A third option, not usually considered by most authorities on REM, stipulates that REM's risky traits are not mere side effects of some other process, but are part and parcel of REM's primary biologic function. REM exists to produce those risky traits that, in turn, perform some service for the organism.

While there is considerable empirical evidence for the first and second options (particularly the second), option three has not been adequately investigated up to now, and thus I present evidence in this book that might help to evaluate option #3. Theories and evidence relevant to the first two options are also summarized.

In order to assess arguments and evidence for the functionality of REM, whenever possible I evaluate the data in light of evolutionary theory. In order to keep the text to manageable size, I focus on effects of evolutionary and genetic conflict, as systems of genetic conflict are known to be associated with production of traits that can impair the health of the organism while simultaneously increasing its chances of getting its genes into the next generation (i.e., its reproductive fitness). The production of costly traits and signals, for example, may serve as indicators of individuals' ability to sustain severe costs and still "carry on." The classic example is the peacock's tail. The peahen often chooses to mate with the peacock who has the most extravagant tail—despite the fact that the tail impairs ability to evade predators and so forth. Apparent handicaps can signal that the bearer of the handicap nevertheless has "good genes" if the bearer still functions in a relatively normal fashion.

Evolutionary conflict theory informs virtually all levels of evolutionary theory. What makes it especially appropriate for the study of REM is that the discipline has generated explicit models, many of them based in evolutionary game theory, of key aspects of animal behavior. Among these behaviors are communication systems, parent-offspring relations, infant attachment strategies, social aggression, and cooperation and mating strategies, to name a few. Conflict theory is therefore more likely to lead to testable predictions regarding REM sleep functions than are other branches of evolutionary theory. I do not claim that this strategy will provide a definitive solution to the problem of the function of REM, but I do believe the approach can provide fresh perspectives and new insights into REM properties and potential functions. I focus on two aspects of conflict theory that appear to be most relevant to sleep and dreams: intragenomic conflict and costly signaling theory.

Intragenomic Conflict

Organisms are composed of multiple genetic entities that do not always share the same interests because they have different modes of inheritance. Different transmission patterns of genes to offspring create the context for conflict or negative fitness covariance between two associated or antagonistic genes. For example, genes that are normally passed on by only one sex, such as mitochondrial genes inherited through the female line, differ in their transmission patterns from Y chromosome genes inherited through the male line, and can therefore enter into conflict with them. If maternal line genes, for example, can increase their likelihood of transmission by decreasing transmission probabilities of paternal line genes, then they will do so.

Genetic conflict can often result in the spread of apparently maladaptive physiologic phenotypes. An allele harmful to male fitness, for example, could spread if it was beneficial to female-line mitochondrial genes. The resultant male phenotypes would be vulnerable physiologically, and thus natural selection would act to create suppressors of the harmful allele in males. Suppression, however, may be only partial ("dose sensitive"), and thus increased expression of the harmful allele may reoccur, creating an evolving cycle of measures and reactive countermeasures by the harmful allele and its suppressors. Effects of the harmful allele on male phenotypes reduces the numbers of males in the population who compete for resources with carrier females, thus increasing the fitness of carriers of the allele (females).

Similarly, conflict can often occur between the genes of parasites and their hosts. The host evolves mechanisms to reduce the damage inflicted by the parasite, and the parasite evolves adaptations to extract resources from the host, despite the host's countermeasures, to improve the chances that its descendants will be transmitted to infect new hosts. Some parasites, such as certain microsporidians in mosquitoes, are only transmitted through females (in the egg cytoplasm). When these parasites find themselves in males, they kill the host and try to get to an alternative host (typically a copepod). In females (daughters) the parasites are harmless. Similarly, in some crustaceans, cytoplasmic bacteria called Wolbachia turn males into females and exploit the "female" to find new hosts to infect.

Another form of genetic conflict called meiotic drive occurs when a gene obtains, during meiosis, a transmission advantage. Meiotic drive can involve both the sex chromosomes and the autosomes. *Segregation distortion* is a form of autosomal meiotic drive that has been intensively studied in the fruit fly, *Drosophila melanogaster*. A similar driving system characterizes the t locus on chromosome 17 in mice. The products of the genes encoded at the t locus are necessary for normal spermatogenesis, and thus when the males are mature they are sterile.

A form of intragenomic conflict that I believe is particularly relevant for expression of sleep states is called genomic imprinting. Genomic imprinting refers to the silencing of one allele of a gene according to its parental origin. The silencing or tagging of the DNA probably involves methylation of CpG-rich domains. Thus, each cell in the progeny recognizes and expresses only one allele of a gene locus, namely either the paternally derived or the maternally derived allele. The pattern-specific monoallelic expression of imprinted genes results in a bias in the inheritance of traits, with some traits inherited down the matriline and others down the patriline. Most of the genes identified to date as imprinted code for proteins that influence early growth, with paternally imprinted or silenced genes tending to inhibit growth and maternally imprinted genes enhancing growth. In sum, paternally expressed loci increase and maternally expressed loci restrain allocation of resources by the mother to offspring.

Haig and colleagues (Haig, 2000, 2002; Haig & Westoby, 1988) provided formal, game-theoretic models of imprinting effects in terms of the opposing effects of patriline and matriline genomes on growth and development. They conceptualized the evolution of genomic imprinting in terms of a process of genetic conflict between the maternal and paternal genomes that obtains whenever there is uncertainty about paternity of offspring (which is considered to be the case for human biology). Because a paternal gene in one offspring is unlikely to be in its siblings or its mother, the paternal gene can increase its chances of getting into the next generation (i.e., its fitness) if it promotes extraction of resources from the mother regardless of costs to the mother or its siblings who, in the context of paternity uncertainty, may carry genes of another male parent. The maternal gene, by contrast, is in all the siblings and thus its fitness is increased by favoring cooperation and sharing of resources.

Thus, paternal-line genes are more likely to foster aggressive prenatal and postnatal growth schedules, while maternal-line genes are more likely to modulate, restrain, or inhibit aggressive rates of growth and development. Because these maternal and paternal genomes act antagonistically with respect to allocation of maternal resources and control of growth schedules, they also tend to promote internal brain and biobehavioral systems that function antagonistically around growth, reproductive behaviors, and adult behavioral repertoires more generally (Tycko & Morison, 2002). I later present evidence for imprinting effects on sleep processes.

Evolutionary conflict can also occur among the autosomal genes of mother and offspring. While not a form of intragenomic conflict, Trivers (1974) pointed out that parent-offspring conflict likely influences a number of traits in mammalian life histories. Parents and offspring share only 50% of their genes. Thus there is plenty of room for conflict. Parental expenditure of time and resources on one offspring has an opportunity cost that means less time and resources are available for other (perhaps future) offspring. Offspring are predicted to attempt to acquire more parental investment and resources than parents are selected to supply. Parent-offspring conflict arises because genes expressed in offspring will evolve to discount benefits and costs to a parent's residual reproductive value relative to costs and benefits to the offspring's reproductive value.

Evolutionary theory predicts increased parent-offspring conflict and sibling versus sibling conflict whenever mating systems depart from strict lifetime monogamy (i.e., whenever females can have offspring by more than one father). If the mother's offspring are sired by different fathers, then any given child will be less related to its siblings than to its father.

While all of these forms of genetic conflict likely impact sleep processes in one way or another, I believe host-parasite interactions and genomic imprinting offer the most immediate payoffs in terms of insight into sleep state functions.

Another form of behavior that arises from genetic conflict is known as costly signaling. Although it emerges from conflict, it may operate to allow for cooperative alliances and honest communication between individuals who may otherwise have conflicting genetic interests.

Costly Signaling Theory

Costly signaling theory first emerged in the context of sexual selection. Sexual selection theory suggests that some traits may have evolved because they signal fitness of the bearer. If, for example, the trait in question is facial symmetry, a feature apparently correlated with attractiveness ratings in humans, then sexual selection theory would predict that the trait "facial symmetry" would likely be correlated with some fitness-enhancing gene such as a disease-resistant gene. Potential mates will then favor reproductive partners who display facial symmetry, and thus the trait "facial symmetry" will increase in the population. Other traits such as large antlers might indicate the presence of parasite-resistance genes in a reindeer or elk. Large antlers will, in effect, advertise presence of these "good genes." This, in turn, creates selective pressures for displaying and enhancing such advertisements. Males without the parasite-resistant gene will not be able to display large antlers, as they will not be able to metabolically grow and maintain the antlers without paying a metabolic cost that in turn will make them more vulnerable to parasite infestation. Thus large antlers, although costly to produce and thus an expensive handicap, will nevertheless constitute an honest signal of good genes, and thus honest communication between potential mates will be possible. In short, costly signaling makes communication possible under adverse conditions; that is, conditions in which the parties have partially conflicting interests.

Game Theory Modeling of Costly Signaling

According to costly signaling theory, a signal is defined as a behavior, expression, or phenotype produced by one individual (the signaler) that aims to influence the behavior of a second individual (the receiver). Under conditions of genetic conflict, the two parties may be motivated to transmit nonveridical, deceptive information in order to obtain an advantage. If one individual can gain an advantage from another by concealing information or by sending misleading information, he or she will do so. In the short run, at least, using deception would sometimes seem to have advantages.

But fundamentally, communication must require that signals be honest and reliable, at least on average. If they were not reliable, the intended receivers would evolve to ignore them. Costly signals appear to have evolved in order to guarantee the reliability and honesty of a communication system. Communication will be stable when the signaler and receiver pursue strategies that together comprise a signaling equilibrium such that neither party gains from unilateral defection to deception or change in strategy. To keep both signaler and receiver in the game, hard-to-fake signals must be utilized.

Grafen (1990) modeled the evolution of a courtship signaling handicap strategy as a "continuous asymmetric scramble game" wherein females have the upper hand (they are the choosier sex) and are thus in a position to choose male partners based on their apparent quality. In Grafen's formal model, males vary continuously (from low-quality to high-quality males) in the qualities females wish to assess. Both females and high-quality males seek to find a way for males to honestly display their qualities and to prevent low-quality males from mimicking high-quality males. Males also vary continuously in at least one feature of interest to females. It may, for example, be intensity of song or dance. Thus, males choosing not to vary their displays (strategy 1) in terms of intensity relative to their quality (i.e., choosing to adopt an uninformative strategy with respect to female observers) will be matched against males who choose to let display intensity vary with quality (strategy 2).

Females, for their part, also adopt two fundamentally different strategies: Some females may choose a skeptical stance, treating all display intensities as the same. Others will use intensity information to rank the males in terms of quality and to make choices regarding mating partners. Male fitness in the model therefore depends on a male's inherent quality, the costs of putting on the display, and the degree to which females use display intensity to rank and choose male partners. The ranking procedure females use defines this game as a scramble competition, as it forces males to compete against other males. The payoff for any one male depends on how well other males perform. Female fitness in the model is maximal when female rankings of male quality are accurate or close to true male quality. Clearly, female fitness rises in proportion to the quality of her choices.

Grafen (1990) showed that this game has two equilibrium points or evolutionary stable strategies (strategies resistant to invasion by other strategies): (1) Males do not display honestly and females ignore all displays, and (2) all or most males are honest and all or most females choose according to display intensity. The second evolutionary stable strategy occurs only if four conditions are met: (1) The higher the perceived quality of a male, the more likely a female will choose him (quality *is* what the females are using to make their choices); (2) signaling must be costly for males, which obtains because a male's fitness decreases while he is performing the display (because all performances require some effort); (3) effort invested in the display/performance must cost less for a high-quality male (he has resources to spare) than for a low-quality male; and (4) both low- and high-quality males receive the same payoffs if they are (due to error) given the same quality ranking by a female.

The condition ensuring signal honesty is number 3 (lower costs incurred by higher-quality males). The payoff to males depends on display intensity, and thus males have an incentive to increase intensity of their displays. This incentive, however, could lead to an arms race in which each male attempts to increase intensity relative to every other male. Thus, every male would be obliged to pay higher and higher display/performance costs to stay in the race. Eventually, costs would exceed benefits of engaging in the scramble competition and this break-even point would occur at a lower total cost for low-quality males than for high-quality males. In short, Grafen showed that costly signaling can be an evolutionary stable strategy under conditions where a skeptical receiver and a potentially deceptive sender must communicate. Such conditions, of course, are almost universal among animals and humans, and thus the application of the costly-signaling paradigm is expected to be extensive.

Grafen's results do not mean that communication systems must employ costly signals in order to ensure honesty, only that employment of costly signals can work to stabilize a communication system if the parties exchanging signals choose to employ costly signals. That choice is more likely under conditions of escalating conflict where arms races might occur, to the mutual ruin of all parties.

Throughout this text, I draw on principles of costly signaling theory to help explain some of REM's paradoxical traits. On the face of it this is a reasonable strategy, as REM clearly is associated with costly physiologic processes. REM is also involved in intense limbic system activation—which suggests that REM contributes to development of emotional expressions. If REM functions to help produce costly signals (e.g., hard-to-fake emotional displays), then some of its paradoxical traits that actually are risky to the organism's health begin to make sense. The production of a system of handicaps can function as signals in a communication game or in a situation of genetic conflict, as in a courtship display and so on.

CHAPTER 2

Patterns of REM Expression Across the Life Span

To discover potential functions of REM, we need to examine its pattern of expression across the life span and whether it correlates with key life history traits.

Sleep in Infancy and Early Childhood

When natural selection works by culling the most vulnerable members of a species, it claims predominantly fetal and juvenile forms of that species. Therefore we stand a good chance of detecting effects of selection by studying the ways in which juvenile forms respond to selective pressures. So strong is the pressure of selection early in development of an organism that much of the behavioral repertoire of the species is formed and set during the fetal and juvenile periods. The ways in which and the effectiveness with which species respond to typical selective pressures encountered early in development predict later reproductive success and so are all-important. It is therefore likely that we will find important clues concerning the evolutionary history and functions of sleep by examining early development of sleep processes.

How does mammalian sleep develop, and does the development of sleep tell us anything about its potential functions?

Sleep Need and Biologic Rhythmicity

In diurnal organisms like humans, the development of sleep is bound up with development of processes that regulate circadian organization. A circadian pacemaker is entrained to the light-dark cycle and promotes the waking state during an active phase of the diurnal cycle and permits sleep during a rest phase of the cycle. A homeostatic process regulates or influences the amount and timing of sleep, possibly via accumulation of adenosine or some other neuroendocrine or neurochemical substance that signals sleep need and sleep debt. The need for sleep accumulates or increases the longer the individual is awake. Need for sleep may also be related to the amount of work or energy used during a waking period. For example, there is some evidence that slow-wave sleep is increased after intense exercise—at least in individuals who are physically fit to begin with. In addition, some indices of sleep vary with metabolic activity in the frontal lobes, suggesting perhaps that sleep replenishes some chemical used up by the frontal lobes during wake-related cognitive work. Interestingly, sleep deprivation seems to be particularly hard on so-called executive functions (executive functions are most vulnerable to impairment after sleep deprivation) that are in turn heavily dependent on the frontal lobes.

Once an individual mammal is asleep, a third cyclic process is activated to control the (ultradian) alternation between REM and NREM sleep states. In the adult human, the ultradian cycle involves sleep onset through NREM sleep stages and sleep offset through REM sleep stages, with NREM sleep states predominating in the first third of the night and REM sleep periods predominating in the last third of the night.

Fetal Sleep

All mammals studied to date exhibit a period of spontaneous and mixed brain activity in utero known as indeterminate sleep that slowly differentiates into distinct sleep states by the middle of the pregnancy. In humans and nonhuman precocial species, this background activity occurs in utero. In altricial species, it occurs both in utero and ex utero. Both quiet sleep (QS) and active sleep (AS) are thought to develop out of this indeterminate sleep.

In humans, development of individual behavioral sleep phenomena such as physiologic cycles of quiescence and arousal into distinct sleep states begins at approximately 28 to 32 weeks gestational age (ga) and is complete by 36 to 40 weeks ga. At about 28 weeks ga, discrete periods characterized by REMs and respiratory movements begin alternating with periods of sustained motor quiesence with no or very low numbers of eye movements. A REM-like sleep state appears between 30 and 32 weeks ga and increases in amount until it comprises approximately 90% of fetal sleep. REM remains at about 90% of sleep until about 1 to 2 weeks of postnatal life, and then it begins a relatively rapid decline toward adult values. That decline occurs at different rates in different infants. By the end of the first year, REM has declined to about 50% of total sleep. By the time adulthood is reached, REM comprises only about 20 to 25% of total sleep. In the human fetus, the amount of NREM sleep initially increases and then stabilizes by 35 to 36 weeks ga and only modest changes are noted in the postnatal period.

Emergence of REM and NREM

There is a controversy as to whether adult REM emerges out of fetal AS and adult NREM emerges out fetal QS. Some investigators argue that behaviorally defined sleep states of altricial species in utero are not homologous to adult sleep states. According to Davis, Frank, and Heller (1999), AS and QS have few features in common with adult REM and NREM. Behavioral AS, for example, is not mediated by the same brain mechanisms responsible for REM. Unlike in the adult, cholinergic blockade has no effect on behavioral AS in the rat, and the adult REM-related atonia is absent in neonatal AS.

Davis et al. argue that behavioral AS and QS in altricial species is similar to presleep indeterminate states in precocial species and humans. The fetal presleep stages of humans and of precocial fetuses and AS behavioral sleep in altricial species are, according to Davis et al., strikingly similar in that cycles of irregular respiration, phasic motor activity, and REMs are poorly coupled in altricial neonates and fetal precocials.

On the other hand, fetal behavioral AS is characterized in both altricial and precocial species by neck muscle atonia, REMs, and generalized muscle twitching—all signs that we are dealing with a precursor form of REM sleep.

Evolutionary Theory I: Sex Ratio Determination

It is not widely appreciated that pregnant females can influence the sex of their offspring via modulation of hormonal and physiologic conditions in utero. Sleep states may play a role in this process. There are good evolutionary reasons to give the mother some control over the sex of her offspring. If the cost of producing one sex is not equal to the cost of producing the other sex (and we know that it is not equal for most mammalian species), then mothers are predicted to find ways to detect the sex of the fetus she is carrying and then to make a "decision" as to whether to carry it to term. Of course, all of this happens in an unconscious manner.

Costs here refer to the amount of resources required to grow a fetus and then a child to reproductive age. If the lifetime reproductive success of the mother can be better enhanced by giving birth to males rather than females, she will give birth to more males than females. If, for example, a male costs twice as much to produce as a female in the context of a population of animals with a 1:1 sex ratio (though humans depart slightly from this 1:1 ratio), then the return on investment to the mother from investing in production of males will be only half that of females. She could instead produce two females for the cost of every male, thereby increasing the chances of getting her genes into the next generation.

Trivers and Willard (1973) argued that because male reproductive opportunities and male lifetime reproductive success are more variable than those of females for most mammalian species, the mother should be selected to invest in males if local conditions (in terms of resources, mortality rates, etc.) are good and in females if local conditions are poor. This argument predicts that the sex ratio should vary to some extent with the social dominance/status of the mother. Mothers high in a dominance hierarchy tend to have greater access to resources, and thus conditions for enhancing lifetime reproductive success of their offspring are good. Pregnant mothers who rank high in a dominance hierarchy should produce more male offspring than female offspring and this result has indeed been reported by at least one research team (Clutton-Brock, Albon, & Guiness, 1986).

Grant (1998) has summarized evidence for maternal influence on determination of sex of offspring in humans. Grant devised a personality measure of dominance and then administered the inventory to samples of mothers. Women whose scores on this inventory were in the top 20% were five times more likely to conceive sons than women in the bottom 20% of the distribution.

The mother's influence on sex of offspring (and therefore on the sex ratio) can be accomplished either in utero or after birth (selective infanticide).

While there are numerous theories (see Krackow, 1995, for review) as to how the mother can determine the sex of the evolving fetus, the common denominator involves modulation of levels of hormones that normally maintain a pregnancy. Sleep states in the mother are known to vary with the trimester of the pregnancy and may influence circulating levels of hormones that maintain the pregnancy. Sleep states may also modulate the mother's ability to maintain a pregnancy regardless of the sex or fitness of the developing fetus.

Evolutionary Theory II: Pregnancy and Genetic Conflict

From the point of view of sleep state biology, pregnancy is, of course, a unique physiologic process wherein the sleep states of two genetically distinct individuals may interact. Haig (1993) has called attention to the fact that the placenta is genetically part of the fetus and not of the mother, and thus there is potential for a divergence of genetic interests between the fetus and the mother. Abnormal triploid fetuses with a double set of the father's genes and a single set of the mother's have a very large placenta, while abnormal fetuses with a double set of the mother's genes and one of the father's have very small placentas and show a retardation of growth. Modeling of genetic strategies of parents and their offspring suggests that with respect to the maternal-fetal interaction, the fetus is selected to extract as much resources from the mother as possible, while the mother is selected to moderate attempts to extract her resources. Her genetic interests lie not just in the present child but in whatever future children she may bear. She needs to be discriminative when it comes to investment of valuable resources in the current child. Future offspring of the mother, therefore, are in direct competition with the current fetus for resources, and the fetus thus attempts to extract as much as it can from its mother.

Given that sleep states are essentially brain states which emit electrical signals that influence an array of neuronal, hormonal, immunological, and behavioral responses, it seems reasonable to suppose that maternal sleep states will influence fetal development. If, furthermore, Haig's (1993) (genetic) conflict theory of human pregnancy is correct, then we can expect that fetal "interests" will include an attempt to target maternal sleep states for modification, given that these sleep states regulate or at least influence fundamental metabolic, hormonal, and immunological systems of the mother.

If the fetus wants to influence transfer of nutrients (e.g., glucose) from maternal tissues to fetal tissues, then the maternal brain (including its sleep states) should become a target for fetal manipulation, particularly in the second and third trimester, when fetal need for glucose is increasing rapidly with fetal brain development. Fetal manipulation of maternal sleep states might also allow the developing child to influence maternal waking behaviors. In many animals, for example, maternal SWS facilitates the milk ejection reflex when an infant suckles. Independent of fetal attempts to influence maternal sleep, the drastic physiologic changes that accompany pregnancy undoubtedly influence maternal sleep states as well. For all of these reasons, we would expect alterations in maternal sleep architecture as the pregnancy progresses.

Fetal strategies are to some extent revealed in placental structure and morphology. Haig (1993) has pointed out that mammalian placentas differ in their ability to invade and modify maternal arterial tissues for the benefit of the fetus. Epitheliochorial placentation is thought to be the ancestral form for eutherian mammals. Here there is little or no invasion of maternal tissue, and fetal nutrition is achieved by diffusion of nutrients across maternal tissue to the placenta and by secretions from maternal uterine glands. Pigs, horses, whales, and lemurs all use forms of epitheliochorial placentation. By contrast, in hemochorial placentation, extraembryonic tissues (which are genetically part of the fetus) breach the walls of maternal blood vessels, and the placenta gains direct access to circulating maternal blood. Examples occur in rodents, lagomorphs, insectivores, bats, apes, and humans. Species with epitheliochorial placentation tend to have shorter sleep times than species with hemochorial placentation, though no one knows why. Clearly in hemochorial placentation, the fetus gains greater access to maternal nutrients than in epitheliochorial placentation. Fetal invasion of the maternal arterial system allows the fetus to directly manipulate maternal physiology by secreting hormones into her blood supply. Decidual reactions occur only in species with hemochorial placentation. Maternal uterine decidual tissues are shed from the maternal body at delivery, miscarriage, or at menstruation, and so Haig (1993) suggested that menstruation could to some extent be seen as a defensive countermeasure against an invasive placenta.

Sleep in Pregnancy

When Lee (1998) reviewed the literature on alterations of sleep architecture in pregnancy, she found less than 20 articles on the topic. When my research assistants and I reviewed the literature in early 2003, we found that the first set of studies (Karacan, Williams, Hursch, McCaulley, & Heine, 1969; Petre-Quadens, DeBrsy, Devos, & Sfaello, 1967) reported much the same findings as the most recent studies (Lee, McEnany, & Zaffke, 2000), namely that time spent in SWS declined over the course of the pregnancy. Now, Schweiger in 1972 found that of 100 women surveyed, 13 complained of substantially poor sleep in the first trimester (T1). Nineteen had altered sleep in trimester 2 (T2), while two-thirds (N = 66) of the group complained of poor sleep in trimester 3 (T3). Sleep was altered throughout pregnancy in 11 women. It was believed that the decline in SWS reported by the early investigators could be attributed to hormonal changes and physical discomfort associated with the changes in the woman's body.

Yet if physical discomfort alone caused the changes in sleep architecture (i.e., decline in SWS), one would expect a more global effect on sleep rather than just an effect on SWS. Lee et al.'s (2000) longitudinal data, furthermore, show that whileof time spent in SWS declined overall, percentage of SWS actually increased in T2 relative to both T1 and T3. Is less physical discomfort expected in T2 relative to T1? If not, then shouldn't SWS be reduced in T2 as well?

Our review of the literature on maternal sleep architecture in pregnancy yielded a total of only 14 studies for the past 50 years (since REM sleep was discovered) of research! These studies represented a combined N of 165 women. Most studies, however, reported data on only a single trimester (typically the third). Only three studies collected data on all three trimesters. Only half of the 14 studies utilized longitudinal designs. But even here there were problems, as most of the longitudinal studies involved very small sample sizes. When sufficient numbers of women were studied with longitudinal designs, a consistent set of findings emerged: there was an overall decline in SWS across the pregnancy, with a transient increase in SWS during the second trimester. REM showed the opposite profile: a decrease in T2 and increase in T3.

Figure 2.1 displays combined results of mean values obtained for each sleep state as a function of trimester across these 14 studies. Typical levels of fetal sleep in the third trimester are indicated as well. It can be seen that

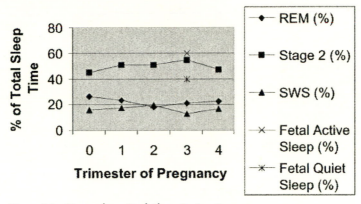

Figure 2.1. Maternal vs. Fetal Sleep During Pregnancy

stage 2 sleep increases slightly across trimesters while SWS decreases—especially in the third trimester. REM is consistently higher than SWS throughout the pregnancy except in T2. SWS percent in T3 declines somewhat relative to T1. Most interesting to us when we studied this data was the apparent crossing of REM and SWS in the second trimester. Assuming that this result can be confirmed by direct study (rather than by retrospective review of the literature), what would be the explanation?

During the first ten weeks of pregnancy, human chorionic gonadotopin (hCG) levels secreted from the trophoblast of the embedded zygote maintains the corpus luteum and its secretions of estrogen and progesterone. These sex steroids together with prolactin (secreted from the pituitary) foster the profound physiologic changes and growth in both the mother and the fetus throughout the pregnancy. Increased levels of progesterone, furthermore, dampen or prevent uterine contractions. hCG falls in T2 as the placenta itself increases its production of placental lactogen (PL), progesterone (P), and estrogen (E). PL is very similar in structure and function to GH. GH is a hormone whose release in males and to a lesser extent in females is intimately dependent on sleep: 95% of daily production of GH occurs in SWS during development. The relation between GH release and SWS is not merely temporal. The SWS state itself stimulates release of the hormone. SWS in females likely plays a similar role but stimulates release of other growth factors in addition to GH. The placenta also releases human placental growth hormone (hPGH). PL, hPGH, and GH are all encoded at 17q22-q24 in a cluster of at least five genes, all derived from an ancestral form of GH gene.

PL acts on maternal tissues, directing them to ensure that enough nutrients are available to the fetus. It also prepares the mother's breasts for lactation after the baby is born. Interestingly, the gene for PL is maternally imprinted (or paternally active) and thus is genetically aligned with paternal interests. PL serves to maintain the pregnancy by reorganizing maternal physiologic resources (e.g., the maternal blood supply is invaded by an extensive capillary network from the placenta that breaks down the walls of the maternal arteries that supply the placenta with nutrients, thus increasing the flow of nutrients to the placenta) in service to the fetus.

One possibility, therefore, is that the decline in maternal REM and the rise in NREM percentage (the crossover effect) in the second trimester reflects the decline in maternal P and the rise in fetal PL hormone during the same period. In addition to all its other effects, PL may act to modulate both REM and NREM processes in the maternal brain. Specifically, it may enhance maternal SWS, which in turn promotes release of maternal hormones that facilitate transfer of maternal resources to the developing fetus and prepares the mother's breasts for postnatal lactation.

PL synthesis, as we have seen, is regulated by a maternally imprinted/paternally active gene, and it has the overall effect of transferring maternal resources to the developing fetus. One example is the following: PL reduces the mother's sensitivity to her own insulin. This means that the mother's blood sugar level stays higher for longer periods of time, giving the fetus longer access to glucose (vital for brain development). The mother counters the rise in PL and the reduction in sensitivity to insulin by increasing production of insulin. SWS is associated with release of insulin, and injection of insulin enhances SWS.

By the end of the pregnancy, the maternal pituitary has ceased to release GH and hPGH has replaced it, becoming the predominant GH in maternal blood. Both PL and maternal SWS decline in T3, while fetal REM increases in T3. If maternal SWS helps to maintain or prolong the pregnancy, then a decline in SWS may signal the end of the pregnancy. The fetus and the mother may therefore struggle over control of maternal sleep states, in particular SWS, because these states influence release of growth factors and other hormones important for fetal development. Typically the fetus loses the battle over SWS intensity by T3, and a well-nourished baby is born at term. Maternal-fetal conflicts over control of maternal SWS intensity may also help explain the correlation found between REM-NREM cycle quotas and length of gestation period (see chapter 3).

Blood pressure changes during pregnancy may also be influenced by these genetic conflicts. The fetus heightens maternal BP in order to increase blood flow to the placenta. Maternal countermeasures to fetal attempts to increase BP may sometimes fail, resulting in a disorder found only in humans—preeclampsia. In this condition, there is severe hypertension with a loss of the normal fall of BP at night. Edwards, Blyton, Kesby, Wilcox, and Sullivan (2000) found that preeclamptic women had markedly altered sleep architecture (relative to nonpreeclamptic controls) with increased percentage of time spent in SWS, increased latency to REM (twice that of controls), and reduced time spent in REM. Because some (not all) of the hypertensive patients in the study were on clonidine for treatment of hypertension, the alterations in REM can probably be ascribed to the medication. But as the authors point out, clonidine normally does not increase SWS during nighttime sleep, and thus the SWS effect seems to be associated with the preeclampsia. Indeed, the four preeclamptic patients who were not taking clonidine evidenced the rise in SWS. Finally, there was no correlation between dose of clonidine and SWS percentage. If preeclampsia can in some way be understood as influenced by genetic conflict over bloodborne nutrients to the fetus, then the rise in SWS percentage may reflect failed fetal attempts to control the mother's SWS intensity, with subsequent effects on release of hormones that impact vascular resistance and other cardiac variables.

The tight coupling of fetal AS and later REM to fetal respiration may also play a role in regulation of maternal-fetal metabolic interactions. Oxygen tension throughout fetal development is known to exert a regulatory influence on placental and fetal growth (Genbacev et al., 1997). Thus, rising fetal REM will impact fetal growth rates.

Dreams of Pregnancy

Krippner, Posner, Pomerance, Barksdale, and Fischer (1974) used the Hall/Van de Castle scoring system to compare dreams of pregnant women (N = 11 volunteer women) to the norms gathered using the Hall/Van de Castle system (see chapter 8). The Hall/Van de Castle norms were based primarily on college students. Krippner had only 33 dreams from the pregnant women in the study. The study is nevertheless valuable because it was the only study I could find that used standardized scoring procedures and in particular used the Hall/Van de Castle system to study dreams of pregnant women. Krippner et al. reported that relative to the norms, dreams of pregnant women contained more social interactions, particularly aggressive interactions, with the dreamer in the role of the aggressor more often than in the normative dreams. The occurrence of anger and aggression in the dream (whether or not the dreamer was the aggressor) was associated with the appearance of small animals. The small animals were typically portrayed as being under threat. Other reports cite these common themes in dreams of pregnant women: themes of being physically or sexually unattractive, emotional conflicts with their own mothers, anxiety themes about the unborn baby such as whether it would be deformed or of unusual size, and so forth. Interestingly, there are anecdotal reports that in the age before use of ultrasound and similar techniques to monitor the developing fetus, when women dreamed about the sex of the child, they most often dreamedt that it was a boy.

Timing of Birth

Among the factors influencing the timing of birth are fetal secretion of ACTH (adrenocorticotropin hormone) and cortisol. In sheep, the most thoroughly studied species to date, cortisol in the fetal blood stimulates the placenta to produce enzymes that convert P into E. Estrogen in turn stimulates production of prostaglandins in the uterine musculature, thus inducing contractions. Recall that P levels act to prevent contractures. The fall in P levels and the associated rise in E levels promote contractions that, when intense enough, will initiate delivery. The mother's pituitary also plays a role. She releases oxytocin, which directly stimulates contractions as well. In sheep and other animals, periodic bouts of activity of the uterine muscle, contractures, occur. These contractures are an important source of input to the fetal nervous system. They cause the fetus to stop "breathing" and they tend to change the sleep state of the fetus. Since the fetus spends the bulk of its time in AS, a contracture typically causes the fetus to switch out of REM/AS. The arrest in breathing and the switch out of REM lowers the amount of oxygen in fetal blood and thus slows growth. The mother appears to be attempting to influence growth of the fetus via control of time spent in AS/REM. It is these contractures that later become contractions associated with birth. Interestingly, in pregnant monkeys the switch from contractures to contractions is related to the onset of sleep in the mother. "Labor" and delivery-related contractions develop over several days and nights. On the first night, contractures last only an hour or so and then revert to contractures during the day. On the second night, contractions are longer and sleep states more intense (Nathanielsz, 1996) until contractions ensue and the baby is born. There is a recurring peak of the nightly contractures. They start to occur early in the night, which would indicate an SWS-related process.

As reviewed above, maternal SWS declines and REM slightly increases in the third trimester before birth. Perhaps the decline in SWS promotes the rise in cortisol (normally the rise in cortisol occurs toward morning), which then promotes contractures.

How does fetal sleep interact with maternal sleep? A review of the available literature suggests that very little is known. The technical difficulties involved in simultaneously recording fetal and maternal sleep patterns are tremendous, and so it is no surprise the studies have only rarely been attempted. I turn now to development of sleep states in the infant after birth.

Evolutionary Theory III: Parent-Offspring Conflict

Postnatal sleep states in the infant develop in the context of mother-infant interactions. From the point of view of the infant, formation of an attachment tie to the mother is all important—else it will not thrive and may even not survive. Development of mother-infant attachment proceeds within a broader context of conflict between mother and child over amount and quality of resources to be invested in the infant. This conflict over provisioning of or investment in the infant is driven by the contrasting genetic interests of the mother versus those of the infant.

Trivers (1974; Trivers & Willard, 1973) pointed out that parents are related to their offspring by a coefficient of relatedness of 0.5; that is, the child carries only half of the maternal genomic complement. Consequently, the genetic interests of mother and child are not identical and offspring will tend to want more from their parents than their parents are willing to give. Offspring in mammals, furthermore, may not share the same father and thus their genetic interests will diverge significantly from those of their siblings. Even if they do share the same father, they are related to siblings only by 0.5 and thus their interests are not identical to those of their siblings. Offspring should therefore attempt to monopolize extraction of resources from the mother regardless of consequences to the mother or to siblings.

One arena where parent-offspring conflict plays itself out in humans is over the quality of the attachment tie formed between a mother and the infant. I return to this issue below and show that sleep states, in particular REM, likely play a role in that conflict. First some basic facts concerning infant sleep development.

Neonatal Sleep

Neonatal AS and then REM is associated with telltale physical signs that can be distinguished by visual inspection (e.g., muscle twitches, rapid eye movements under closed eyelids, etc.—REM was, after all, discovered by visually observing a sleeping infant). Early bouts of crying and vocalizing are known to occur while the infant is in REM (Wolff, 1987). When recorded polygraphically, AS/REM sleep is characterized by a low-voltage, fast EEG, activation of limbic brain sites, rapid and irregular heart and respiratory rates, rapid saccadic eye movements under closed lids, and, later in infancy, inhibited peripheral muscle tone. In addition, facial grimaces, smiles, and distal limb twitches can be observed. In contrast, NREM sleep is characterized by slow, synchronized, high-voltage EEG patterns, regular and slowed respiratory and heart rates, and the absence of eye movements and other peripheral body movements.

In sharp contrast to the adult pattern of entering sleep via an NREM episode, normal, full-term newborns enter sleep through a REM-like state rather than an NREM-like state. The newborn, furthermore, spends approximately 18 hours per day asleep, with short periods of wakefulness interrupting sleep every 3 to 4 hours. That is, there are typically 6 to 8 regularly occurring sleep periods in a 24-hour day for a typical newborn (Coons & Guilleminault, 1984). Significant variability exists, however, so that some newborns, for the first few days after birth, sleep for 18 to 20 hours while others sleep for only 10 to 12 hours in a 24-hour period (Sadeh, Dark, & Vohr, 1996).

Table 2.1. Sleep Changes from Infant to Adult Period

	Infant	Adult
%REM/NREM	50/50	20/80
REM/NREM cycle	50-60 minutes	90-100 minutes
Sleep onset state	REM	NREM
Temporal organization of sleep states	REM/NREM cycles equally throughout sleep period	NREM predominates in first third of night; REM predominates in last third of night
Sleep architecture	1 NREM stage	4 NREM stages

Reprinted from *Principles and Practice of Sleep Medicine in the Child* by R. Ferber (ed.). Copyright 1995, with permission of Elsevier.

Within the first month following birth, sleep-wake state organization begins to adapt to the light-dark cycle and to social cues.

During the first 3 months of life, infants spend 50% of their sleep time in AS (the REM-like state) and the other 50% in QS (or the NREM-like state). The infantile precursor sleep states (AS and QS) begin to approximate adult forms of REM and NREM by about 6 months. With increasing maturity, the proportionate amount of time in REM sleep diminishes. The 2- to 3-year-old child spends approximately 35% of sleep time in REM sleep, while the adult spends about 20 percent in REM sleep. After 3 months of age, REM periods continue to recur with a periodicity of 50 to 60 minutes; however, the amount of REM sleep in each cycle begins to shift. REM sleep predominates in the later sleep cycles of the night and NREM sleep predominates during the earlier cycles, especially NREM stage IV sleep. By 3 years of age, the temporal organization of sleep during the night resembles that of adult sleep except for the sleep cycle periodicity, which does not lengthen to the 90-minute periodicity of adults until adolescence (table 2.1).

In contrast to REM, where the maturation of electrographic features are quite prolonged (e.g., PGO waves are not present in the kitten until 3 weeks postnatally), the maturation of NREM brain activity (slow waves in the delta bands 0.5–4.0 Hz and sleep spindles at 7–14 Hz) is completed in a relatively short time. EEG slow waves are generally reported to develop as isolated slow waves in a burst suppression EEG pattern, called trace alternant in the human infant. This pattern in turn is replaced later with a more continuous slow-wave pattern during the course of development. Sleep spindles appear later as well.

Relation of Infant REM to Altriciality

The overabundance of REM during infancy relative to the adult state is found in other animals as well. Virtually every species studied demonstrates the pattern of high amounts of REM in infancy versus the adult state (see Zepelin, 2000, for a recent review). Zepelin (1989), for example, found that REM sleep "quotas correlated significantly with degree of altriciality ($r = -.45$), neonatal brain weight ($r = -.55$), and gestation period ($r = -.39$) across a large range of mammalian species. Opossums and ferrets, for example, are born in an extremely immature state. These animals devote about 30% of their total adult sleep time to REM. Adult humans spend a little less time (24% of total sleep time) in REM sleep relative to opossums/ferrets, and a little more time in REM than the precocial horses/elephants (who spend approximately 22% of their total sleep time in REM). In some extremely precocial species (e.g., the bottlenose dolphin), EEG signs of REM (though not behavioral signs such as penile erection) may have disappeared altogether (Mukhametov, Supin, & Polyakova, 1977).

The striking quantitative relationships between REM quotas and measures of juvenile development have led a number of evolutionary and comparative analysts to suggest that REM may have evolved, in part, to support some aspect of mammalian infant development (Mirmiran, 1995; Roffwarg, Muzio, & Dement, 1966; Zepelin, 2000) but that function still has not been identified. The function most favored by investigators who specialize in this field is brain development. Juvenile REM, however, may also be shaped by and influence the infant's most important relationship: its relationship to the mother.

In any case, REM's prominence in early development suggests that it may influence formation of long-term behavioral strategies in the child and then the adult. For example, the quality of the early attachment tie of the infant to the mother likely influences the adult's approach to intimate relationships later in life. If REM affects infantile attachment formation, then it will also potentially influence development of adult reproductive strategies. I present arguments and evidence for this claim below.

Impact of Early Experience on Adult Functioning

In mammals and birds, adult reproductive behaviors and strategies appear to be strongly influenced by events during the juvenile period. In humans, it is known, for example, that early indicators of familial stress are associated with poor parenting styles and subsequent behavioral problems in the children (Bronfenbrenner & Crouter, 1982; Burgess & Draper, 1989; Emery, 1988; McLoyd, 1990). For girls, father absence and early family conflict predict earlier menarche even when body weight is controlled for (Graber, Brooks-Gunn, & Warren, 1995; Smith, Udry, & Morris, 1985; Surbey, 1990). Nonhuman primates who undergo early maternal deprivation do not behave normally sexually as adults (Hrdy, 1999; Kraemer, 1992). Similarly, Bischof (1997) has shown that early experience in avian species in the forms of song exposure/learning, filial imprinting, and sexual imprinting determine later reproductive behaviors and mating strategies. Sexual imprinting, in particular, is a process whereby adult mate preferences are affected by learning at a very young age, usually using a parent as the model.

Evolutionary Theory IV: Life History Theory

According to life history theory (Clutton-Brock, 1991; Stearns, 1992), life cycle traits such as gestation length, size and number of offspring, age at first reproduction, lactation/weaning period, ongoing reproductive strategy, and length of life are all influenced by local ecologic context and contribute to reproductive fitness. Individuals develop mechanisms or biobehavioral strategies that help them solve problems of infant survival, childhood growth, adult development, and reproduction across the life span. Perceptual-emotional information about current environmental conditions (e.g., local mortality rates) is used to make (unconscious) decisions about optimal allocation of limited resources.

Trade-offs have to be made between time and energy devoted to "somatic effort" (i.e., investing in growth and development of the body) versus time and energy devoted to "reproductive effort" (i.e., funneling effort toward producing and raising offspring). Similarly, the developing organism needs to "decide" whether to invest in reproduction sooner (an early maturity) as opposed to some later more propitious time. Reproductive effort has two further components: mating effort (locating, courting, and retaining a suitable mate) and parenting effort (i.e., gestating, giving birth, and engaging in postnatal care). In short, when it concerns the developing organism, life history theory deals with how juvenile individuals unconsciously and optimally allocate somatic versus reproductive effort now versus in the future, given an assessment of current life circumstances. Given the impact of developmental sleep processes on brain development, it is possible that sleep processes may figure in unconscious decisions concerning somatic development as well as development of behavioral strategies to support reproductive effort (parent-offspring relations and mating strategies).

Evolutionary Theory V: Attachment Theory and Ecologically Contingent Behavioral Strategies

Several investigators (e.g., Belsky, Fish, & Isabella, 1991; Chisholm, 1999; Simpson, 2000) have suggested that for the neonate and the juvenile, evaluation of local ecologic conditions reduces to their experience of their caregivers. The neonate does not make conscious decisions, and thus its decision-making processes must occur unconsciously or automatically. Bowlby and others in the field of attachment theory have called attention to the importance of infant-mother attachment relationships in development of infant cognitive, emotional, and social skills. If the neonate/child can form a secure emotional attachment to the mother, the child will "conclude" that the local environment will support a long-term reproductive strategy of delayed maturity and high investment in a few high-quality offspring. If, on the other hand, the child meets a cold, rejecting mother or faces threats of abandonment, and so on, then a strategy of rapid maturation and early reproduction with greater numbers of offspring, and so forth, will most likely obtain. Thus, development of adult reproductive strategies depends crucially on the juvenile's early experience of attachment.

The Belsky et al. Model

Belsky, Steinberg, and Draper (1991) developed one of the first models of childhood attachment patterns as they relate to later reproductive behaviors. Belsky et al. suggested that early environmental factors in the family of origin (e.g., the amount of stress, spousal harmony, and financial resources) affect early child-rearing experiences (the level of sensitive and responsive caregiving). These child-rearing experiences then affect psychological and behavioral development of the child (e.g., patterns of attachment, the nature of internal working models of self and of others), which influences both somatic development (how quickly sexual maturation is reached) and development of reproductive effort.

Behavioral and reproductive strategies are conceived as ensembles of cognitive, brain, physiologic, and social processes and behaviors that implement a series of adaptive behaviors that increase reproductive fitness. Two developmental trajectories are conceived, eventuating in two reproductive strategies in adulthood. One strategy involves a short-term opportunistic orientation toward mating and parenting in which sexual intercourse with multiple partners occurs earlier and romantic relationships are short-term and unstable. This orientation is geared toward increasing the quantity of offspring as early as possible. The second strategy involves a long-term investing orientation in which sexual intercourse occurs later in life with fewer partners, pair bonds are long term and more stable, and personal investment is greater. This orientation is associated with delayed maturity and with maximizing the quality of offspring.

The Chisholm Model

Building on the work of Belsky, Steinberg, and Draper (1991) and Stearns (1992), Chisholm (1993, 1996, 1999) noted that local mortality rates may act as a proximal environmental cue that directs people toward different developmental/reproductive strategies. When mortality rates are high in an area, the optimal reproductive strategy should be to start early and maximize current fertility rates. When local mortality rates are low, the best strategy involves deferred long-term reproduction in which fewer offspring are given better and more long-term care. In environments with abundant resources, a delayed maturation/high investment reproductive strategy should increase the total number of descendants over multiple generations by minimizing the variance of surviving offspring between generations. Parental indifference or insensitivity may be used by children as cues or indicators of local high mortality rates, leading them to develop, for example, avoidant attachment styles better suited to facilitating fitness in harsh environments. In addition, parents' inability or unwillingness to invest in offspring would be used as indicators of harshness of the local environment.

Chisholm reconceptualizes the three classic attachment patterns (secure, ambivalent, and avoidant) in terms of parent-offspring conflict and how the behavioral pattern might maximize the child's later reproductive interests. Secure attachment is seen as the resultant of having parents who are both willing and able to invest in the child. Avoidant attachment is an adaptation to parents' unwillingness to invest regardless of ability, and ambivalent attachment is an adaptation to parents' inability to invest (most likely because of limited resources) regardless of willingness. Using Chisholm's logic, we might advance a final attachment outcome correlated with parents who are both unwilling and unable to invest adequately in their offspring. For children in this particularly harsh situation, what behavioral strategy would be most adaptive? Perhaps this kind of harsh social environment might result in so-called disorganized attachment patterns, where the child's attachment and later reproductive behaviors are unpredictable and disorganized.

REM Sleep and Unconscious Appraisals of Ecologic Context

The Belsky, Steinberg, and Draper (1991) and Chisholm (1993) models of developmental attachment processes suggest that there must be a physiologic process by which assessment of current life circumstances is made early in life. REM is a viable candidate for such a process as it involves very high activation levels of the amygdala and associated structures (Maquet et al., 1997). There is now abundant evidence that the amygdala specializes in processing of emotion, particularly negative emotions, and functions as the "decisional" or "appraisal organ" of the mind (Bechara, Damasio, Damasio, & Lee, 1999; Davidson & Irwin, 1999; Ledoux, 1996). In addition, along with hippocampal sites, it apparently supports both emotional memory formation and reactivation of emotional memories during REM (Wagner, Gais, & Born, 2001; Wilson & McNaughton, 1994). It also contributes to regulation of other brain structures such as the hypothalamus that, in turn, regulate ongoing neuroendocrine processes in the developing organism (Davis & Whalen, 2001; Ledoux, 2000). Finally, the amygdala is implicated in development of key cognitive components (e.g., "theory of mind") of the attachment process in the child (Siegel & Varley, 2002). Thus, early in life when REM predominates over NREM sleep, REM-related amygdaloid activation may signal the processing of unconscious appraisals or assessments of current ecologic conditions (e.g., maternal sensitivity to the child). REM then takes these assessments and

uses them to implement appropriate adjustments in somatic versus reproductive effort.

Impact of Developmental Sleep on Adult Functioning

Interestingly, sleep processes appear to play a crucial role in physiologic
mechanisms whereby early experience shapes adult reproductive strategies.
In birds, paradoxical/active sleep (REM is sometimes called paradoxical
sleep or PS in nonhuman species) may mediate certain aspects of sexual
imprinting. The total amount of time spent in PS, as well as the number of
PS episodes, increase significantly following an imprinting session in the
laboratory. Solodkin, Cardona, and Corsi-Cabrera (1985) demonstrated that
the effect was selective for PS sleep as no changes occur in SWS after an
imprinting session. There is also evidence which suggests that blocking
REM early in life yields sexual dysfunction later in life in mammalian species. Mirmiran et al. (1983), for example, found that masculine sexual responses (mounts and ejaculations) were significantly impaired in rats that
had been treated early in life (when neonates) with REM suppressant agents
(e.g., clomipramine). Early REM deprivation may also be associated with
profound anatomic and metabolic lesions later in life. Mirmiran et al. found
significant reductions in volume in the cerebral cortex and medulla oblongata in rats that had been treated as neonates with REM suppressant agents.
These data are consistent with the large literature on effects of attachment-
related early psychosocial stress on later adult functioning and health including adult cortisol levels, adult stature, and sleep quality (see Maunder &
Hunter, 2001, for review).

In a series of well-controlled studies, Vogel and Hagler (1996) demonstrated that administration of the REM suppressant and antidepressant
drugs clorimipramine, zimeldine, or desipramine to neonatal rats produced
abnormalities at maturity including depressive symptoms and sexual dysfunction. Although these three drugs affect different neurotransmitter systems, all cause REM sleep deprivation (RSD). This suggests that RSD is the
causative factor in the adult depressive syndrome and sexual dysfunction.
To test that idea, Vogel and Hagler administered iprindole to neonates.
Iprindole is an antidepressant drug that does not produce RSD. When the
iprindole-treated rats matured, they evidenced no sexual dysfunction or
depressive symptoms.

REM in Promotion of Brain Development

Brain activation is important for neural development, and REM sleep
may provide endogenous brain stimulation at times when wake amounts are
very low. Correlative studies have shown associations between the amount

of REM sleep, or REM sleep phasic activity, and brain development. When juvenile cats are placed in enriched environments, the weight and synaptic densities of their brains increase, and these changes are associated with increased REM sleep. In rats, phasic REMs increase in duration and intensity during REM near the time of eye opening. This elevation in phasic activity is also observed in dark-reared rat pups and is believed to represent preparatory activations of the visual system prior to waking experience. Davenne, Fregnac, Imbert, and Adrien (1989), Oksenberg et al. (1996), and Pompeiano, Pompeiano, and Corvaja (1995) have independently demonstrated a possible role for REM in the developing visual system. PGO activity, which is maximally expressed during REM, was abolished in neonatal kittens by bilateral lesions of brain stem PGO centers. The loss of PGO activity during development resulted in smaller lateral geniculate neurons and lowered their responses to optic stimulation. These findings suggest that the phasic activity of REM sleep may be important for the development of lateral geniculate neurons.

In summary, early experience can significantly influence adult brain, behavioral, and sexual functioning. Impairment in neonatal or juvenile active sleep (but not SWS) can significantly influence later adult functioning, including brain, mood, and sexual functioning. Juvenile REM may therefore contribute to formation of long-term behavioral strategies including reproductive strategies. The outcome of these early formation processes will depend on the early experiences of the infant/child and the ability of the infant to consistently extract quality resources from its mother.

Costly Signaling in Mother-Infant Relations

Given the fact that selection pressures are most acute during the dependent infancy period, the juvenile must use all of its available resources to survive. Thus the infant will attempt to manipulate the mother to gain vital resources of food, warmth, and protection in the context of siblings who are competing for the same resources. How does the mother decide to allocate her energies? Her genetic interests do not necessarily lie in providing equal amounts of care to each child. Rather, she likely adjusts her level of care depending on infant needs and infant fitness. Will it help her or her other children to expend copious amounts of care on an infant that will not survive? She would be in danger of losing all of the children if she did not allocate resources as efficiently as possible. How then does she make such decisions?

The mother must use cues about each child's vigor, health, neediness, and so on to assess fitness of each child. She must to some extent use signals that the child produces to assess fitness of the child. The child (or the child's genes) "wants" to send a signal indicating, "I am fit so don't abandon me—but I am not so fit that I don't need you for some things." The child must advertise his or her fitness. As discussed in chapter 1, such advertisements, however, are open to error or even being faked. The mother must assess the accuracy and honesty of the child's signals and she must do so on the basis of phenotypic markers. If an attribute is a marker of heritable fitness, selection should promote the ability to fake the valued feature, even in individuals who do not actually have high fitness. Thus, "cheaters"— individuals who display the selected phenotypic traits or behaviors but do not have high fitness—may invade the population. How will the mother be able to discern honest from dishonest signals?

The signals may need to be costly for the child to produce in order to be judged as honest by a caretaker. If the infant can produce costly signals and still thrive, it must be fit. In the context of mother-infant communication, costly signals likely include high-pitched vocalizations, begging displays, and crying bouts in humans.

While mothers must make decisions concerning allocation of resources, they must do so typically with an infant who spends the bulk of its time in the first few months of its life asleep. This means that mothers must use sleep-related cues (along with cues derived from the child's waking behavior) to assess infant fitness and that infants in turn will use sleep physiology to signal fitness. Infants cannot afford not to use sleep-related cues to signal fitness if mothers are using such cues to make decisions concerning investment of resources. If mammalian mothers use sleep-related cues to assess fitness or need in offspring, then infant sleep states will evolve specializations to effectively signal fitness or need and to manipulate levels of maternal investment. The activated brain state of AS/REM is the sleep state most likely to evolve the relevant specializations.

In what follows, I summarize evidence which suggests that mothers use REM-related cues to make investment decisions in offspring and that infants may use REM processes to elicit maternal care. I show that (1) AS/ REM values vary with offspring physical state and need (and thus can be used by mothers to assess infant fitness); (2) maternal investment in young varies with AS/REM levels; (3) neurophysiological characteristics of REM are compatible with processing and activation of filiative drives/needs in the infant; (4) REM is associated with night wakings and thus with attachment-related behavioral signaling; and (5) existing cross-sectional studies on sleep and attachment in human infants support a physiologically significant relationship between the two systems.

Active Sleep/REM sleep Values Vary With Offspring Physical State and Need

Significant variability in percentage of total sleep time spent in REM exists, thus allowing REM times to vary with the physiologic state of the infant. Available data confirm that typical or normal infant REM sleep varies considerably in the first year of life (Burnham, Goodlin-Jones, Gaylor, & Anders, 2002). Using videosomnography to measure percentage of total sleep time spent in AS and QS, and measuring from 1 month of age to 12 months of age, Burnham et al. reported a great deal of variability in AS percentage from night to night and at each age. For example, although the mean of AS percentage was 66.2% (SD = 9.4) at 1 month, it ranged from a low of 41.0% to a high of 92.5%. Similarly, by 12 months, the mean was 41.0% (SD = 8.8), with a range of 20.0% to 68.5%. In general, mean AS percentages were higher earlier in life, but variability was high across the entire first year of life.

Infant sleep states are tightly coupled with developmental metabolic, respiratory, thermoregulatory, and neurphysiologic systems (Bach et al., 2002; Curzi-Dascalova & Callamel, 2000), and thus sleep patterns necessarily reflect the overall physiologic state of the infant. Absolute and relative amounts of sleep correlate with physical state in many mammalian species. Comparative analyses of "sleep quotas" (i.e., percentage of total sleep time spent in AS/REM vs. NREM sleep) reveal that AS/REM sleep quotas, in particular, correlate strongly with developmental indices of dependency in juveniles. As mentioned previously, AS/REM quotas, for example, vary systematically with the altriciality rating of a species (Elgar, Pagel, & Harvey, 1988; Meddis, 1983; Zepelin, 1989). The greater the immaturity of the young at birth, the longer the time spent in AS/REM sleep (Zepelin, 1989).

Studies of the effects of maternal separation on developing rats (Hofer, 1975, 1984; Hofer & Shair, 1982) and monkeys (Reite, Kaemingk, & Boccia, 1989; Reite, Kaufman, Pauley, & Stynes, 1974; Reite, Short, & Seiler, 1978; Reite, Short, Seiler, & Pauley, 1981; Reite & Short, 1978) provide a dramatic illustration of how AS/REM values are linked with infant need for something the mother provides. These studies have conclusively shown that measures of AS/REM sleep (but not NREM or SWS) are selectively influenced after maternal separation. There is an initial increase in AS/REM times and then a dramatic reduction after separation. This effect is predicted by the costly signaling evolutionary framework described above: there is no sense in signaling need in the absence of the mother. It is more adaptive to conserve resources and wait.

Maternal Investment in Young Varies With AS/REM Levels

In a comparative analysis of the relation of sleep quotas to maternal energetic investment in offspring as measured by milk yield, McNamara, Dowdall, and Auerbach (2002) found that while indices of milk content (dry matter and protein) across a variety of mammalian species correlated significantly with both QS times and AS times, maternal energetic investment at peak lactation (milk yield) correlated significantly with AS time ($r = .65$, $p = .039$) only, indicating a selective role for AS/REM in extraction of resources from the mother.

In addition, infant rats prefer to nurse while they are in AS/REM sleep, with the amount of AS/REM sleep displayed by the infant rat varying systematically with the length of the nursing bout. Lorenz (1986) and Lorenz et al. (1998) found that the amount of AS/REM sleep displayed in the suckling rat pup increased as the volume of milk received from the mother increased up to 4% of the pup's body weight. Lehtonen (2002) reported that infant breastfeeding is associated with a significant increase in the amplitude of the infant's brain activity in the occipital-temporal-parietal area.

Neurophysiology of REM Is Compatible With Processing and Activation of Filiative Drives/Needs in the Infant

If mothers use REM-related cues to make investment decisions in offspring, then offspring will come under selective pressures to use REM processes to manipulate maternal investments. REM physiology should include processes that can support emotional processing and expression as well as vocalizations that can signal distress and manipulate maternal responding. Several recent PET and fMRI studies have demonstrated that AS/REM sleep is associated with high activation levels of the amygdala, hypothalamus, and associated limbic forebrain structures (reviewed in Maquet & Franck, 1997) in the adult. These amygdaloid and limbic sites are anatomically active in the neonate (Daenen, Wolterink, Gerrits, & Van Ree, 2002) and implicated in the neurobiology of emotional expression, vocalization, and maternal-infant attachment processes (Bachevalier, Malkova, & Mishkin, 2001; Steklis & Kling, 1985). For example, surgical removal of the amygdala during the first week of a macaque monkey's life results in reduction of social affiliative responses, reduction in vocalizations after maternal separation, and increased social withdrawal and avoidance (Bachevalier et al., 2001; Malkova, Mishkin, Suomi, & Bachevalier, 1997). Similarly, pharmacologic suppression of AS/REM sleep during early development in rats results in social withdrawal and a later syndrome reminiscent of depression in the human (see review in Vogel, Feng, & Kinney, 2000). Perhaps both processes (amygdaloid lesions and AS/REM suppression) selectively affect filiative circuits in the developing infant brain as well as signaling capacities in the infant.

Moreover, AS/REM sleep appears to play a role in the regulation of select neuroendocrine circuits such as those involving release of the growth and attachment-related hormones, prolactin and oxytocin, that control development of behavioral interactions and affectional ties between the mother and the infant (Forsling, 1993; Insel, 1992; Insel & Young, 2001; Van Cauter & Speigel, 1999). In summary, REM constitutes an endogenous source of periodic activation of precisely those brain regions implicated in processing and expression of attachment-related needs.

Association of REM With Night Wakings and Attachment-Related Behavioral Signaling

Burnham et al. (2002) reported significant variability in number of night wakings/arousals in the infant. At 1 month, infants woke an average of

4.12 (SD = 2.57) times, with a range from 1 to 11 times. At 12 months, infants were waking an average of 2.62 times (SD = 2.03), with a range of 0 to 10 times. Night wakings are known to be sensitive to maternal factors: Scher, Tirosh, Rubin, Sadeh, and Lavie (1995) and Scher (2001) reported that level of separation anxiety in the mother at the beginning of the infant's life (3 months) predicted frequency of infant night wakings at 9 months. When nighttime awakenings are followed by a signaling episode such as crying, they are more likely to elicit a maternal intervention than when no signaling occurs. Several forms of nighttime signaling can influence attachment processes, including crying, sucking, nursing, smiling, grasping, twitches, cooing, babbling, and other vocalizations. All of these behaviors are more likely either to occur in, or to emerge from, REM rather than NREM sleep (Curzi-Dascalova & Callamel, 2000; Dreyfus-Brisac, 1975; Emde & Koenig, 1969; Giganti & Toselli, 2002; Salzarulo & Ficca, 2002; Wolff, 1987).

Cross-Sectional Studies on Sleep and Attachment in Human Infants Suggest a Significant Relationship Between the Two Systems

In a study of 20 infants judged insecurely attached to mother, Benoit, Zeanah, Boucher, and Minde (1992) reported that 100% of these children evidenced severe sleep disorders. When Sagi, van Ijzendoorn, Aviezer, Donnell, and Mayseless (1994) studied effects of sleeping arrangements in Israeli kibbutzim (communal vs. home) on attachment security, they found that 52% of communal-sleeping infants (i.e., those who slept away from their parents' home) and only 20% of home-sleeping infants were later classified as insecurely attached.

Sleep-wake patterns of securely attached 1-year-olds can be summarized from data reported in Scher (2001): There is a short sleep onset time (mean of 15 minutes), with about one awakening per night, averaging about 11 minutes. Scher also studied sleep patterns in nonsecurely attached infants. Scher (2001) reported that 55% of secure and 60% of insecure (almost exclusively resistant) infants were described by their mothers as night wakers, though this difference was not confirmed by actigraphic data. Whereas only 6% of the mothers of insecurely attached infants thought that their child had settling difficulties when going to sleep, 43% of "dependent secure" (i.e., B4: secure infants who nevertheless exhibit some ambivalence as well) and 23% of the mothers of other secure infants reported that their infants had settling difficulties. Infants with frequent night awakenings scored higher on contact maintenance in the Strange Situation than non-night-waking infants. Unfortunately, Scher (2001) did not report percent AS as a function of attachment status. In addition, Scher could not study infants classified as avoidant, given their very low frequency in Israeli samples.

REM and Cosleeping

We have seen that REM percentage is associated with altriciality. Zepelin (1989) points out that altriciality evolved in mammals in conjunction with new methods to regulate body temperature. Altriciality may have reduced the energy requirements for maturation by reducing gestational periods and by relying on parental body heat for temperature regulation in the young. But this innovation, of course, placed a premium on parental care of the infant for survival, and thus the increasingly sophisticated infant attempts to elicit care from an adult (i.e., attachment). The need for an infant to attach to a caregiver is linked not only to its need for food and protection but also to its need for warmth. The altricial infant uses the body heat of the mother to begin to regulate its own body temperature. This is particularly important during REM because REM is a partially poikilothermic state. For the neonate to benefit from its mother's thermal and other resources during REM sleep, it needs to be in close proximity to its mother. Mammalian maternal care is often associated with building a nest where the mother can suckle the young and sleep in close physical contact with the young. Thus, mammalian maternal care usually takes the form of cosleeping, with the neonate sleeping next to the mother and nursing during sleep. Interestingly, cosleeping is a near universal mammalian practice and is practiced in virtually every human culture, with the sole exception being 20th- and 21st-century industrialized cultures (McKenna, Mosko, Dungy, & McAninch, 1990; McKenna et al., 1993).

It is through sleeping next to the mother that the helpless neonate can best elicit nutritional and thermal resources from the mother. As the infant grows, it can add to its care-elicitation repertoire new and emerging capacities and behaviors such as distress vocalizations in the rat and mutual eye gazing in humans.

Attachment in the neonate can also be fruitfully understood as entrainment or attunement of physiologic and behavioral processes between mother and infant. These attunement processes may occur most optimally while the infant and mother sleep. Among the interactive processes executed during sleep are heat transfer, touch, grooming, suckling in the infant, milk ejection in the mother, gut filling in the infant, PS activation in the infant, arousal overlaps, hormonal rhythm overlap, temperature cycle entrainment, breathing cycles, and so on. Hofer and others (e.g., Stern, 1985) call these exquisitely timed sleep interactions between mother and infant "attunement behaviors" or examples of synchrony between behavioral and biologic rhythms in the mother and infant.

The mammalian neonate is an open system that depends upon the mother to set regulatory values of internal physiologic rhythms and organization (Hofer, 1984; Hrdy, 1999; Reppert, Duncan, & Weaver, 1987; Rosenblum &

Moltz, 1983; Stern, 1985). These neonatal physiologic systems become organized through interaction with or attachment to the mother. As the work of McKenna et al. (1990; McKenna & Mosko, 1994) has shown, cosleeping facilitates the development of infant physiologic systems as well as entrainment of biologic rhythms in the infant to the mother. The mother acts as a kind of zeitgeber for the infant, and the mutual entrainment of rhythms occurs both during sleep and during waking behaviors. Synchrony and attunement of physiologic variables such as autonomic indices and EEG waveforms may help each member of the attached pair to better regulate their own internal physiologic systems. Beebe, Gertsman, and Carson (1982) and Belsky and Nezworski (1988), among others, have documented the role of synchrony in the attachment process (in humans) between mothers and infants. Several experts on the psychobiologic mechanisms of attachment (Field, 1985; Hofer, 1987; Reite & Capitanio, 1985; Stern, 1985) have argued that attachment can be understood as psychobiologic attunement or synchrony between individuals. From this perspective, attachment *is* synchrony of behavioral and biological rhythms between individuals. Field (1985) cites a long list of behavioral and biologic variables that have been documented to display synchrony of one kind or another in organisms undergoing attachment. Among these variables are sleep states and EEG waveforms.

If the physiologic basis of attachment involves mechanisms of behavioral and physiologic synchrony, then attachment in the neonate and the child can plausibly occur while the infant is sleeping next to the mother. If so, we would expect to find that REM variables would vary systematically as a function of cosleeping status. Fortunately, data are available on sleep variables as function of cosleeping status, and they tend to confirm the prediction. McKenna et al. (1990, 1993) and McKenna and Mosko (1994) studied both routinely cosleeping mother-infant pairs and mother-infant pairs who do not routinely cosleep. A number of physiologic parameters were measured in both mothers and their infants when they coslept and when they slept alone. McKenna et al. found that (a) bed-sharing mothers and infants exhibited high levels of "arousal overlap," meaning, presumably, that arousal times were synchronized; (b) infants exhibited more frequent stage shifts (i.e., they moved from one stage of sleep to another more frequently) when bed-sharing; (c) they spent more time in the same sleep stage as their mother when bed-sharing (another example, possibly, of synchrony); and (d) they spent less time in stages 3 and 4 and more time in AS or REM when bed-sharing. In addition, during the bed-sharing night, infants faced toward the mother during most of the night (between 72 and 100% of the time) and they almost doubled their number of breast-feeding episodes during the bed-sharing night (relative to the solitary sleeping night when mothers were available in the next room for breastfeeding if the infant cried, etc.).

Nursing and Sleep States

Hofer (1987) and his colleagues have shown that nursing (the paradigmatic attachment behavior) in the rat is controlled by an elaborate set of cues, all embedded in sleep. Infants sleep while they are nursing and suck while they are asleep. Their sucking induces milk ejections (via oxytocin release) to occur in the mother. However, oxytocin release in the mother cannot occur unless she is in SWS (Hofer, 1984; Lincoln et al., 1980; Voloscin & Tramezzani, 1979). The infant, on the other hand, must be in AS at the point of milk ejection, since it begins a pattern of rapid rhythmic sucking once the teat is engorged with milk. Lorenz and associates (Lorenz, 1986; Lorenz et al., 1998) find that the suckling rat pup responds to receiving the milk by displaying PS. Indeed, the amount of PS displayed increases as the volume of milk increases to 4% of the pup's body weight. Gut loads of milk and a warm ambient temperature (from a cosleeping mother or littermates) appear to work in an additive manner to enhance PS duration.

This review of the literature on REM sleep and socioemotional development of the infant (in terms of maternal-infant attachment formation) has revealed that many mammalian infants nurse while they are asleep and there are indications that they are in AS when they nurse. REM values vary systematically with cosleeping status in human infants. REM is associated with anatomic activation of brain sites that are implicated in attachment processes—namely amygdala and limbic cortex. Disruption of the attachment bond leads to a selective effect on REM: REM processes are inhibited or even lost altogether, while no significant changes occur in NREM/SWS values. Infant signaling (vocalizations, crying, smiling, etc.) typically occurs while the infant is asleep in REM or when it awakens from REM. The mother may use these hard-to-fake signals as indicators of infant fitness.

Sleep and Dreams in Childhood

Sleeping children, from the toddler years up to and including teens, are extremely difficult to arouse. If you fit these children with headphones that deliver sounds as loud as a large revving motorcycle (123 decibels), you will find that these children will nevertheless not awaken. Sounds any louder than 123 decibels might actually damage their eardrums. When children sleep, they are "dead to the world." This deep sleep state appears to be associated with increased SWS values in children and teens relative to the adult state (Carskadon & Dement, 2000). Although the infant "prefers" AS/REM, the child "prefers" NREM/SWS. The first NREM period in children may last as long as an hour, and instead of awakening from a REM period they often awaken out of NREM. Arousals from NREM/SWS give rise to confusional states that may be due to only partially arousing from SWS. It takes a child a longer period of time and perhaps greater effort relative to an adult to arouse from SWS. The amount and intensity of SWS peaks around age 4 in humans. This is interesting as age 4 is the traditional weaning age in humans, a period of intense parent-offspring genetic conflict. It is certainly easier for a mother to wean a child if the child is asleep and not demanding attention.

The dreams of children from age 3 up to the teen years were studied by Foulkes (1982). Dream content appears to track very closely children's developing cognitive abilities. Dreams of children between 3 and 5 years do not tell a story and so have no clear narrative structure. They are typically brief visual scenes or pictures, but they only rarely portray the self. The child himself or herself does not participate in the scene. The self character typically appears by age 7, along with clear narratives and reports of emotional experiences (that are typically appropriate to the storyline). The most frequently reported characters in these children's dreams are their parents and friends. Aggressive social interactions are rare. Animal figures are abundant, particularly in young children, and Foulkes suggests that they may be a stand-in for depiction of the self, as their appearances diminish as the self character becomes more prominent. Interestingly, the best predictors of dream recall in children are performance on visual-spatial neuropsychological tests (such as the block-design test) rather than performance on verbal memory tasks.

Sleep and Dreams in the Teenage Years

The average sleep time declines from a high of about 10 hours per day during childhood to about 8 hours in the teenage years, but this decline may be due to erratic sleep schedules of modern teens rather than to any decline in sleep need. Indeed, sleep need may actually increase with the onset of puberty. Time spent in SWS declines, but there is variability in time spent in REM. Latency to first REM period after sleep onset appears to decrease in boys. Virtually all of the growth hormone released during these years occurs during sleep, and many of the hormones controlling onset of puberty are also influenced by sleep processes. The phenomenon of nocturnal emission typically occurs at this time in boys. Indeed, boys are likely to experience their first orgasm as part of a dream experience.

Disorders That May Be Linked to Sleep Changes in Adolescence

As mentioned above, adolescence is associated with a decline in percentage of total sleep time composed of SWS. This means that there may be a corresponding increase in REM. The profile of reduced SWS and variable or increased REM is associated with a number of disorders, including depression and suicide. Sabo, Reynolds, Kupfer, and Berman (1991) compared EEG sleep measures of major depressives with and without a history of suicidal behavior. They found suicide attempters had longer sleep latency, lower sleep efficiency, and fewer late-night delta wave counts than normal controls. They also demonstrated that nonattempters, as compared to attempters, had less REM time and activity in the second REM period, but more delta wave counts in the fourth non-REM period. In the United States, suicide is the third cause of death among adolescents. Across all age groups, suicidal ideation is most common among adolescents. One factor that might contribute to adolescent suicidal ideation as well as suicidal attempts is the previously cited decline in SWS along with an increase in REM. Reduced delta wave counts may be a potential predictor of risk for suicidal ideation, but the issue has not been well studied. Given its clinical importance, the links between sleep changes in adolescence and the elevated risk for suicide in this group of children should be better studied. Anecdotal evidence suggests that suicidal attempts or plans are often preceded by dreams involving harm to the self, including so-called masochistic dreams.

Adolescent anorexia may be another disorder involving severe reductions in the amount of SWS. Nobili et al. (1999) documented significant reductions in SWS amounts in 10 adolescent anorectic girls relative to 10 age-matched healthy controls. Interestingly, most of the slow-wave activity in the anorectic girls occurred in the first NREM-REM cycle, with little or no NREM in the later portion of the night. Nobili et al. also reported that body mass index of the anorectics was correlated with the amount of slow-wave activity, strengthening the case for a relationship between changes in SWS and anorexia.

Dreams in Adolescents
Very few systematic studies have been conducted on dreams of teens. Nielsen et al. (2000), however, reported a high prevalence of disturbing dreams during adolescence, particularly in girls.

Sleep Entrainment of Gonadotropins During Sexual Maturation
During childhood, gonadal and certain adrenal functions are under tonic inhibition mediated by hypothalamic and other forebrain sites. The onset of puberty is triggered by disinhibition of hypothalamic regulatory centers resulting in gonadotropin (e.g., gonadotropin-releasing hormone [GnRH], luteinizing hormone [LH], and follicle-stimulating hormone [FSH]) release. Under the influence of these hormones, secondary sexual characteristics emerge. Morphological changes include height gains, breast development, genital development, hair growth and redistribution, muscle development, and cellular changes in selected brain areas including the hypothalamus. The timing of onset and the morphologic effects of puberty differ for boys and girls, with girls typically maturing earlier than boys.

Using an ultrasensitive immunofluorometric assay (DELFIA) to measure plasma LH and deconvolution analysis to depict LH secretory characteristics, Wu, Butler, Kelnar, Huhtaniemi, and Vehdhuis (1996) compared nocturnal pulsatile LH secretion in 16 boys in midchildhood, 8 prepubertal boys, 8 early pubertal boys, and 8 young adult men. They reported that the first increase in sleep-entrained GnRH/LH secretion occurred some 2 years before the clinical onset of puberty. From midchildhood to sexual maturity, LH production rate increased 39-fold. GnRH/LH pulse frequency showed only a relatively small (1.8-fold) increment from midchildhood to the clinical onset of puberty. The authors suggest that the puberty-inducing increment in LH plasma concentration from childhood to sexual maturity could be accounted for by an amplification of a preexisting ultradian rhythm of secretion. This amplification of a preexisting LH rhythm results in an increased mass of LH molecules secreted per burst. The amplification of existing LH secretion bursts may be accomplished by linking the existing LH rhythm with sleep state activation. Presumably, selected cellular rhythms (as yet unidentified) associated with sleep state activation stimulate a GnRH pulse generator in such a way as to modulate frequency and amplitude of GnRH/LH secretory bursts.

REM and Sexual Functions in the Adult

I review other aspects of REM expression and REM dreams in the adult in other chapters of this book. Here I focus on the impact of REM on sexual functions in the adult.

Anecdotal Evidence for a Relation Between Sexuality and Sleep

Converging lines of evidence implicate REM in development and maintenance of normal sexual function. REM deprivation early in life is associated with later impairment in sexual functions in the adult, at least in the rat and the monkey. There is also the long-standing observation (confirmed experimentally in rats; Vazquez-Palacios, Bonilla-Jaime, Retana-Marquez, & Velazquez-Moctezuma, 2002) that copulatory activity leads to increased sleepiness—at least in males.

Although large-scale analyses of dream content across hundreds of dream reports gathered from hundreds of participants find little or no overt sexual content in dreams, these same dream content studies reveal that when men have sexual dreams, they report content involving multiple anonymous sexual encounters more often than do women. Women, for their part, are more likely to report sex involving a familiar partner. These sex differences in content are not likely due to reporting biases induced by social desirability effects, given that these reports are anonymous. In addition, men more often report aggressive encounters with unknown male strangers than do women. These patterns in dream content, as Brubaker (1998) has pointed out, are consistent with sex differences in mating strategies.

Finally, there is the well-known phenonenon that nocturnal penile erections regularly and invariably occur in phase with the REM cycle. These facts and others I explore below raise the question of whether a functional relationship might exist between sexual function and REM sleep.

REM Deprivation and Sexual Function

Conflicting findings abound in the REM deprivation (REMD) literature with respect to its effects on sexual function. While Hicks, Bautista, and Phillips (1991) report no effects of REMD on rat sexual behavior, Velaquez-Moctezuma, Salazar, and Retana-Marquez (1996) reported that even when effects of the stress associated with the REMD procedure in rats are controlled, sexual behavior is radically impaired in male rats after selective REMD. When compared to control rats, REMD rats evidenced an increase in mount, intromission, and ejaculation latencies and in mount frequency as well. There was also a decrease in ejaculation frequency. Thus, while some measures of sexual drive (mount frequency) might increase after REMD, sexual function as measured by intromission and ejaculations may decline after REMD. Ferraz, Ferraz, and Santos (2001) also reported that REMD reduced sexual drive behaviors in rats by decreasing mount and intromission latencies, but increased sexual function behaviors by increasing copulatory efficiency and intromission rates.

Hormonal Effects

REM may contribute to recruitment and activation of sexual functions and related behavioral strategies via its modulation of key neuroendocrine systems (Van Cauter & Speigel, 1999). Prolactin release, for example, is related to REM, with its levels rising rapidly at sleep onset and peaking around 3 to 5 a.m. when REM predominates. Its release can be blocked by sleep deprivation. Prolactin is known to be crucial, not only for development of mammaries and synthesis of maternal milk proteins, but for development of reproductive and sexual behaviors as well (Bole-Feysot, Goffin, Edery, Binart, & Kelly, 1998). It stimulates an array of testicular functions in males and ovarian functions in females.

Oxytocin also displays a sleep-sensitive pattern of release in humans, with peak levels occurring at about 4 a.m., when REM sleep begins to predominate over NREM (Forsling, 1993). When injected centrally, oxytocin induces several of the behaviors associated with social bond formation in mammals, including maternal-infant contact, nursing in infants, caretaking behaviors in the mother, and species-typical reproductive behaviors in adults (Argiolas & Gessa, 1991; Insel, 1992). Oxytocin release may also be implicated in ability to orgasm.

Sex-related hormones are sleep sensitive as well: testosterone levels vary with the stages of sleep. Testosterone levels in males, for example, are highest at the transition from NREM stages to REM (Borbely & Tobler, 1989).

Melatonin

Melatonin is a hormone produced in the pineal gland and linked to onset of seasonal estrus in seasonally reproducing animals. It is released primarily during the night in both diurnal and nocturnal animals and thus can be used by seasonal breeders as a measure of day length. As day length increases in the spring, the longer light period inhibits melatonin production, leading to shorter durations for nighttime peak values. These changes in nocturnal melatonin levels then disinhibit the release of gonadotropins, bringing the animal into reproductive mode.

In humans, melatonin release begins to increase at around 10 p.m., with CNS levels peaking around 3 a.m. (when REM predominates) and then declining to very low levels by 8 a.m. Daytime levels are almost undetectable. Circulating levels of melatonin decrease dramatically in prepubertal children and may contribute to disinhibition of gonadotropins and to development of nocturnal entrainment of release of these gonadotropins. When melatonin is administered to humans, its primary effect is to increase sleepiness.

REM-Related Penile Erections

Fisher, Gross, and Zuch (1965) first reported the cyclic occurrence of penile erections with REM sleep periods. Later, Karacan (1966) reported that these REM-related erections could be observed in boys as young as 3 years old. Total times (mean of 190 minutes) spent in tumescence peaked in peripubertal boys and declined to a mean of 100 minutes in men in their seventies. Subsequent research revealed that appearance and duration of REM-related erections was not necessarily related to whether men were sexually active or not. Sleep-related erections (SREs) occur in all men, regardless of recent sexual activities. Nor are erections related to erotic content of dreams. The erections occur in association with all types of dream content. These facts, along with the fact that REM-related erections occur in both young children and in elderly men, argue against a purely reproductive function for this phenomenon.

Other findings suggest as well that REM-related genital arousal may not be confined to males. A number of reports have demonstrated similar REM-related genital arousal in females (Karacan, 1966; Van de Castle, 1994) such as increased circulatory activity in the genital area, clitoral erections, and increased pelvic thrusting in females during REM.

Brain regions responsible for sexual function overlap those that control sleep processes. A partial listing of these overlapping regions includes the paraventricular nucleus, the medial preoptic area, the bed nucleus of the stria terminalis, the amygdala, and the hippocampus. The medial preoptic area and the lateral preoptic nucleus of the hypothalamus are known to be implicated in sleep regulation, as lesions in these sites result in long-lasting insomnia. Stimulation and single-unit studies in the rat suggest that the preoptic area participates in generation of SWS and inhibition of wakefulness.

Schmidt (2000) has shown that REM-related penile erections are dependent upon specialized neuroanatomical regions in the basal forebrain and in the lateral preoptic area of the hypothalamus (LPOA). They found that lesioning the LPOA in rats disrupts nocturnal but not waking erections. LPOA lesioning also resulted in long-lasting insomnia characterized by a significant decrease in SWS amounts, but REM sleep architecture was not affected. Do these data imply that REM-related erections are in response to or generated from SWS neurophysiologic mechanisms? Whatever the case may be, it is clear that while SREs most often occur in tandem with REM sleep processes, SREs can be dissociated from REM. Lavie (1990), for example, reported intact penile erection cycles in a man who had sustained brain injuries, resulting in a drastic reduction in his REM sleep times (REM averaged 2% of total sleep). Penile erection cycles are also reported to occur in dolphins, who otherwise show no electrophysiologic signs of REM.

REM-related erections have been observed in all mammalian species where they were looked for, with the interesting exception of the nine-banded armadillo (Affani, Cervino, & Marcos, 2001). It is not clear why SREs are NREM-related rather than REM-related in this species. One possibility is that the armadillo differs from most other mammals in terms of its reproductive behaviors. Armadillos exhibit a rare reproductive phenomenon or strategy called polyembryony, which results in offspring that are genetic clones of one another. Among other things, polyembryony should reduce genetic conflict between siblings.

REM Across the Menstrual Cycle

Figure 2.2 depicts changes in the menstrual cycle in nonpregnant women. A word about the physiology of the menstrual cycle: the entire monthly cycle is driven by hormonal changes that are largely controlled at the level of the hypothalamus. At puberty, LH is secreted only during sleep, though it is not clear whether its release is associated with REM or NREM. In any case, the hypothalamus releases GnRH, which in turn stimulates the pituitary to release LH and FSH. In the first half of the cycle during the follicular stage, estrogen levels increase with the development of the follicle. LH levels decrease and FSH increases. Ovulation occurs at midcycle. Some authors report an increase in REM percentage (time spent in REM) during the follicular stage, but most studies find no significant changes in sleep architecture during the follicular stage. During the luteal stage, the corpus luteum secretes progesterone and estrogen. If fertilization does not occur, the corpus luteum regresses and menses occur. It can be seen from figure 2.2 that very little change in the amount of REM and SWS occurs throughout the monthly cycle. Stage 2 NREM sleep appears to increase during the luteal stage, probably at the expense of stage 1 light sleep, as REM and SWS percentages do not change appreciably across the cycle.

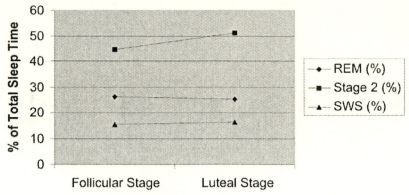

Figure 2.2. Sleep in the Menstrual Cycle

Sleep and Dreams in the Elderly

The most consistently reported change in the sleep architecture of healthy elderly persons is a decline in percentage of sleep composed of SWS (Bliwise, 2000). In some cases, SWS may occupy only 5 to 10% of total sleep. While there is great variability, REM percentage tends not to decline with age. One of the most interesting things about sleep patterns in the elderly is the great freedom with which they dream. While systematic studies are scarce, there appear to be increased themes surrounding "possible selves" and fulfillment of and striving after long-standing personal goals. While the elderly have their share of unpleasant dreams, as well as dreams of loss of resources and loved ones, wisdom themes as well as so-called transcendent and epic dreams are more likely to emerge in old age. More than the dreams of any other population, dreams of the elderly support Jung and Adler's contention that dreams reveal "purposes"—that our lives are guided more by personal purpose than by previous history.

CHAPTER 3

Phylogeny of Sleep

Some form of sleep is found in all mammals and birds and may be present in reptiles and even in invertebrates. The study of variation in sleep patterns in animals is the best method we have for studying potential adaptive functions of sleep. It is the only method we have for inferring its evolutionary history. Particularly important for an analysis of sleep's evolutionary history is to identify changes in sleep patterns as a function of divergences between species in evolutionary pathways. Modern mammalian and avian lineages, for example, are thought to have diverged from their reptilian ancestors about 250 million years ago. Modern extant forms of reptiles may retain some of the sleep characteristics of their ancestors who flourished before the rise of the mammals. Thus, studies of modern reptiles may reveal the form of sleep from which mammalian and avian sleep evolved. Before we can study comparative patterns of sleep expression, we must agree on what can count as sleep.

Definition of Sleep

Sleep is composed of behavioral, functional, physiologic, and electro-physiologic traits (see table 3.1). For most animals, sleep can only be identified via measurement of its behavioral and functional sleep traits, as their nervous systems do not support what has become known as full polygraphic sleep. Full polygraphic sleep refers to electrophysiologic measures of both REM and NREM sleep stages 1–4 identified via the EEG. It has become common, however, to use the term "full polygraphic sleep" to refer to an animal who exhibits most or all of the other three major components of sleep in addition to the electrophysiologic measures. When an animal exhibits all four major components of sleep, including the behavioral, electrophysiologic, physiologic, and functional components, then it is said that the animal exhibits full polygraphic sleep. Full polygraphic sleep, in this sense, has so far been documented only in primates (including humans).

Table 3.1. Criteria for the Definition of Sleep

1. Behavioral
   - Typical body posture
   - Specific sleeping site
   - Behavioral rituals before sleep (e.g., circling, yawning)
   - Physical quiescence
   - Elevated threshold for arousal and reactivity
   - Rapid state reversibility
   - Circadian organization of rest-activity cycles
   - Hibernation/torpor
2. Electrophysiological
   EEG
     NREM: high-voltage slow waves (quiet sleep)
     - spindles in some animals
     - K-complexes in some primates
     REM: low-voltage fast waves (REM, paradoxical sleep or active sleep)
     - hippocampal theta; PGO waves
   Electro-oculogram
     NREM: absence of eye movements or slow rolling eye movements
     REM: rapid eye movements
   EMG
     - Progressive loss of muscle tone from waking → NREM → REM
3. Physiological
   - REM: instabilities in heart rate, breathing, body temperature, etc. Other: penile tumesence
   - NREM: reduction in physiologic/metabolic processes; reduction of about 2°C in body temp
4. Functional
   Compensation of sleep deficit (homeostatic regulation):
   - enhancement of sleep time
   - intensification of the sleep process (e.g., enhanced EEG power in the delta range)

Adapted from Moorcroft, W. H. (2003). *Understanding Sleep and Dreaming*. Used with permission of Kluwer Academic/Plenum Publishers.

While REM and NREM have been identified in a large number of mammalian species, NREM in most of these species cannot be differentiated into four distinct stages as it is in several primate species.

Behavioral measures of sleep include a species-specific body posture and sleeping site, reduced physical activity (quiescence), reduced muscle tone, reduction in neck/nuchal muscle tone, paralysis of the antigravity muscles in some species, increased arousal threshold, and rapid reversibility to wakefulness. Physiologic indices of sleep include significant reductions in temperature and metabolism during NREM and significant lability in ANS, cardiovascular, and respiratory measures during REM, along with increases in metabolism. Electrophysiologic measures of REM include low-voltage fast waves, rapid eye movements, theta rhythms in the hippocampus, and PGO waves. Electrophysiologic measures of NREM include high-voltage slow waves (HVSW), spindles, and k-complexes. Functional indices of sleep include increased amounts of sleep after sleep deprivation, and increased sleep intensity after sleep deprivation.

Methodologic Issues in the Study of Comparative Sleep

Comparative Analyses

Comparative analyses have long been the cornerstone of evolutionary and functional hypothesis testing in biologic science. Within sleep science, findings from comparative analyses have formed the basis for several extremely fruitful and influential theories of mammalian sleep function, such as the "ontogenetic" hypothesis, where developmental REM sleep was theorized to be crucial for normal development of the brain, or the "energy-conservation" hypothesis, where NREM sleep quotas (durations) were thought to be linked to the need to conserve energy and to regulate metabolic rates. While these early hypotheses stimulated several lines of research that deepened our understanding of sleep function as well as clinical aspects of sleep disorders, they were necessarily limited by the comparative databases and comparative analytic techniques available at the time.

Inferences Concerning Sleep's Evolutionary History Based on Comparative Analyses

Rattenborg and Amlaner (2002) point out that thinking on the evolution of sleep has to some extent been distorted by an assumption that mammals are more advanced than nonmammals. Yet in some respects, birds have developed innovations in cortical laminar structure not observed in mammals. Similarly, reptiles have developed quite complex neural systems specialized to transduce light information into neural impulses that regulate rest-activity cycles (e.g., a parietal eye, a complex pineal system, a brain site homologous to the suprachiasmatic nucleus (SCN), etc.). Clearly, we should not be seduced by evolutionary stories that inevitably lead to big-brained species who sit at the top of the ladder and are the most fit or successful. Nor should we deny the fact that certain evolutionary transitions were crucial for development of big brains and therefore full polygraphic sleep in primates. One can identify such transitions and innovations without necessarily assuming that earlier steps in the pathway represent evolutionary dead ends in the taxa in which those transitions occurred. Rather, it is highly likely that sleep traits in those taxa continued to develop, sometimes slowly, sometimes rapidly, depending on selective pressures faced by the animals. Thus, differences in sleep traits across different taxa may, as Rattenborg and Amlaner point out, "actually reflect alternative means of fulfilling similar functions, rather than indicating different levels of sleep evolution" (p. 7).

On the other hand, when one or more of the behavioral, physiologic, electrophysiologic, or functional components of primate sleep are identified in taxa whose divergence from primates along the evolutionary tree can be accurately estimated (using molecular phylogenies and other phylogenetic techniques), then we can make some reasonable estimates concerning when selected traits of REM and NREM emerged in the line leading to the primates. Furthermore, when selected sleep traits are found to be associated with significant ecologic, life-history, or physiologic traits across taxa with similar biologies and brain structure, then it is reasonable to investigate those associations in hopes of revealing functional relationships. In short, comparative phylogenetic analyses of sleep variation can help us discern when a trait evolved, in how many lineages, how long it survived over evolutionary time, and what its consistent functional relationships might be.

Comparative analyses are typically carried out on large-scale databases that contain data points on dozens of variables, both sleep variables and variables hypothesized to be related to sleep, such as body size, metabolic rates, brain size, and so on. Previously constructed comparative databases suffered from a number of shortcomings related to the reliability and validity of the data contained in the databases. To begin with, the number of species represented in the databases was relatively small, usually between 50 and 80 species. The smaller the number of species, the lower the statistical power investigators had when analyzing the data sets. A related problem was that species represented in the database were not a randomly selected sample. Mammals were overrepresented.

The last comparative databases constructed on sleep variables, however, appear to have been those of Elgar et al. in 1988, and Zepelin in 1989. In order to see if the data abundance and representiveness problems had improved since then, my colleagues and I conducted a search of the relevant literature. The search revealed sources for data on daily sleep quotas (percentage of total sleep time spent in each sleep state) in at least 148 taxa (species and genera) representing 18 orders, 56 families, and 148 species. While data from rodents (N = 42 species and 13 families) and primates (N = 28 species and 8 families) were somewhat overrepresented, all extant orders of mammalia were represented, with more than one data source available for many species. This means that a new, updated comparative database on sleep in mammals, containing an N large enough to give it statistical power and representativeness, should now be possible.

Another shortcoming of previous sleep databases was that they had no ratings on the quality of the data contained in the database. Was the data gathered under reasonably similar conditions? Was it gathered on animals in the wild or in the laboratory? If in the laboratory, the animal may have been restrained in order to record EEG sleep changes. Restraint for animals may be very stressful, and this could affect the sleep recordings. What were ambient temperature conditions when sleep recordings were made? Sleep variables are known to be sensitive to small temperature changes. Was recording accomplished under light or dark conditions? Light inhibits some components of the sleep response (e.g., secretion of melatonin or other hormones) in some animals. It is also important to note that some animals are active during the dark period while others are not. All of these variables are known to affect an animal's sleep, and thus they need to be taken into account when using data compiled in these comparative databases.

To assess quality of the comparative data (sleep quotas) currently available, we studied 53 randomly selected articles from a list of 130 that turned up in our literature search. The 53 selected articles contained data on 84 species (i.e., some studies examined more than one species). Each study was given 1 point for each of the following procedures: (1) at least 24 hour EEG recordings, (2) EEG conducted under normal (for the animal) light-dark schedules, (3) EEG conducted only after the animal was adapted to the laboratory and recording procedure, (4) normal ad libitum diet, (5) normal ambient temperature (normal for the animal), (6) whether the animal was allowed to move freely (was not restrained), and (7) whether behavioral sleep data were recorded. Thus, the total possible score was 7 points. Results showed that mean data quality score was 5.09 (SD = 1.9). Most often studies lost points because they did not mention whether the animal was restrained or whether behavioral signs of sleep were recorded. This analysis indicates generally very high quality data obtained from these studies and available for inclusion in a comparative database. In addition, it shows that relatively uniform data collection procedures were employed by the bulk of the authors whose work involved collection of sleep data from animals.

Representativeness of Laboratory-Obtained Data

What about the problem of whether lab-obtained values on sleep measures truly reflect the sleep of these animals in the wild? Since EEG recordings are difficult to perform in the wild, sleep data are typically obtained outside of the animal's natural habitat. As reviewed by several authorities (Campbell & Tobler, 1984; Meddis, 1983; Walker & Berger, 1980b; Zepelin, 1989), sleep values obtained in the lab are not arbitrarily related to sleep values obtained in the wild but rather represent the animal's maximum capacity for sleep. When sleep values obtained in the lab are compared to values obtained in the wild for the same species, the lab-obtained values are invariably slightly longer than those obtained in the wild. Thus, most authorities conclude that lab-obtained values are predictably related to the animals' natural sleep processes and thus comparative analyses will not yield arbitrary findings with respect to relative sleep times across species or with respect to correlations between sleep times and nonsleep variables such as physiologic, ecologic, and life-history traits of the animals. The crucial condition for obtaining valid, nonarbitrary, and representative values is that lab conditions approximate (in terms of light-dark schedules, ambient temperature, diet, etc.) natural conditions for the animal in question. Most important, the animal must be adapted to the lab and recording procedures before sleep recordings are made. We have seen that the majority of available studies satisfy these minimal criteria (i.e., lab recording procedures approximate natural conditions for the animal and recordings are virtually never conducted until the animal is adapted to the lab). Thus, we can be reasonably confident that available data on sleep quota variation in mammals are a reasonable approximation to sleep variation in the wild.

Nevertheless, data obtained in the wild are preferable to data obtained in the lab when considering questions of sleep variation. It turns out that there are a number of studies that utilized telemetry to measure sleep architecture and sleep times in the wild. Data from telemetric recordings obtained under natural conditions are available for a number of species, for example: oppossums (Snyder, Bugbee, & Douthitt, 1972), hedgehogs (Snyder et al., 1972), baboons (Bert, Balzamo, Chase, & Pegram, 1975), lemurs (Vuillon-Cacciuttolo, Balzamo, Petter, & Bert, 1976), chimpanzees (Bert, Balzamo, Chase, & Pegram, 1970), rats (Borbely & Neuhaus, 1979), and rock and tree hyraxes (Snyder, 1974). Telemetric techniques have also been used to study the sleep of a number of marine mammals who were allowed to swim freely while recording was conducted (Lyamin, 1993; Lyamin, Manger, Mukhametov, Siegel, & Shpak, 2000; Lyamin et al., 1994; Mukhametov, 1984; Mukhametov et al., 1977; Ridgway, Harrison, & Joyce, 1975).

In summary, detailed analyses of data availability and data quality suggest that the sleep data now available for construction of a comparative database on sleep include (1) sleep quotas on at least 150 mammalian species, (2) data points (sleep quotas) that were collected under relatively uniform and rigorous data collection procedures, and (3) data points obtained under either natural conditions or recording conditions that approximated natural conditions for the animals. Thus, the available data appear to be reasonably valid indices of sleep processes in the animals studied and are reliable and usable for the kinds of comparative analyses discussed above.

Unfortunately, no such database has recently been constructed and analyzed. As mentioned above, the last such databases were constructed by Elgar et al. back in 1988 and by Zepelin in 1989. Thus, we are left with evaluating analyses of previously constructed databases. It should be kept in mind that even though many data quality problems were addressed by the scientists who gathered the data that appeared in these databases, other data quality problems were overlooked. Berger (1990) and Zepelin (2000), for example, argued that some of the data in comparative databases were questionable. Some body mass estimates in Elgar et al. (1988) differ from other published estimates by a factor of two to three. Most important, previous analyses did not adequately control for what is called phylogenetic independence of data points in the database and for body size.

Allometric and Phylogenetic Corrections

A large proportion of the variance in comparative biological variables is commonly associated with two factors: body size and phylogeny. Allometry is the study of how a trait scales with body size. Previous studies of sleep quotas have found negative correlations with body size (Zepelin, 1994), but little attention has been paid to establishing quantitative scaling relationships, despite the fact that regularities in these relationships may be important for understanding sleep variation in general.

With regard to the issue of phylogeny, the problem arises because comparative analyses look for similarities in traits across taxa in hope of discovering trends and function. But the degree of similarity between organisms is partly a function of their phylogenetic propinquity. Indeed, in order to properly describe even the allometric scaling of a trait, it is necessary to take phylogenetic effects into account (Harvey & Pagel, 1991; Nunn & Barton, 2000, 2001). Hence, analysis of scaling and of phylogenetic effects must go hand-in-hand. Properly conducted phylogenetic and allometric analyses can help us answer three fundamental questions about the evolution of sleep. First, do phylogenetically close species share similar REM and NREM times and proportions? Second, which sleep-related traits are evolutionarily primitive for mammals and birds, which are derived, and which similarities have arisen by convergent evolution? Third, do groups of taxa exhibit different scaling relationships? A deeper understanding of allometric patterns can be accomplished through understanding such "grade shifts" (Nunn & Barton, 2000). Finally, we can ask whether particular taxa evolved distinctively different patterns of sleep, and, if so, how these patterns might relate to other features of their biology.

Findings of Previous Comparative Analyses of REM and NREM in Mammals

Zepelin and Rechtschaffen (1974) compiled the first extensive database on sleep quotas and constitutional variables in a large number of mammalian species. Data were compiled on 53 species and included total sleep time per day, total QS time, total AS time, the active-quiet cycle length, and percentages derived from these basic quantities. Constitutional variables included basal metabolic rate, body weight, brain weight, and gestation period. They found that sleep cycle length and total sleep time were significantly correlated with all of the constitutional variables, but with brain weight emerging as the best predictor of sleep cycle length. This finding may be due to the fact that larger brains can support longer sleep cycles, or it may be due to something more fundamental about sleep biology. Perhaps

large brains require long sleep cycles because sleep performs a function
for the brain rather than for the body. On the other hand, large bodies are
often associated with large brains, so once again we return to the need to re-
analyze these comparative data using adequate phylogenetic and allometric
corrections.

Allison and Cicchetti (1976) later added a number of new ecologic
variables to Zepelin and Rechtschaffen's original database. These new
variables were designed to capture the extent to which a given species was
vulnerable to predation. Analyses on 39 species with complete data revealed
small but significant correlations between sleep parameters and the new
ecologic variables. Only gestation time, however, predicted AS. Next,
Zepelin (1980) and Meddis (1983) added new ecological and constitutional
measures to this growing database, including measures of diet, neonatal
brain weight, and altriciality (or immaturity at birth). Active sleep was
found to be significantly correlated with both gestational period and altriciality. Zepelin (1980, 1989) later replicated these findings, reporting significant correlations between AS times and altriciality. Meddis (1983), too,
confirmed this association, as well as an earlier documented association with
predatory threat. The latter finding, however, may be complicated by dis-
agreements concerning classifications of predators and prey.

Elgar et al. (1988) reevaluated these earlier analyses and added new
ecologic measures and new species (for a total of 69 species) to previously
constructed data sets but failed to find significant associations between sleep
quotas and most constitutional variables after controlling for body weight.
They did, however, find an inverse association between QS and metabolic
rate, indicating that the higher the metabolic rate, the less time spent in QS.
They also confirmed the association between altriciality and AS times
documented in previous studies. Subsequently, this study was criticized by
Berger (1990) on the grounds that a number of the species estimates were
highly questionable. Elgar, Pagel, and Harvey (1990) reanalyzed their data,
omitting the data points Berger objected to, and largely replicated their
original findings using a substantially reduced sample (42 species, giving
actual sample sizes of up to 30 families). However, one major difference
in the reanalysis was that REM duration was no longer associated with
altriciality after removal of the effects of body size. This may have been due
to a reduction in statistical power/sample size when reanalysis was conducted. In any case, Zepelin (1989) later found a relation between altriciality
and REM duration in an updated data set containing 84 taxa. The correlation between REM and altriciality remained even after adjusting for body
size. Thus, the relation between altriciality and AS has survived repeated
enlargements of the database and increasingly sophisticated statistical tests
of the association.

I turn now to a survey of comparative sleep patterns focusing on mammals
but with a short excursus on sleep in reptiles and birds. Before I detail

electrophysiologic patterns of sleep among these animals, I first want to touch on some of the other indices of sleep that figure in the broad definition of sleep summarized in table 3.1.

Circadian Organization

The placing or occurrence of the sleep period during the 24-hour day varies greatly in mammals. In primates, sleep is usually monophasic or consolidated into one long sleep period at night. In most mammals, sleep is polyphasic, with bouts of sleep occurring during the day and night. In species such as the cat and the guinea pig, sleep occurs in short bouts at virtually any time of the day or night. The factors responsible for the different patterns of phasing remain unclear.

Sleep Postures and Closed Eyes

In most terrestrial mammals, sleep occurs with the animal in a recumbent position and with eyes closed. It is not at all clear why eyes are closed in most species when they sleep. Indeed, many animals sleep with their eyes only half closed (ruminants) or with one eye open (some aquatic mammals and some birds). The phenomenon of unilateral eye closure during sleep makes it more difficult to argue that open eyes are incompatible with sleep due to the arousing effects of the sensory barrage that would occur with open eyes. On the other hand, studies have shown that an open eye in animals who sleep with one eye open is usually contralateral to the hemisphere that is asleep, and thus the open eye is transmitting information to an awake hemisphere in these animals. If it can be confirmed that the open eye is always transmitting information only to the awake hemisphere, then we can more safely conclude that animals sleep with their eyes closed in order to avoid being awakened by arousing stimuli. On the other hand, we also need to establish that in species with unilateral eye closure, the incoming sensory information is prevented from traveling to sites in the sleeping hemisphere that could arouse the animal. If the animal is in SWS, then it is likely that information reaching cortical sites could not arouse the animal, but if information reached subcortical sites, the incoming stimulus may be able to arouse the animal.

While unilateral eye closure is often thought to be related to predator detection, it also occurs in species without natural predators, such as whales. Similarly, it is not clear why most animals sleep in a recumbent position. While REM-related paralysis is incompatible with standing, some ruminants sleep while standing. But this may be a special case, and these animals may obtain many of the benefits of sleep from an intermediate sleep state known as drowsiness.

In aquatic mammals, sleep may occur in a quiescent state underwater near the ocean floor or may occur while the animal is swimming. Sea otters, on the other hand, prefer to sleep floating on the ocean's surface. In both cases, the animal may keep one eye open—depending on which hemisphere is asleep. In birds, sleep may occur in a quiescent state, again with one eye open and with the head or bill resting inside a wing. Other birds may sleep while on the wing, though this has been difficult to verify. Still other birds may sleep while hanging upside down from a branch of a tree. Bats, too, sleep while hanging upside down from a cave wall. Sleep for bats is a social process in that nutrients (e.g., blood in vampire bats) may be passed from bat to bat during sleep or at least during a quiescent state. Many juvenile mammals sleep next to siblings or to mothers, thus deriving heat from these relatives. Sleep is not a passive process in mammalian juveniles, as they can grasp, suck, and snuggle while asleep. The juvenile rat, for example, "expects" a social environment and appears to be adapted to sleeping in groups near a mother who provides heat, protection, and nutrients. Adult rodents sleep curled up within a hidden niche or a burrow. Many hoofed animals evidence both typical sleep patterns and drowsiness while standing. They typically sleep lying on their side with legs stretched out. In ruminants, sleep occurs while the animal is standing, with eyes blinking or partially open, and ruminating persists into SWS but not REM sleep.

Effects of Social Conflict on Sleep Sites

Sleep sites vary systematically with social organization in primates (Anderson, 1998). Social relationships among individuals in a group influence arrangements of sleeping clusters in primates. Kin relations, reproductive status, and dominance relations influence spatial and huddling relations during sleep. Internest differences, nest architecture, and nest use also vary with social relationships. In macaques (e.g., rhesus and bonnets), for example, the most frequent huddle size is two and composed primarily of male-female consortships, mother-infant pairs, or same-sex individuals. Individuals among baboons, gorillas, and orangutans prefer to sleep next to their mothers until well into subadult years. Juveniles vigorously protest rejection when they request being received into a huddle, whether or not the huddle is with their mother. Protest includes loud and persistent vocalizations until the juvenile is accepted into some huddle for the night. While galago males and females do not typically sleep together, galago females sleep together in relatively large groups (Bearder, 1987). Nest sites may reflect female dominance patterns in some primates, while predator detection may drive gibbon site selection (Fruth & McGrew, 1998).

Ramakrishnan and Coss (2001) reported that adult Nilgiri langurs, Hanuman langurs, and bonnet macaques preferred to sleep in tall trees with high boles, presumably to discourage predators. On the other hand, dominant adult males (langurs) usually slept on higher branches than adult females who, in turn, slept above subadults. Langurs usually slept alone on separate branches, while macaques slept in clusters. Noser, Gygax, and

Tobler (2003) reported that sleep duration was correlated inversely with social rank (increasing with decreasing rank) in females and juveniles in gelada baboons. Di Bitetti, Vidal, Baldovino, and Benesovsky (2000) reported that tufted capuchin monkeys preferred to sleep in tall emergent species of trees with large crowns and many horizontal branches. As in other primate species, adult females typically slept with their kin and infants.

Fruth and Hohmann (1993) and others (Fruth & McGrew, 1998) have noted that among the great apes, a number of filiative and cooperative interactions such as play, grooming, sexual encounters, and mother-infant nursing take place in the nests at sleep sites. This suggests that sleep processes themselves may also be influenced by social factors in the primates. Reite, Stynes, Vaughn, Pauley, and Short (1976) showed that in the pigtail macaque, infants of dominant females had shorter latency to sleep onset times and that REM sleep was selectively inhibited after maternal separation. The suppression of REM sleep (with a concomitant increase of NREM) persisted in peer-reared juveniles.

Yawning

In primates, yawning may be contagious or a signal meant to synchronize sleep times. Yawning is associated with sleepiness and appears to occur in all mammals and in some birds, and may even occur in reptiles. Yawns are involuntary openings of the mouth, inspiration of a breath, closing of the eyes, and stretching of torso and limbs. Like REM sleep, yawning is associated with cholinergic excitation and dopaminergic inhibition. Oxytocin and testosterone infusions can induce yawns as well. Interestingly, when oxytocin is injected into paraventricular nucleus or the hippocampus, it induces both yawning and penile erections. Yawning occurs in the fetus and throughout the life span.

In humans, at least one form of yawning is contagious—just the sight of another person yawning can trigger a yawn, suggesting a social function for yawning. When yawning functions as a signal (as in the case of contagious yawning), then it may acquire costly traits (placing the yawner in a vulnerable position, etc.). In that case, receivers will tend to use the signal to infer the current status of the sender. According to costly signaling theory, the yawn would then convey a message that implies that the sender is currently handicapped ("I am not fully aroused and my attentional skills are flagging, etc., and therefore I am vulnerable"). But it is far from clear whether such an analysis helps us to understand the functions, if any, of contagious yawning. A far more likely explanation is that the contagious yawn serves to synchronize sleep behaviors of a group of primates.

Comparative data on other forms of (noncontagious) yawning in relation to sleep variables are lacking and thus not much can be said about their functions and potential relation to sleep. Nevertheless, the yawn's wide taxonomic distribution in the animal kingdom suggests an ancient lineage as well as an important functional relationship with sleep states. It would be interesting to know whether manipulations of yawning (i.e., inhibiting or enhancing rates of yawning) have systematic effects on either REM or NREM (or both). It would further be interesting to know whether yawning occurs in species with little or no REM.

Homeostatic Regulation of Sleep Varies Across Taxa and Indicates That It Has an Adaptive Function

Sleep is a need and whether we like it or not we eventually succumb tosleep. It is an involuntary physiologic function. Following SD in mammals, there is a compensatory rebound in some aspect of sleep such that a relatively constant daily amount of sleep is maintained over the long term. This homeostatic component of sleep may not be confined to mammalian sleep as once believed. Compensatory increases in sleep amount and sleep intensity have now been demonstrated in some nonmammalian species. The manifestations of sleep rebound phenomena, not surprisingly, vary across species. In mammals, the deprivation of NREM sleep leads to a remarkable increase of EEG slow waves. REM sleep is also homeostatically regulated, but it is unclear whether an intensity dimension exists for REM sleep. This homeostatic component of sleep regulation is morphologically and functionally distinct from the circadian regulatory sites and processes. While both are linked to hypothalamic networks, the circadian system depends on the suprachiasmatic nucleus, while the homeostatic system does not. Varying the duration of SD showed that the increase in slow-wave activity (SWA; mean EEG power density approximately 0.75–4.0 Hz) is a function primarily of the duration of prior waking. Because SWA in mammals is determined by duration of prior sleep and waking when sleep is initiated, SWA should occur before other forms of sleep, and amount of SWA should decline as the need for sleep dissipates. It is not currently known what wake-related process or agent is being homeostatically regulated. Whatever the process is, however, it must be adaptive for the organism (otherwise the organism would not need to regulate its amount). Thus, one question to be investigated in studies of the adaptive functions of sleep is what is being regulated in species that evidence a homeostatically regulated sleep process.

Hibernation and Torpor

Hibernation and torpor are not typically considered part of the definition of behavioral sleep—yet intuitively most investigators feel that hibernation and torpor are states closely related to sleep. Surely investigation of hibernation and torpor may yield clues to the functions of sleep.

Several orders of mammals contain hibernating species or species that enter torpor, including the monotremes (echidna), the marsupials (murine opposum), insectivora (hedgehog), chiroptera (brown bats), primates (dwarf lemur), and rodents (Kilduff, Krilowicz, Milsom, Trachsel, & Wang, 1993). According to Nedergaard and Cannon (1990), no mammals larger than a marmot (about 5 kg) hibernate, despite the substantial energy savings that come from hibernation. The reason is that as body size increases, metabolic rate (MR) increases at a fixed rate (MR = 3.34 × [body mass(kg)]$^{0.75}$) and not in proportion to body mass. Thus, potential energy savings from a maneuver like hibernation decrease as body mass increases. Bears appear to be a counterexample to this rule. However, they are not true hibernators. During winter their body temperature does not decrease beyond the level of normal sleep, and the bear remains alert and active in the den. Typically it is the pregnant female who retires to the den for the entire winter. She gives birth to her cubs and nourishes them, often while in a state of sleep. To accomplish this feat, she bulks up during the feeding season and lives off fat reserves during the winter.

A hibernation bout is entered through SWS. Body temperature drifts to ambient temperature until it is below 10°C. Metabolism shifts to lipid catabolism in a kind of slow starvation. Both REM sleep and wakefulness are suppressed. During the hibernation season, the hibernator will regularly arouse and then return to the hibernating state. It is not known why hibernators arouse regularly from hibernation, particularly if the function of hibernation is to conserve energy. Arousals are costly in energetic terms. Moreover, the animals arouse from hibernation and promptly go into SWS, prompting some investigators to question whether they are sleep deprived. At the end of a bout of hibernation, the animal rapidly warms itself up, relying mostly on nonshivering thermogenesis associated with brown adipose tissue to do so.

Whatever the function of hibernation, the fact that the hibernator regularly arouses to go into SWS suggests that the function of SWS may not simply be to conserve energy, as a hibernating animal expends no appreciable amount of energy.

Survey of Findings on the Electrophysiologic Features of Sleep in Reptiles, Birds, and Mammals

Reptiles
Unlike birds and mammals, polygraphic signs of active/REM sleep appear to be absent in most and perhaps all reptiles. Some investigators have assumed that because avian and mammalian sleep exhibit electrophysiologic signs of both REM and NREM while reptiles do not, sleep processes in birds and mammals may reflect common descent from a reptilian ancestor

with similar sleep patterns. Alternatively, the similar sleep processes of birds and mammals may be due to convergent evolution. Convergent evolution would suggest that similar sleep patterns of birds and mammals occur because these animals developed similar solutions to common problems. Both birds and mammals are endothermic species. Sleep processes are implicated in temperature regulation, at least in mammals, and therefore the evolution of similar REM and NREM sleep processes in birds and mammals may be due to the emergence of the need for complex thermoregulatory processes to support endothermy in these animals.

On the other hand, some authorities hold that reptiles are not a monophyletic group and do not share a common ancestor. In any case, if birds descended from a common reptilian stock, they would be most closely related to the crocodilians. Life history characteristics of crocodiles are more similar to life history characteristics of birds than any other reptilian species. Burghardt (1998) for example, claims that crocodiles show postnatal parental care of young, along with complex vocalization systems that signal contact and separation distress. Some reptilian species also show elements of juvenile play. These considerations predict that if full polygraphic REM was a mammalian innovation linked to altriciality and related factors, then crocodilians should exhibit some elements or protoforms of REM. We will see below that some reptilian species exhibit sharp spikes in the context of HVSW activity during their quiescent states.

The similarities between mammalian and avian sleep, in any case, are not as deep or clear as once thought. REM sleep is fleeting and NREM sleep may not be homeostatically regulated in birds. The dissimilarity of sleep processes in birds and mammals, of course, does not rule out convergent evolution of sleep in these animals. Rather, it suggests caution when extrapolating REM's evolutionary history from supposed similarities of REM-like processes across taxa.

While behavioral signs of sleep are clearly observable in reptiles, correlations between these behavioral signs of sleep and selected EEG indices are difficult to evaluate, given the complexities of recording sleep EEGs from the reptilian scalp and brain. Early studies by Flanigan and others reported an association between behavioral sleep and intermittent high-voltage spikes and sharp waves recorded from various brain structures in crocodilians, lizards, and turtles. Other investigations found no such association between behavioral sleep and high-amplitude spikes and sharp waves in the same animals. Hartse (1994) argued that high-amplitude spikes and sharp waves define a reptilian sleep state homologous with mammalian SWS.

High-voltage slow waves superimposed on the waking and sleeping EEG in reptiles has been proposed as a precursor of SWA found in the sleep of mammals. The equation of reptilian HVSW with mammalian SWA is supported by findings (Flanigan, 1973) of compensatory rebound of sleep-related processes including EEG spikes after SD in reptiles. The latency to behavioral sleep was increased and the duration of behavioral sleep was increased as well after SD in reptiles.

With respect to REM, the consensus at this point is that reptiles do not exhibit it. When Frank (1999) reviewed the literature on reptilian sleep, he concluded that no convincing evidence had yet been produced of REM-like states in reptiles. Rattenborg and Amlanar (2002) also called the evidence for REM in reptiles "equivocal." Even when investigators claim to have found signs of REM in a reptile, they have hitherto failed to report whether those signs were observed while the animal was unresponsive to the environment (i.e., whether arousal thresholds were elevated) or other crucial signs of behavioral sleep. Thus, it may be that putative REM-like episodes in reptiles were actually brief arousals into waking or some form of waking. On the other hand, crocodilian sharp waves and spike activity in the context of HVSW may be a kind of indeterminate or mixed form of what is called in mammalian species REM and NREM, and thus these reptiles may exhibit protoforms of REM.

Monotremes

Composed of three extant species (two species of echidna and the duck-billed platypus), monotremes are thought to have diverged from the main mammalian line prior to the divergence of marsupials and placental mammals. Allison, Van Twyver, and Goff's (1972) original polysomnographic study of the short-beaked echidna (*Tachyglossus aculeatus*) revealed unequivocal SWS but no EEG signs of REM. Siegel, Manger, Nienhuis, Fahringer, and Pettigrew (1996) investigated activity of brain stem reticular neurons in the same species. Patterned reticular neuronal activity varies consistently in REM and NREM states. Discharge rate is high and irregular during REM and low and regular during SWS. Siegel et al. found irregular reticular discharge patterns during SWS in the short-beaked echidna (i.e., a mixture of REM and NREM signs). Rapid eye movements were also later recorded in the duck-billed platypus despite no overt EEG signs of REM. Thus, the monotremes appear to exhibit a mixed, indeterminate form of sleep containing elements of both REM and NREM mammalian sleep states. Siegel and others have suggested that mammalian sleep states emerged out of this primordial hybrid state of indeterminate sleep with SWS and REM segregating into independent brain states dependent on CNS organization of the animal.

Nicol, Andersen, Phillips, and Berger (2000) reported that they could detect REM characterized by concurrent cortical activation, reduced tonic EMG activity, and rapid eye movements in short-beaked echidnas under low, thermo-neutral, and high-ambient temperatures. Some investigators have suggested that the REM sleep episodes reported by Nicol et al. actually reflect a quiet waking state in these animals. These studies of REM in monotremes have forced us to admit that some REM-like electrophysiologic activity occurs in these animals, but the work also confirms previous impressions that full polygraphic REM without signs of SWA does not occur in monotremes.

Aquatic Mammals

Members of three different orders that contain aquatic mammals—cetaceans (dolphins, porpoises, and whales), carnivores (seals, sea lions, and otters), and sirenians (manatees)—typically engage in unihemispheric sleep. Cetaceans exhibit a clear form of unihemispheric SWS (USWS). EEG signs of REM are absent, but cetaceans show other behavioral signs of REM including rapid eye movements, penile erections, and muscle twitching. The two main families of pinnipeds, Otariidae (sea lions and fur seals) and Phocidae (true seals), show both unihemispheric and bihemispheric forms of sleep. Phocids sleep underwater (obviously holding their breath) while both hemispheres exhibit either REM or SWS. Amazonian manatees (*Trichechus inunguis*) also sleep under water, exhibiting three sleep states: bihemispheric REM, bihemispheric SWS, and USWS. Both hemispheres awaken to surface and breathe.

Sleep deprivation in an animal exhibiting unihemispheric sleep may evidence unihemispheric sleep rebound, prompting some authorities to claim that sleep serves a primary function for the brain rather than the body. It appears that sleep rebound effects may occur only for local regions of the forebrain. The data on unihemispheric sleep in marine mammals also suggest that REM and NREM serve distinct functions, as animals without full polygraphic REM can survive. In addition, when REM occurs in marine mammals, it is always bihemispheric. The bilateral nature of REM may be considered one of its costs, and the brain structure of certain marine mammals, apparently, cannot bear these costs.

Despite the lack of cortical activation characteristic of REM, cetaceans show other behavioral signs of REM including rapid eye movements, penile erections, and muscle twitching. Interestingly, even when full polygraphic REM occurs in aquatic mammals, it never occurs unihemispherically.

Explanations of the loss of EEG signs of REM and the emergence of unihemisphericity of SWS in some aquatic mammals tend to reference the supposed incompatibility of REM-related muscle atonia and breathing while underwater. Yet, as just described, other seagoing mammals with similar ecologic constraints (e.g., Phocidae) evidence bihemispheric REM sleep even while underwater. Given the alternative means of sleeping and breathing in water observed in pinnipeds, one would expect manatees (order Sirenia) to display either of these strategies. Surprisingly, however, Amazonian manatees (*Trichechus inunguis*) hold their breath underwater during REM sleep, bihemispheric SWS, and USWS, and awaken both hemispheres to surface to breathe. Thus, unlike that in dolphins and Otariidae seals, USWS in manatees is not clearly linked to surfacing to breathe. Nor does the relatively advanced nature of the cetacean brain help explain USWS and the absence of EEG REM in cetaceans. Other mammals with equally developed brains (such as primates) express abundant REM.

As in birds, unihemispheric sleep in aquatic mammals is associated with keeping one eye open during sleep—typically the eye contralateral to the hemisphere that is asleep. Goley in 1999 (quoted in Rattenborg & Amlaner, 2002) reported that when a group of sleeping Pacific white-sided dolphins (*Lagenorhynchus obliquidens*) swim slowly side-by-side in a group, they preferentially direct the open eye toward the other dolphins, as if watching to maintain contact with the group. Interestingly, when the sleeping dolphins switched, on an hourly basis, from one side of the group to the other, the side with the open eye switched accordingly, as if allowing each hemisphere a turn to sleep. Many male dolphins who swim in groups do so in order to monopolize access to a fertile female. Therefore, the open eye may be keeping an eye on the herded female.

Avian Sleep

As is the case with mammals, birds can be either monophasic (with one consolidated period of sleep per day) or polyphasic sleepers (with several short episodes of sleep per day). Birds appear to exhibit a special form of SWS and very little REM-like sleep. SWA in birds does not appear to be homeostatically regulated. SWA in NREM sleep in pigeons does not decline in the course of the dark period, suggesting that SWA in these animals is not building up some chemical that was depleted during waking. Moreover, SWA does not appear to increase after SD. Unlike mammals, sleep spindles are absent during NREM in birds. In addition to conventional SWS, birds also display sleep states that simultaneously combine features of both wakefulness and SWS. As in aquatic mammals, unilateral eye closure and USWS also occur in birds (reviewed in Rattenborg, Amlaner, & Lima, 2000).

Avian REM-like sleep states are associated with desynchronized EEG, impaired thermoregulation, and higher arousal thresholds, but they last only seconds and are cumulatively only one-quarter the amount typically reported for mammalian species. Moreover, there appears to be no REM rebound following REM sleep deprivation. Thus, while REM-like episodes occur in birds, full polygraphic REM probably does not.

Conclusion

Although not reviewed in this chapter, it should be mentioned that fish and amphibians exhibit some behavioral signs of sleep, though not of two types of sleep, as in mammalian REM and NREM. This fact, along with the evidence presented in chapter 5 concerning solid signs of behavioral sleep in the fruit fly, suggests that sleep is a very ancient adaptation indeed and that its benefits outweigh the risks associated with quiescence and reduced responsiveness to the environment. We do not see evidence, however, of the emergence of distinct sleep states until we come to the reptiles. The presence of HVSW as well as sharp spikes in the reptilian sleep EEG suggests that what is now called SWS in mammals first appeared in reptiles. The fact that some aspects of EEG sleep in reptiles appear to exhibit rebound effects after SD supports the argument that some form of SWS is present in reptiles. REM, however, does not occur in reptiles, with the possible exception of the crocodiles.

Consistent with the idea that SWS is present in reptiles is evidence that they may engage in some form of unihemispheric sleep. Rattenborg and Amlaner (2002) point out that many reptiles keep one eye open during behavioral sleep, suggesting that sleep may occur unihemispherically in these animals. The discovery of some form of unihemispheric sleep in reptiles would be significant because it would suggest that typical mammalian sleep (which is bihemispheric, with both eyes closed in most mammalian species, excluding a minority of aquatic mammals) is the exception among animals rather than the rule and that mammals could bear the costs associated with bihemispheric sleep while most other animals could not. It may be that REM is a mammalian innovation and that only mammals engage in full polygraphic REM. REM, furthermore, appears to always engage both hemispheres, and therefore bihemispheric sleep always involves REM.

The costs of bihemispheric sleep (and by inference REM) must be considerable, given that some mammals revert to unihemispheric sleep when the environment (e.g., the ocean) makes it more costly. It would be interesting to know if unihemispheric sleep occurs in any terrestrial mammal. To date, no such evidence has emerged. Indeed, in all mammals studied to date, both REM and NREM appear and are bihemispheric. Theoretically, unihemispheric sleep might occur in mammals who have little or no REM. There are, however, no cases of terrestrial mammals without REM that I am aware of. On the other hand, one report (Bert et al., 1975) suggests that stage 4 SWS is reduced or absent in baboons due to their precarious sleeping sites high up in the forest canopy. If this report can be confirmed, then it appears that at least one terrestrial mammal dispenses with SWS rather than with REM when forced to curtail its sleep. If the precarious sleeping site is the reason for the reduction in stage 4 in this animal, one wonders why REM rather than SWS is not curtailed, given the motor paralysis associated with REM. One further wonders if there is any evidence for unihemispheric sleep in the baboon that dispenses with SWS. Until the case of the baboon is settled, it appears that we must conclude that unihemipheric sleep does not occur in terrestrial mammals.

Why did mammals give up the ability to facultatively switch from bihemispheric sleep to unihemispheric sleep when needed? Apparently, some aspect of the biology of mammals (excepting again the aquatic mammals who exhibit unihemispheric sleep) prevents the switch to unihemispheric sleep. Mammals prefer to engage in REM despite its costs. Consideration of the distribution of unihemispheric sleep in all advanced animals except ter-restrial mammals, as well as the fact that full polygraphic REM only seems to occur bihemispherically (and therefore does not occur in reptiles, birds, and selected aquatic mammals), suggests that full polygraphic REM is metabolically costly and is an invention of the mammalian order.

The discovery that a form of unihemispheric SWS potentially exists in reptiles suggests that SWS emerged prior to REM sleep in evolutionary history. With the appearance of protomammals, the monotremes, signs of REM begin to appear in the sleep EEG. With the appearance of marsupials and placental mammals, full polygraphic REM emerges along with bihe-mispheric sleep. Avian REM and NREM are substantially different from mammalian sleep states, as the avian versions do not exhibit sleep rebound effects after sleep deprivation. Reptilian HVSW, on the other hand, does ex-hibit signs of sleep rebound effects. Thus, avian sleep appears to be an exam-ple of independent evolution of sleeplike states.

Although I have emphasized the differences in avian and mammalian sleep, other investigators are impressed with their similarities. Both forms of sleep, REM and NREM, for example, seem to exist in birds and mammals, whereas only mixed or hybrid combinations of features of REM and NREM appear to exist in reptilian and monotreme sleep states. The lack of distinct sleep states in reptiles may reflect the lack of an enlarged laminated cortical structure in reptiles, similar to the neocortex in mammals or wulst in birds. On the other hand, monotremes exhibit advanced cortical structure (including a relatively enlarged prefrontal cortex in the echidna), yet they do not exhibit two clearly segregated and distinct sleep states.

I have argued that SWS appeared before REM and that mammalian REM and NREM emerged from a hybrid combination of REM and NREM that first appeared in monotremes. This position is similar to that of Karamanova (1982) and to Siegel et al. (1996). Both Siegel and Karaman-ova, on the other hand, place the appearance of a mixed indeterminate form of sleep before the appearance of the monotremes, that is, in reptiles.

CHAPTER 4

REM-NREM Signaling and Interactions

I have reviewed a number of ontogenetic and phylogenetic factors that appear to influence expression of REM. In addition to the brain circuits responsible for REM regulation (summarized in chapter 1), one other factor strongly influences REM expression: NREM physiology. Some of the properties of REM sleep and REM dreams are influenced by processes of NREM sleep and NREM dreams, and vice versa. The two sleep states appear to have evolved out of the same hybrid or indeterminate form of sleep seen in reptiles and monotremes. In addition, REM and NREM are known to emerge developmentally from an indeterminate sleep state that seems to combine features of both REM and NREM. It may also be the case that when one sleep state is impaired in association with some neuro-psychiatric or neurologic disorder, the other sleep state will often be affected as well and often in an inverse fashion, suggesting that the two sleep states are in some kind of mutual inhibitory balance. When, for example, REM processes are enhanced in depressive disorders, certain NREM sleep indices (such as delta count) are reduced. Finally, aside from pathology, NREM sleep always appears before REM. This suggests that some portions of REM's expression appear in response to something that occurs in NREM. Benington and Heller (1994) have called attention to the fact that REM amounts and the interval between REM periods is related to the amount of NREM that has elapsed since sleep onset—not only the amount of wake time, again suggesting that something in REM undoes or responds to some-thing in NREM. I summarize evidence which suggests that the two sleep states interact in mammals and that this interaction is functional: that is, it promotes certain physiologic processes. It is also possible that the dream content of one sleep state influences dream content of the other sleep state. However, as yet very few data are available on this issue. I nevertheless review what data are available in hopes of learning something new about formation of REM dream content and of stimulating more research in this area.

Physiologic Interactions of REM and NREM

The two major mammalian sleep states, REM and NREM, are, to some extent, in mutual inhibitory balance with one another such that activation of NREM inhibits activation of key REM processes and vice versa. Selected processes of REM and NREM also appear to operate conflictually by opposing one another's physiologic effects on certain growth factors. While, for example, NREM acts to enhance release of GH, REM is associated with enhanced release of SS, a growth hormone inhibitor (Van Cauter et al., 1998). Similarly, while corticotropin-releasing hormone (CRH) suppresses NREM, it enhances REM sleep indices, including rebound effects after REM sleep deprivation (Steiger, 2003).

REM-NREM interactions may operate antagonistically with respect to other functions as well. While NREM enables an enhanced response to infectious challenge, REM seems to impair immunoregulatory functions (Krueger, Majde, & Obal, 2003). Fever and thermogenesis are difficult to mount during REM, and several proinflammatory cytokines such as interferon alpha, interleukin 1 (IL-1), and tumor necrosis factor (TNF) enhance NREM but suppress REM in rabbits (Inoue, Honda, Kimura, & Zhang, 1999; Obal & Krueger, 2003). While autonomic, cardiac, renal, and respiratory functions are stable in NREM, they are quite unstable in REM (Orem & Barnes, 1980; Parmeggiani, 2000). While thermoregulatory capacities are intact (but downregulated) in NREM, they are mostly absent in REM (Szymusiak et al., 1998). While cerebral blood flow volumes are downregulated in NREM, they are enhanced in REM (Maquet & Phillips, 1999; Orem & Barnes, 1980). While muscle tone is intact in NREM, it is absent in REM (Lai & Siegel, 1999). While the EEG is synchronized in NREM, it is desynchronized in REM (Steriade & McCarley, 1990).

Antagonistic Cellular Interactions in Regulation of REM

Hobson and Pace-Schott (2002), Steriade and McCarley (1990), and others have presented a great deal of experimental evidence which suggests that regulation of REM is governed by two major neural ensembles that act in an antagonistic fashion to turn on or turn off REM. Briefly, REM is generated by cholinergic neurons originating within the peribrachial regions known as the laterodorsal tegmental and pedunculopontine tegmental (LDT/PPT) nuclei, and is inhibited by noradrenergic and serotonergic neurons in the locus coeruleus and dorsal raphe, respectively. Activation of cholinergic REM is due to removal of inhibition of cholinergic cells in the LDT/PPT normally sustained by aminergic efferents. In sum, REM expression is regulated by antagonistic cellular groups with aminergic cell groups inhibiting expression of REM and cholinergic groups promoting expression of REM. When cholinergic REM-on cells are activated, aminergic REM-off cell groups are inhibited, and vice versa.

McCarley and Hobson (1975) presented a mathematical model of these REM-on and REM-off interactions. They found that REM-NREM interactions could be accurately captured using the classical Lotka-Volterra equations that describe conflict between predator and prey populations in field and ecological biology. Typically, the growth of the predator group depends upon and occurs at the expense of the prey group. Growth of the predator population is slow at first, but then exponential when prey are abundant. When the food supply grows scarce, the predator population crashes, and predators remain rare. When the prey population recovers, the cycle repeats itself. In the mathematical model, the REM-off cells are the predators, as they inhibit/suppress the prey population of REM-on cells. Levels of activation in the two (REM-on and REM-off) neuronal groups represent population levels of the prey and predators. As inhibitory aminergic neurotransmitter levels decline, the activation levels of cholinergic REM-on cells recover and so forth. The equations describing reciprocal interactions between the two cell groups accurately predicted the cyclical alterations in firing rates observed in the two populations of neurons responsible for REM-on/REM-off dynamics in the cat pontine brain stem.

More recently, several groups have presented a picture of sleep state regulation involving opposing cellular interactions occurring in the hypothalamus and basal forebrain (Lu et al., 2002; Morrison et al., 1999; Zaborszky & Duque, 2003) that initiate and terminate a REM period. This indicates that REM and NREM regulatory networks interact at several hierarchical levels of the neuraxis from the brain stem up to the forebrain. I summarize only the findings for opposing interactions at the level of the hypothalamus, as the hypothalamus is known to be crucial for sleep, growth, and a number of other fundamental regulatory functions (Nishino, 2003).

Lu et al. (2002) found that lesions to a group of sleep-active cells in the ventrolateral preoptic (VLPO) nucleus of the hypothalamus decreases NREM, while lesions to cells in an area dorsomedial to the VLPO (the extended VLPO) decreases REM but not NREM. In dark-treated rats with increased REM times, Fos-positive cells (indicating activation) in the VLPO were correlated with REM but not NREM times, while Fos-positive cells in the extended VLPO were correlated with NREM but not REM times. It appears that neurons in the VLPO promote REM via GABA-ergic inhibition of nearby hypothalamic and thalamic arousal systems.

Saint-Mleux et al. (2004) reported that Ach inhibited VLPO neurons (and presumably REM) through a nicotinic receptor at presynaptic sites. These receptors are known to play a role in sleep mechanisms, as they are implicated in the disorder known as nocturnal frontal lobe epilepsy (Provini, Plazzi, Montagna, & Lugaresi, 2000; Rozycka, Skorupska, Kostyrko, & Trzeciak, 2003; Sutor & Zolles, 2001). Mendelson, Lantigua, Wyatt, Gillin, and Jacobs (1981), furthermore, reported that piperidine administration enhanced sleep-related GH secretion rates. Thus, hypothalamic nicotinic receptors may play a role in regulation of REM and NREM interactions.

The apparent functional opposition of REM and NREM described at various levels of the neuraxis does not arise simply because one sleep state lacks the functional capacities of the other. Rather, these functional contrasts arise because in key respects the two sleep states actually oppose one another's functional effects. REM, for example, is not associated with rises in the levels of just any hormones. Rather, it is associated with rises in levels of a group of hormones (such as SS, CRH, prolactin, sex steroids, etc.) that directly suppress or inhibit products associated with NREM stimulation (GH, TNF, IL-1, insulin, insulin-like growth factor 1, etc.). Similarly, it is not only that the EEG and physiologic correlates of REM are different from those of NREM, but rather that the EEG and physiologic correlates of REM act to suppress or undo those of NREM.

Benington and Heller (1995), for example, have pointed out that a substantial amount of evidence derived from studies of REM rebound effects after varying periods of partial or total sleep deprivation suggests that regulation of REM is accomplished via accumulation of a REM need or propensity that builds up during NREM rather than during waking. If REM reverses some process that occurs during NREM, then it seems reasonable to suppose that the physiologic processes of the two sleep states in some ways conflict with one another and that this conflict may hold important clues to the biologic functions of both REM and NREM.

Endocrine Interactions in REM and NREM

Slow-wave sleep of NREM is associated with a major surge in GH release (Mueller et al., 1999; Van Cauter et al., 1998). GHRH promotes NREM sleep, while SS inhibits NREM and GH and GHRH release while enhancing REM.

Effects of GH Depend on REM and SS Release

Physiologic and growth-promoting effects of GH in the rat and in the human depend on pulsatile release of GH (Mueller et al., 1999; Veldhuis, 2003). But pulsatile release of GH, in turn, depends on SS-ergic activity. Available data support the model of GH release originally proposed by Tannenbaum and Ling (1984). In this model, SS is released in a sinusoidal pattern. When GHRH is released during a trough period of SS release, it induces pulsatile release of GH, while a rise in SS release reduces GH release to baseline levels, thus allowing a new cycle of GH-SS interactions to begin. Fluctuating levels of SS release are therefore required to sustain pulsatile release of GH. Similarly, after reviewing available data, Veldhuis (2003) proposed a "final-common-pathway" model of GH release emphasizing interactions between GHRH, the GH-releasing peptide ghrelin, and SS. In the model, intermittent exposure of somatotropes to fluctuating levels of SS sensitizes somatotropes such that stimulation by ghrelin or GHRH results in increased pulsatile GH secretion rates as well as an elevation of the mass of GH secreted in GH secretory bursts. In sum, SS release is crucial for obtaining pulsatile release of GH and therefore the growth-promoting effects of GH release. Because SS release is associated with REM activation, REM levels may be correlated with growth-promoting effects of GH.

Interactions between REM and NREM with respect to GH release and levels may be reflected in dynamics of sleep homeostasis. Rates and amounts of GH release influence sleep amounts, as evidenced by sleep rebound effects after sleep deprivation. SS release, for example, in the rat causes an accumulation of GHRH in the rat hypothalamus (Gardi et al., 2001), suggesting that NREM rebound amounts after sleep deprivation involve the discharge of stores of GHRH/GH. Toppila et al. (1996, 1997) have reported that sleep deprivation in the rat increases both SS and GHRH mRNA levels in the hippocampus. Antisera to SS or GHRH can block sleep rebound effects after sleep deprivation (Obal & Krueger, 2003).

One other growth-related hormone linked to REM sleep is prolactin. Prolactin release is partially dependent on sleep: Its levels rise rapidly at sleep onset but peak around 3 to 5 a.m. when REM predominates (Borbely & Tobler, 1989; Inoue et al., 1999). Prolactin's release can be blocked by sleep deprivation.

In summary, REM and NREM processes (1) interact at cellular and physiologic levels, (2) interact antagonistically in certain respects and in such a way as to (3) influence release of a number of physiologically active hormones. These conclusions suggest that through their effects on circulating levels of key hormones, REM-NREM interactions can influence waking behavior.

NREM-REM interaction effects on brain activation patterns may also influence dream content. But what evidence is there for interaction effects on cognitive and dream content?

Memory Processing Depends on NREM-REM Interactions

Many authors have suggested various ways in which NREM interacts with REM in processing of memories. Sejnowski and Destexhe (2000) provided a model of the sleep-related consolidation process that depends on spindle oscillations during early SWS and an alternating pattern between slow-wave complexes and brief episodes of fast oscillations as SWS deepens. Giudditta et al. (1995) suggested that NREM selects memories that will be consolidated, and then consolidation occurs under REM. Stickgold and his associates have drawn on the work of Buzsaki (1996) and their own empirical findings in analyses of dream content (Fosse, Fosse, Hobson, & Stickgold, 2003) to suggest that one can "see" aspects of the process of memory consolidation as a function of REM-NREM interactions by looking at dream content. During slow-wave NREM sleep, memories of life episodes and events are consolidated into episodic memories and transferred to the cortex for storage. During REM sleep, hippocampal outflow to the cortex is blocked. Instead, the hippocampus receives information from cortical networks, thus preventing transfer of newly consolidated episodic memories to the cortex. Thus, one should not see instances of fully formed episodic memories in REM dreams, and that is what Fosse et al., in fact, found. Instead, semantic and procedural aspects of memories are thought to be processed during REM. Consistent with the Stickgold et al. model, Cavallero, Cicogna, and Bosinelli (1988) elicited dreams from the onset phase, from NREM and REM sleep, and asked their subjects to freely associate to individual dream segments. Associations to REM dreams were more often related to general knowledge, whereas dream onset and NREM dreams were more closely related to memories of life episodes.

REM-NREM Interactions and Emotional Processing

Dreams are filled with emotion. That popular conception about dreams, at least, appears to be correct. Fully 80% of dreams contain at least one emotion (a negative emotion, unfortunately). Although Strauch and Meier (1996, p. 92) write that "emotions are not a consistent feature of the dream experience," they nevertheless report that specific emotions were part of every second dream in their series. Another quarter of the dreams in their series were accompanied by a generalized mood state, according to the persons who had the dreams. Only one-quarter of the Strauch and Meier dream series had no emotions associated with them. Merritt, Stickgold, Pace-Schott, Williams, and Hobson (1994) asked their subjects to specifically indicate, on a line-by-line basis, the presence of one or more specific emotions. Using this method, Merritt et al. found that 95% of all their dream reports (N = 200 reports) contained at least one emotion and that each dream report averaged about 3.6 emotions per dream. Thus, specifically asking subjects to describe their dream emotions reveals that dreams are filled with emotions—at least spontaneously recalled dreams (probably REM dreams).

Early reports of content differences between REM and NREM suggested that REM dreams were more emotional than NREM dreams. NREM dreams were characterized as being less vivid and more thoughtlike than REM dreams. Strauch and Meier (1996, p. 138) comment that in their dream series, "barely every second NREM dream featured the dream self emotionally related to the dream situation, whereas four out of every five REM dreams involved the dreamer emotionally in its events."

The differences in emotional content between REM and NREM suggest potential emotional processing specializations in REM and NREM. Several authors in the psychoanalytic tradition (French & Fromme, 1964) suggested that dreams at the beginning of the night (we now know that these would be NREM dreams) would announce an emotional wish or emotional conflict that dreams later in the night would pick up and work with in an attempt to contain or resolve the emotional conflict. Trosman, Rechtschaffen, Offenkrantz, and Wolpert (1960) analyzed both manifest dream content and subjects' associations to their dreams after repeated awakenings from consecutive REM periods. The authors suggested that their data revealed an accumulation of tension around disguised wishes in early dreams of the night that then is discharged in subsequent dreams late in the sleep period. Later dreams represent attempts at resolution of the conflict announced in earlier dreams.

Interestingly, Trosman et al. noted that there was a tendency for specific dream scenes or elements to occur in similar positions in the dream sequence (e.g., REM period 2) on separate nights. For example, one subject dreamed of an obese woman in the third dream of a dream sequence on three separate occasions. Another subject dreamed of observing an athletic event in the first dream, experienced rejection by a friend in the second dream, and freed a buried object from the ground in the third dream of a sequence, on two successive nights. Later, Offenkrantz and Rechtschaffen (1963) found similar repeating sequences in another subject, but I could find no recent reports on the phenomenon. At a minimum, these kinds of phenomena would suggest cognitive and emotional processing specializations for each stage of sleep.

Domhoff and Kamiya (1964) assessed dream content of 22 college students from each of the first three REM periods. Aggressive content and number of characters tended to increase as the night progressed. Similarly, Hall and Van de Castle (cited in Van de Castle, 1970) examined dream content of 15 males across several REM periods of the night. Although an increase in "misfortunes" in later REM periods was noted, no other major differences in content as a function of late versus early REM periods were noted.

Offenkrantz and Rechtschaffen (1963) studied the sequential sleep patterns and dreams of a patient in psychotherapy for 15 consecutive nights. They noted that scenes from childhood memories never occurred early in the night but did occur on 8 of the 15 nights in dreams late in the night, after 4:30 a.m. They also noted that all the dreams of a night tended to be concerned with the same emotional conflict or a small number of such conflicts. They also claimed that they found evidence that the organization of a particular dream depended on the results of the dream work of the preceding dream, such that dream wishes required less and less disguise as the night progressed. NREM dreams were not examined.

Offenkrantz and Rechtschaffen's 1963 article was the first study, and remains one of the few studies, to explicitly look for REM-NREM interactions in the manifest content of dreams. They studied sequential NREM-REM dreams within a single night in three subjects who had previously demonstrated good dream recall from NREM sleep. They restricted themselves to noting only obvious connections between dreams in sequence rather than analyzing "latent" content or asking for the dreamer's associations to his or her dreams. They found repeated instances of dream elements recurring throughout the dream sequence. For example, the image of a street corner appeared in the first NREM dream of the night. It later appeared as the place where the dreamer met a girl. Other repeating elements noted in dream sequences of other subjects included: riding a bicycle, looking at a photograph, attending an outing, picnic, or camping trip, taking exams, sensing a sunny day, and so on. These elements, settings, or themes recurred throughout dream sequences in the three subjects studied by Rechtschaffen et al. There was no clear evidence that the content of one dream depended on work done on content of a previous dream, except in the trivial sense of use of the same images, as mentioned above. Thus, if REM and NREM are interacting to produce manifest content of dreams, then the interactions must involve production of some nonobvious dream element such as "change in feeling tone or affect" or some other unidentified element. On the other hand, the authors did not perform quantitative analyses of the frequency of selected content categories such as number of aggressive versus friendly social interactions, density of characters per social interaction, number of unknown versus familiar characters, and so forth. It is likely that more systematic study will yield interesting relationships.

Kramer (see review in Kramer, 1993) has conducted a systematic program of research of mood-regulatory aspects of dreaming. He theorizes that dreams function to contain a surge of emotion associated with REM. He also claims that content changes systematically across the night in successive REM periods and that this content change is correlated with a reduction in "unhappy" mood scores from night to morning. Interestingly, Kramer reported that the content variables that showed statistically significant change across the night's dreams and that were most predictive of mood improvement in the morning were three character variables. In other words, the number and variety of characters in a dream changes systematically from dream to dream throughout the night, and this change is related to the mood state of the dreamer. Both Kramer's and Domhoff's results on the role of unknown male characters as signals for danger or threat (see chapters 6 and 7) suggest that these dream elements may function as signaling elements (concerning emotional changes) used in interactions between REM and NREM and with measurable effects on waking mood.

REM-NREM Interactions as Signaling Systems

REM-NREM interactions in the physiologic sphere suggest that both the thematic content of dreams and the formal features of REM-related dreams cannot be understood in isolation from NREM dreams. If dreams of REM are in interaction with dreams of NREM, then some elements of dream content of REM should be in response to, or linked to, or refer to elements of dream content of NREM, and vice versa. In other words, NREM and REM content should be in some kind of communication: they should signal one another. We have seen that there is some preliminary empirical evidence for this. Given that such an exchange of signals is actually taking place, then this exchange will likely help to structure the formal cognitive properties of the systems that are communicating with one another. This signal exchange, in other words, should obey design rules of animal communication systems more generally and in doing so should, in the context of sleep states, help yield formal properties of dreams such as narrative structure, visual imagery, simulations of social interactions, and so forth.

Hockett's Criteria and Dream Elements

The literature on animal communication systems is vast, and findings from that literature have, as far as I know, never been applied to human sleep mentation. Thus, the following discussion can only represent an initial foray into the task of situating sleep signaling into the biology of animal communication systems. First, to bolster our confidence that dream elements might function as biologic signals, it is worth briefly reviewing Hockett's design features of animal communication systems in order to identify features of dream content that satisfy Hockett's criteria.

These criteria include such factors as sender/receiver interchangeability, semanticity (the extent to which signals carry information and refer to objects), discreteness, and displacement (reference to unseen objects or to future events). Most investigators of the dream would agree that many and perhaps most dreams exhibit semanticity and displacement but would be unsure about interchangeability and discreteness. Dreams exhibit semanticity because they are about something; they refer to objects that have significance for the dreamer. Domhoff (1996, 2003) has conclusively demonstrated that the dreams of an individual contain themes that are consistent throughout that individual's lifetime. The same significant persons show up, and conflicts with those persons are simulated in ways that reflect waking realities vis-à-vis those persons. In short, the images and themes that occur in dreams are not random with respect to emotional concerns of the dreamer. Intentional states are also certainly depicted: the dreamer intends, struggles, desires, fears, plans, thinks, and so on.

What is more, dreams also can refer to unseen objects and to future states. Dreams can escape slavery to the concrete. Dreams, in short, can refer and therefore exhibit the property of displacement. Indeed, dreams should be considered to be the arena in which displacement really takes off. The figurative language of dreams certainly surpasses that seen in daily conversation of most persons when they are awake.

Sender-receiver interchangeability and discreteness are less obvious features of dream images. While dream images appear to come in discrete units, they also blend and fuse in such profusion, at least in some dreams, that discreteness probably does not apply to dreams. As to sender-receiver interchangeability: Who would be the receiver of signals produced in a dream? Unless we suppose that the mind is not a unity, then the question is absurd. But at least in one sense, the mind clearly is not a unity: it has two distinct, functional brain/mind states in sleep: REM and NREM. These two states, furthermore, exchange cellular, hormonal, and neuronal signals. There is no reason why this exchange of signals should not include dream elements.

If the receiver of a signal emanating from REM is a component process or element in NREM and vice versa, then sender-receiver interchangeability is a necessity. The signals have to be "readable" on both ends. If, for example, high-amplitude pulses in GH release in NREM are associated with a corresponding increase in release of cortisol or of somatostatin in REM, then there is sender-receiver communication or interchangeability between REM and NREM, since an exchange of signals (neuronal firing intensities associated with amplitude or intensity of hormonal release) result in physiologic change. Now, if we assume further that neuronal firing patterns associated with GH release are in turn associated with duration of an NREM episode (and we know that it is), and duration of an NREM episode is associated with longer dream reports from NREM stages, then elements of the dream from these NREM stages could encode the intensity signal. Conversely, if intensity of phasic REMs translates into density of individual elements or characters in a dream or plot changes in a REM dream, then once again elements of the dream (in this case a REM dream) could encode intensity signals of phasic REMs.

Other dream codes are imaginable as well. If, for example, we take the presence and number of unknown male characters in a dream to be an index of threat and aggression (see chapter 8 for justification of this equation), then the number of unknown male characters in REM and NREM dreams should rise and fall as a function of emotional changes in dream content through the night. Kramer (1993) shows something close to this in his findings of systematic changes in character density as a function of early or late REM periods. If interactions are taking place between REM and NREM, number of unknown males should, furthermore, vary in response to the preceding number in a REM or NREM dream. If an NREM dream, for example, "wagers" two or three unknown characters at the start of a night's dreaming, then one of the following REM episodes should enter a counterwager: perhaps five or six unknown characters, and so on. These simplistic suggestions are not meant to be anything more than devices designed to raise potential issues, if interaction is a reality and a factor in the formation of dream content.

In addition to Hockett's features of communicative signaling, Bradbury and Vehrencamp (1998) urge consideration of other features. Such features include the temporal or spatial range over which signals must communicate, the "duty cycle" of a signaling bout ("on" time of a signal relative to its "off" time, or signal duration divided by signal plus intersignal duration), and the "locatability" of a signal, including its sender or receiver. Senders apparently often adjust signal properties in order to make it more difficult to locate the sender, and thus make it easier to manipulate the receiver. The "modulation potential" of a signal specifies the range from stereotyped to graded over which a signal can vary in order to carry relevant information. Graded signals, for example, can vary in intensity, frequency, amplitude, and repetition rate. Finally, signals can vary in the degree to which signal form is linked to or dependent on signal content. All of these properties of signaling and communication systems may apply to dream elements. For example, if we continue with the example of the "male stranger as signal for threat" dream element, then we might imagine the following analyses: If we suppose that an on-time of the male stranger signal could be measured accurately in terms of a percentage of dream content containing male strangers, then there may be significant changes in the characteristics of the duty cycle of this signal in consecutive REM and NREM dreams as the night progresses. The duty-cycle pattern, in turn, would tell us how much of the content of REM and NREM interactions concerns this dream element, as well as how this content changes quantitatively across the night.

Modeling Potential Interactions

Signals, however, should not be considered mere bearers of information. Signaling can be manipulative and therefore may bear disinformation. In waking life, emotional signals, in particular, are often designed to effect a change in the person observing an emotional expression (Russell, Bachorowski, & Fernandez-Dols, 2003) of another. A smile may be emitted in order to encourage an interlocutor to continue to divulge information. A liar may smile to hide a lie. A coward may feign rage so as to not have to fight. Likewise, an animal facing a fight with a superior opponent may emit a display that hides its poor qualities and emphasizes its threatening qualities. A bird wishing to obtain a mate may advertise his ability to provision the female by singing an elaborate song that ends up having little or no correlation with later provision of resources. A juvenile wishing to stave off the weaning process emits extravagant begging displays that bear no true relationship to physiologic need, and so on.

Given that senders often have an interest in sending deceptive signals, the relationship of signal form to signal content is often arbitrary. In order to prevent being deceived, receivers have had to evolve a means or test with which they could gauge the truth content of a signal. As discussed in chapter 1, Zahavi (1975) suggested that receivers settled on the handicap principle: Receivers will tend to insist on signals that are hard to fake and are costly (metabolically, energetically, or behaviorally, etc.) to produce. In producing such signals, the sender is actually handicapped, since he or she must invest valuable resources in production of the signal. The peacock's feathers are the classic example: The production of such fine feathers advertises his abilities (good genes) to invest in high-cost signals. Therefore he must have genes good enough to produce such a signal. Therefore, the signal is not a deception: he can be trusted to have good genes. Females (peahens) will choose to mate with him. The production of hard-to-fake costly signals helps the females to identify the best mates. These same signals force the males to engage in production of ever more costly signals until some limit is reached beyond which the costs become too great (the tails are so elaborate that the animals cannot escape predators, etc.).

Thus, in situations of conflict, one can expect sender-receiver signaling bouts that are fraught with deceptive moves and countermoves along with costly signaling in order to move toward conflict resolution. Of course, all kinds of outcomes are possible depending on what type of conflict is involved. In the case of REM-NREM signaling bouts, costly signaling is probably involved, given the physiologic aberrations associated with REM (see chapter 1). We can model the signaling interactions of REM and NREM with game theory techniques. It seems reasonable when doing so to begin with the simplest possible verbal model, test it against dream content data, and then adjust as needed. Eventually, quantitative modeling of interactions involving dream elements of REM versus NREM should be possible.

REM-NREM interactions will involve a minimum of two players (REM and NREM), and the game is conflictual, so one might begin with a simple discrete, symmetrical contest game like the "take game," in which two players compete over some limited resource. In REM and NREM interactions, the resource might be level of release of or, in the cognitive realm, number of characters per social interaction, and so on. Players in such a game may develop costly signals as method of communicating trustworthy signals and optimizing interactions in service to attaining waking behavioral goals.

Given this kind of contest between REM and NREM processes, what might we expect in terms of formal features of dreams and in terms of thematic content? If signaling or communication is, in fact, occurring, what is being signaled? If we assume, for example, that REM and NREM engage in a contest over control of selected chemical/hormonal signaling systems of the organism, then each should try to neutralize or silence the other's influence over the hypothalamic-pituitary axis and ultimately waking behavior. We should not expect honest signaling, and we should expect escalating displays of greater and greater intensity as the night progresses. The object of all of this intensity and signaling should be to silence elements of the opponent's signaling system and to gain control over the behavioral goals of the dreamer. Alternatively, both players in the interaction can cooperate in some common goal (energy conservation or memory consolidation, where orderly interactions between the two states are required, perhaps), or either or both players in the conflict can defect or opt out of cooperative interchange using elements of sleep mentation to inhibit signaling in the opposing state or to increase the length of a sleep episode and therefore dominate the interaction. Sleep state interactions can therefore theoretically approximate the prisoner's dilemma game, in which defection is always a better strategy for one player, yet mutual cooperation makes both players better off.

CHAPTER 5

REM Sleep and Genetic Conflict

We have seen that REM sleep exhibits a number of paradoxical physiologic traits (chapter 1) that depart from equilibrium. These paradoxical traits may even impair the health of the organism. In addition, we have seen (chapter 2) that emergence of fetal AS and QS may be influenced by maternal-fetal conflict over growth schedules and the like. In the adult, furthermore, REM and NREM sometimes interact in an antagonistic fashion to regulate levels and release of growth factors. We have, furthermore, seen that REM itself appears to be regulated via similar antagonistic cellular interactions at each level of the neuraxis up to the cortex. Finally, REM and NREM seem to express functionally antagonistic traits and processes across a spectrum of functional states (see table 5.1). All of these data raise the issue of the extent to which REM and NREM are regulated by separate sets of genes with opposing genetic interests and thus whether the evolution of REM biology was influenced by processes of genetic conflict.

Genes and Sleep

Model systems for genetic dissection of sleep include work in fruit flies (*Drosophila*). The fruit fly periodically becomes quiescent and exhibits reduced responsiveness to stimulation during the quiescent state, rapid reversibility to activity, and a kind of sleep rebound after deprivation of rest, thus satisfying several behavioral and functional criteria for sleep. In addition, pharmacological agents, such as caffeine, that affect sleep in mammals through their action on the Al adenosine receptor, had a similar effect on sleep in flies. Shaw, Tononi, Greenspan, and Robinson (2002) demonstrated that the clock gene mutant cyc(01) showed a reduced expression of heat shock genes after sleep loss and died after 10 hours of sleep deprivation. Activating these heat shock genes in cyc(01) flies before sleep deprivation was imposed on them protected the flies against the lethal effects of sleep

Table 5.1. REM-NREM Characteristics Suggesting Opposing Functional States

	REM	NREM
Mouse strains indicating separate genetic influences	C57BL and C57BR are associated with increased REM and short SWS episodes	BALB/c is associated with short REM and long NREM episodes
Prader-Willi syndrome (paternal deletions/maternal additions on C15) Excessive sleepiness	Decreased	Increased
Angelman syndrome (paternal additions/maternal deletions on C15) sleeplessness	Increased	Decreased
Nursing (rat)	Neonate typically in REM during nursing and REM% increases during milk ingestion up to 4% of body weight	Mother must be in NREM-SWS for milk ejection to occur
Percent of total sleep time in adult	20-25%	75-80%
Distribution during sleep phase	Predominates in last third of night	Predominates in first third of night
Response to infection	Decreased	Increased
Sleep deprivation-related rebound (both REM and NREM)	Increases SS and GHRH mRNA. Antisera to GHRH prevent sleep rebound after SD	(Repaid before REM)
Cerebral blood flow	Increased	Decreased
Arousal thresholds	+	++
Eye movements	Rapid eye movements with occasional bursts or clusters of REMs	Slow rolling eye movements
EEG	"Desynchronized" Phasic events: REM bursts, muscle twitching, middle ear muscle activity, hippocampal theta waves Tonic events: muscle hypotonia or atonia, especially in the anti-gravity muscles, penile tumescence	Synchronized
		Stage I (light falling asleep)
		Stage II (light sleep with K-complexes and spindles)
		Stage III and IV slow wave sleep with delta waves

Table 5.1. (continued)

	REM	NREM
Muscle tone	Decreased	Intact
Cortical activation	Increased (except in dorsolateral prefrontal cortex and posterior cingulate)	Decreased but with complex variations
Subcortical activation	Limbic, hypothalamic, amygdala	Thalamic inhibitory efferents (which globally inhibit cortex)
Metabolic rate under thermoneutral conditions	Increased	Decreased
Durations when sleeper is exposed to temperature changes outside of thermoneutral zone	Decreased	Increased
Effect of antifever meds	?	Decreased
Thermoregulatory reflexes	Decreased to absent	Present
ANS	Increased variability/ANS storms/increased HR and BP	No significant changes
Neurochemistry	Cholinergic REM-on cells 5HT and NE REM-off cells	GABA important for NREM onset
Parasomnias/sleep disorders	Nightmares, narcolepsy, REM sleep behavior disorder; suicide; depression	Sleep terrors, sleepwalking, i.e., arousal parasomnias
Mentation	Vivid dreams	Ruminative
Hormones	Somatostatin Prolactin	Growth hormone GHRH

deprivation, suggesting a role of sleep in thermoregulation. Similarities of behavioral and functional aspects of sleep in flies and mammals suggest that these aspects of sleep are regulated by genes and have been conserved over evolutionary time.

Tafti and Franken (2002) have shown that inbred mice strains C57BL and C57BR are associated with increased REM and short SWS episodes, while the BALB/c strain is associated with short REM and long NREM episodes, indicating separate genetic influences on REM and NREM sleep amounts.

Electrophysiologic measures of sleep in humans are also influenced by genes. Studies of sleep EEG in twins reared apart show stronger correlations on EEG indices among monozygotic twin pairs as compared to dizygotic twin pairs (see reviews in Tafti & Franken, 2002; Taheri & Mignot, 2002).

Recently, it was discovered that mutations in the orexin 2 receptor gene was associated with the canine and a murine form of narcolepsy (Chemelli et al., 1999; Guilleminault & Anagnos, 2000). Orexins (hypocretins) are hypothalamic peptides known to be involved in feeding and energetic balance. It is unclear how disturbances in the orexin system give rise to sleep-related problems. In humans, in sporadic cases (particularly those with onset in the adolescent years), narcolepsy-cataplexy is associated with specific mutations in a major histocompatibility complex, HLA class II allele DQB1*0301. Narcolepsy may therefore be due in part to an autoimmune targeting of hypocretin cells in the hypothalamus.

Sleepwalking and night terrors are disorders emerging from SWS and generally occur in children. There is strong evidence that the disorders run in families, and twin studies reveal a high degree of concordance for the disorders among monozygotic pairs. Hublin, Kaprio, Partinen, and Koskenvu (2001) used self-reports of childhood parasomnias among twins as well as structural equation modeling of data obtained from these self-reports to estimate proportion of the total phenotypic variance attributable to genetic factors. They found that variance attributable to genetic effects for such disorders as sleepwalking, sleep talking, bruxism, and nightmares varied between 36% and 80% when adults were queried.

Klein-Levin syndrome affects mainly young males and, like Prader-Willi syndrome (PWS, described below), is characterized by bouts of hypersomnia, compulsive eating, cognitive changes, signs of dysautonomia, and, unlike Prader-Willi, episodes of hypersexuality. Tafti and Franken (2002) report that HLA DQB1*0201 allele frequency may be elevated in these patients and their families.

A disorder involving insomnia is fatal familial insomnia (FFI). In FFI, the patient develops a form of insomnia involving the loss of NREM sleep and eventual permanent insomnia until death occurs. Lugaresi et al. (1986) described FFI and later showed that FFI is related to a point mutation at codon 128 or 129 of the prion protein gene on chromosome 20.

There can be little doubt, then, that basic sleep processes are influenced by genes, and it may be that separate sets of genes regulate expression of REM and NREM.

Genetic Conflict

As mentioned in chapter 1, individual organisms are composed of multiple genetic entities that obey varying transmission or inheritance patterns that create the context for intragenomic conflict (Partridge & Hurst, 1998; Pomiankowski, 1999) between two associated or antagonistic genes or genomes. The phenomenon known as genomic imprinting (Nicholls, 2000; Tycko & Morison, 2002; Verona, Mann, & Bartolomei, 2003) is considered by many to be an example of intragenomic conflict. In this case, the genomes in conflict are paternally derived and maternally derived alleles, as imprinting involves the inactivation or silencing of one allele of a gene, depending on its parental origin. Expression of the associated allele likewise depends on whether it was inherited from the father or the mother. Haig's (2002) game theoretic models of the ways in which these genomes interact to produce development of a normal baby suggest that the paternally derived alleles act to enhance growth of a developing fetus or child regardless of its effects on the mother or siblings of the child, and that maternally derived alleles act to restrain transfer of resources to any given offspring. In this chapter, I examine the evidence for effects of imprinting on sleep biology.

Effects of Imprinted Genes on Physiologic Systems Implicated in Growth

Use of knockout mice models has revealed how intimately these imprinted genes shape internal physiologic systems supporting growth and reproductive behaviors. The paternally expressed genes *Peg1* and *Peg3*, for example, are both expressed in the hypothalamus and influence regulation of CNS and neuroendocrine functions. Female heterozygous mice that inherited the knocked-out *Peg1* gene from their father failed to build nests and to retrieve and care for pups. *Peg3* knockouts not only failed to retrieve and care for pups but also could not effectively suckle their pups. Histological examination of the brains of these mothers revealed a significant reduction in oxytocinergic neurons in the hypothalamus. Given that oxytocin release is required for milk letdown in mice, offspring of these *Peg3* knockout mice failed to gain weight and grow normally. These results are consistent with the idea that paternally expressed genes function to promote growth by controlling reproductive and parenting behaviors of mothers. Specifically, *Peg1* and *Peg3* appear to influence oxytocinergic circuits of the hypothalamus involved in care and nursing of pups.

Sleep state activation is linked with these hypothalamic oxytocinergic circuits. Activation of NREM SWS in the mother, for example, is required for oxytocin release (in rats and presumably in mice as well). As discussed in chapter 2, infant rats, on the other hand, prefer to nurse while they are in AS/REM sleep. The AS/REM state, apparently, facilitates transfer of relatively large volumes of milk from the mother to the pup (Lorenz, 1986; Lorenz et al., 1998). Thus, nursing in the rat may typically occur when all parties (mother and pups) are asleep, but in different sleep states: the mother in NREM SWS and the pup in AS/REM. Imprinted genes (*Peg1* and *Peg3*) play a key role in this nocturnal interchange by influencing hypothalamic circuits that promote both wake-related and nursing-related maternal behaviors in the mother.

Effects of Imprinted Genes on Functional Brain Systems That Have Been Directly Implicated in Sleep Processes

Keverne, Martel, and Nevison (1996) showed that functionally distinct regions of the brain may reflect the distinct contributions of the maternal and paternal genomes. They examined embryological development in mice possessing only maternal (parthenogenetic, PG) or paternal (androgenetic, AG) chromosomes. They produced a chimeric mouse containing a mixture of cells with either the single parent or normal complement of chromosomes (wild type). When they compared AG to PG wild types, they found that the distribution of PG and AG cells formed strikingly reciprocal patterns. Whereas PG cells were concentrated in cortical and striatal structures but excluded from hypothalamic, septal, basal forebrain, and preoptic areas, AG cells showed the opposite pattern. These data may have implications for sleep state biology, as REM sleep is associated with activation in hypothalamic, preoptic, basal forebrain, and limbic areas (i.e., areas with high paternal-line AG cell concentrations), and deactivation in selected cortical structures (i.e., areas high in maternal PG cell concentrations).

In summary, imprinted genes shape internal CNS physiologic systems concerned with growth, reproduction, and related behaviors. Given that both REM and NREM directly influence release and levels of a number of growth-related factors including GH, SS, and gonadal steroids (Inoue et al., 1999; Obal & Krueger, 2003; Van Cauter et al., 1998), it seems reasonable to suppose that imprinted genes might exert a significant impact on selected properties of REM and NREM.

Genomic Imprinting and Sleep State Biology

Before summarizing evidence for links between imprinted genes and sleep state biology, we need to briefly review key aspects of sleep state biology. REM sleep is promoted by cholinergic neurons originating within the LDT/PPT. REM sleep may be inhibited by noradrenergic and serotonergic neurons in the locus coeruleus and dorsal raphe, respectively. Activation of cholinergic REM (including phasic REM) is related to removal of inhibition exerted by these aminergic efferents on cholinergic cells in the LDT/PPT. When the aminergic neurons decrease their firing, cells of the LDT/PPT are released from inhibition and increase their firing. The release of acetylcholine from terminals of LDT/PPT cells triggers the onset of REM by activating brain regions that control various components of REM, including brain stem sites, hypothalamus, the limbic system, amygdala, and the basal forebrain. Cholinergic collaterals to the locus coeruleus and dorsal raphe nuclei exert an indirect excitatory effect on aminergic cell groups in these nuclei. As REM proceeds, this excitatory effect eventually reaches a threshold wherein their activation results in a feedback inhibition on REM-on cells of the LDT/PPT, thus ending the REM period. The initiation of NREM sleep may be a GABA-ergic-mediated process characterized by loss of wake-related alpha waves and slowing of EEG frequency.

Imprinting Clusters and Control Centers

An intriguing characteristic of imprinted genes is that they often cluster on a chromosome, forming large imprinted domains. In humans, areas near 20q13.2, 11p15.5, and 15q11–13 are examples of imprinting domains. This clustering has suggested to many that there are imprinting control regions that function in a domainwide manner to establish imprinting and/or parent-of-origin effects for all genes in or near that cluster. Thus, it is essential to look at several genes in a given imprinting-related domain when attempting to discover new genes that may be imprinted under certain conditions. This strategy, in fact, has been successfully used to discover new imprinted genes. Thus I look at genes in the above three domains to identify genes that are either (1) known to be imprinted and sleep-related, or (2) may be both imprinted and sleep related.

Area 15q11–13

Area 15q11–13 is sometimes called the Prader-Willi/Angelman region because genes responsible for these disorders are located in this region. Angelman and Prader-Willi are neurodevelopmental syndromes that involve opposite contrasting sleep state changes. Prader-Willi syndrome is associated with maternal additions/paternal deletions of alleles at chromosome 15q11–13 and is characterized by poor sucking response, temperature control abnormalities, and excessive sleepiness. Sleep architecture changes have also been noted in children and young adults with PWS, most specifically REM sleep abnormalities such as sleep onset REM periods, REM fragmentation, intrusion of REM into stage 2 sleep, and short latencies to REM (Hertz, Cataletto, Feinsilver, & Angulo, 1993; Vela-Bueno et al., 1984; Vgontzas et al., 1996).

Conversely, Angelman syndrome is associated with paternal additions/maternal deletions on chromosome 15q11–13 and is characterized by prolonged sucking, severe mental retardation, and reductions in sleep. These children may sleep as little as 1 to 5 hours a night, with frequent and prolonged night wakings (Clayton-Smith & Laan, 2003; Zhdanova, Wurtman, & Wagstaff, 1999). I could find no EEG studies of sleep in children with Angelman syndrome, but the well-known association between night wakings and REM sleep in infants (night wakings typically emerge from REM; Salzarulo & Ficca, 2002) suggests that children with Angelman spend a disproportionate amount of their sleep in REM. One of the genes thought to be responsible for Angelman syndrome is *UBE3A* or ubiquitin-protein ligase E3A, which is expressed only from the maternal allele in certain brain tissues. These are the hippocampus and Purkinje cells of the cerebellum. This fact may be important for models of sleep and hippocampal memory function, given that *UBE3A* is expressed biparentally in all other tissues.

At area 15q11.2-q12 are genes that code for GABA receptors. GABA, an inhibitory neurotransmitter with both subcortical and cortical effects, has long been suspected to play a role in the promotion of sleep (Gottesmann, 2002; Mallick, Kaur, Jha, & Siegel, 1999). Conversely, decreased GABA-ergic inhibition may contribute to insomnia. Mallick et al. (1999) have reviewed the evidence for a role of GABA projections in regulation of REM sleep via inhibition of pontine REM-off neurons. Forebrain GABA-ergic efferents exert inhibitory control over serotonergic neurons in the dorsal raphe nucleus during REM sleep, thus placing them in a position to regulate downstream REM processes in the pons which receive DRN neurons.

While GABA A receptors are not believed to be imprinted, some GABA B receptors may be maternally imprinted/paternally expressed (Meguro et al., 1997) and involved in sleep regulation. Meguro et al. (1997) demonstrated that three human GABA receptor subunit genes, *GABRB3*, *GABRA5*, and *GABRG3*, appear to be expressed exclusively from the paternal allele.

Buhr et al. (2002) found in a family of persons who suffered insomnia a G to A transition in exon 6 of the *GABRB3* gene, resulting in an arg192 to his (R192H) change in the mature beta-unit-3 subunit. Mice lacking this beta-3 subunit lose the sleep-inducing response to oleamide (Laposky, Homanics, Basile, & Mendelson, 2001). Juhasz, Emri, Kekesi, Salfay, and Crunelli (1994) showed that blockade of GABA B receptors could inhibit EEG synchronization and, by implication, NREM sleep.

GABA B receptors may play a role in generation of REM (Ming-Chu, Morales, & Chase, 1999). As mentioned above, serotonergic cells regulate REM-on cells such that when serotonin systems fall silent (i.e., when serotonin inhibition is removed), LDT/PPT cholinergic REM-on cells start firing. What removes aminergic and local inhibitory input on REM state-on cells? One possibility is GABA-ergic inhibition of aminergic inhibition (and thus facilitation) of REM-on cells of the brainstem. When GABA-ergic agents that activate GABA B receptors are injected into the peribrachial region, signs of REM activation occur, including increases in the frequency of PGO waves.

Area 20q13.2

Using recombinant and inbred strains of mice, Franken, Chollet, and Tafti (2001) identified quantitative trait loci for a trait that modifies the rate at which need for SWS (or delta power) accumulates. A QTL (quantitative trait loci) on mouse chromosome 2 homologous to human chromosome area 20q13.2 was identified. This region is known to be an imprinting control region. Franken et al. point out that several genes at or near this locus likely participate in SWS regulation. Among these are the gene-encoding brain glycogen phosphorylase, an enzyme that converts glycogen into glucose-1-phosphate during metabolic demand. Bennington and Heller (1995) have argued that SWS functions to restore brain energy homeostasis by replenishing glial glycogen stores that are depleted during waking. Two other genes (S-adenosyl-homocysteine hydroxylase and adenosine deaminase) near this locus participate in regulation of adenosine levels. Adenosine depletion and restoration has been implicated in regulation of SWS need (Porkka-Heiskanen, Strecker, & McCarley, 2000). Franken et al. point out that the genes for GHRH and the somatostatin receptor are also localized near 20q13.2. Along with GH, these hormones participate in regulation of both NREM and REM sleep processes. GH is released during NREM, while somatostatin is released during REM. Varying levels of somatostatin exert varying effects on GH release. When somatostatin reaches trough (but not zero) levels, pulsatile release of GH is facilitated, while high levels of somatostatin are associated with inhibition of GH release and NREM sleep.

A number of sleep disorders are associated with genes encoded in the 20q13.2 region. Anokhin et al. (1992) identified a locus at 20q13.2 linked to so-called low-voltage EEG disorder, which involves a gradual loss of alpha waves in the EEG. Under normal physiologic conditions, alpha waves gradually diminish as a person falls asleep and descends into each successive stage of NREM. Another sleep-related disorder linked to a gene at 20q13.2–q13.3 is nocturnal frontal lobe epilepsy. Here the patients undergo seizures during the night whose focus is localized to the frontal lobes (Provini et al., 2000). Interestingly, the seizures typically occur during the light stages (stage 2) of NREM sleep (Scheffer et al., 1995). Steinlein et al. (1994) suggested that the location of *CHRNA4* in the 20q13.2 region made it a possible candidate gene for either benign neonatal familial convulsions (EBN1) or the electroencephalographic variant pattern 1 (EEGV1). Finally, Ondine's curse or central hypoventilation syndrome (which manifests during sleep), as well as congenital failure of central ANS control, have been linked to markers at 20q13.2. Given REM's respiratory and ANS instabilities (see below), the link is interesting.

With respect to imprinted genes at 20q13.2–q13.3, *GNAS1* likely influences sleep state biology. The gene encoding the Gs alpha subunit is known as *GNAS1*. *GNAS* encodes the alpha subunit of a major heterotrimeric Gs signaling protein. The stimulatory G protein couples multiple hormonal receptors with adenyl cyclase. It comprises 13 exons encoding a 394-amino acid protein. Although Gs alpha is encoded by the nonimprinted exons 1–13 of *GNAS1*, two upstream alternative promoters are found in this locus, and these sequences are oppositely imprinted, with *NESP55* being maternally expressed and the XL alpha s paternally expressed. Both of these protein products are involved in formation of neuroendocrine secretory granules. Mutations of *GNAS1*, for example, are associated with pseudohypoparathyroidism and a number of other endocrine disorders that also affect sleep functions (Polychronakos & Kukuvitis, 2002).

Area 11p15.5

Another large imprinting domain in humans is at 11p15.5. The subtelomeric region of 11p (11p15.5) contains three genes, *IGF2*, *INS*, and *TH* (tyrosine hydroxylase), that lie in an interval of less than 50 kb, all of which have been implicated in sleep mechanisms, risk for cardiovascular traits, and a neurodevelopmental disorder called Beckwith-Widemann syndrome (BWS). BWS is characterized by somatic overgrowth in the neonate and a predisposition to tumor in the early years. Among patients with BWS, 25 to 50% have duplication of the active paternal copy of *IGF2*. Another 50% have an epigenetic mutation resulting in loss of imprinting of a transcript called *KCNQ1OT1* (Weksberg, Smith, Squire, & Sadowski, 2003). *KCNQ1OT1* is a paternally expressed antisense transcript within *KvLQt1*, otherwise known as *KCNQ1*. *KCNQ1* is a potassium channel gene involved in the long QT syndrome. It is maternally expressed in several tissues but not in the heart. Five genes make up the KCNQ potassium channel gene family. *KCNQ2, 3*, and *5* are widely expressed in neurons of the CNS and may underlie the M current in rat CA1 neurons of the hippocampus. These neurons, of course, are crucial for memory functions. Benington, Woudenberg, and Heller (1995) reported that apamin, a potassium channel blocker, suppressed REM sleep. No compensatory rebound of REM was noted when apamin-related REM suppression was lifted.

The human insulin gene has been localized to 11p15.5. Aside from its role in glucose regulation, insulin also enhances NREM sleep in rats (Inoue et al., 1999). There is some evidence for imprinting effects at *INS*. Le Stunff, Fallin, and Bougneres (2001) reported that paternal transmission of the Class I insulin VNTR (variable number of tandem repeats) allele predisposes to childhood obesity. *INS* is paternally expressed in mouse yolk sac. Insulin-like growth factors I and II are single-chain polypeptides that share an amino acid sequence homology of about 47% with *INS*. Their functions include mediation of growth hormone action, stimulation of growth of cultured cells, stimulation of the action of insulin, and involvement in development and growth. *Igf1* mediates many of the effects of growth hormone in tissues and it may also stimulate NREM sleep. No data are yet available on potential effects of *Igf2* on sleep. The maternal allele of *Igf2* is silenced and the paternal allele is active in fetal tissues.

Aside from these relatively large imprinting domains, several other imprinted genes may have important effects on sleep. I discuss only one, but it is crucially important for REM.

The 5HT2A Receptor

The serotonin 2a receptor (5HT2AR) at 13q14–q21 appears to be expressed from the maternal allele through polymorphic imprinting of the gene and may be the rule in the adult human brain (Kato et al., 1996). Many of the new generation of antipsychotics target this receptor, and thus it may also be implicated in pathogenesis of schizophrenia. Indeed, linkage and genetic association studies have pointed to polymorphisms in the gene as a contributing factor to schizophrenic symptomology (Dean, 2003). Antipsychotic agents antagonize the 5HT2A receptor, thereby improving prefrontal cortical function and schizophrenic symptomology. REM sleep is associated with deactivation of the prefrontal cortex. That deactivation may be mediated by 5HT2A receptors, given the fact that 5HT2AR antagonists activate prefrontal functions or, in the case of schizophrenia, improve prefrontal function.

Several studies have directly linked the 5HT2A receptor to regulation of sleep mechanisms (Amici et al., 2004; Kirov & Moyanova, 1998; Landolt et al., 1999; Mayer, 2003; Monti & Monti, 1999), including regulation of REM. 5HT2 receptor sites have been found on cholinergic REM on-off neurons in the LDT/PPT. Amici et al. (2004) locally microinjected the 5HT2A agonist DOI [(+/−)-1-(2,5-dimethoxy-4-iodophenyl)-2-aminopropane HCl] and the 5HT(2) antagonist, ketanserin, in LDT in rats. DOI (the agonist) was found to decrease and ketanserin (the antagonist) was found to increase the number, but not the duration, of REM sleep episodes. It appears, therefore, that 5HT2A receptors in the LDT function to inhibit REM, while blockade of these receptors at the level of the LDT enhance REM. These receptors may also interact with GABA-ergic interneurons, as 5HT2A receptors are found on interneurons that express calbindin, which are mainly GABA-ergic.

REM has often been associated with memory and learning functions (see review in Pace-Schott & Hobson, 2002). It is therefore interesting that recent reports have linked activation of the 5HT2A receptor to learning and memory functions (de Quervain et al., 2003; Harvey, 2003). These receptors may also interact with GABA-ergic interneurons, as 5HT2A receptors are found on interneurons that express calbindin. We have seen that GABA receptors (both the A and B subtypes) are intimately involved in sleep regulation. Finally, the 5HT2AR receptor has been implicated in glycogen breakdown into glucose (Azmitia, 2001), a function crucial for brain energy stores.

Summary

Several imprinted sleep-related disorders and sleep-related genes emerge from this brief review of the imprinting literature. At 15q11–13: PWS and

Angelman syndrome are neurodevelopmental syndromes that exhibit opposite imprinting profiles and opposite sleep phenotypes. PWS is associated with maternal additions/paternal deletions and exhibits a hypersomnic profile with REM abnormalities. Angelman syndrome, by contrast, is associated with paternal additions/maternal deletions, frequent night wakings, and insomnia with probably enhanced REM. These data are consistent with a genetic conflict model of sleep regulation where REM is aligned with patriline genetic influence and interests.

Genes that code for GABA B receptors are found at 15q11. What little evidence exists suggests that they are paternally expressed. Evidence summarized above (e.g., Amici et al., 2004) implies that maternally expressed 5HT2A receptors mediate aminergic inhibition of REM-on cells in the PBL region, but that paternally expressed GABA B receptors may mediate inhibition of these aminergic inhibitory effects on REM, thus facilitating REM expression. Thus these data are consistent with a conflict model of sleep, again aligning REM with patriline interests.

At 20q13.2 are genes that likely contribute to both REM and NREM expression. *Gnas1* is crucial for expression of the whole series of G-protein receptors and thus neuroendocrine functions. The *GNAS* locus contains both paternally expressed and maternally expressed alleles. Franken et al. (2001) identified a QTL that is implicated in regulation of the need for SWS. The disorder of loss of alpha EEG is linked to 20q13.2, as is nocturnal frontal lobe epilepsy and Ondine's curse, which involves sleep-related respiratory and ANS dysfunction. These data are neutral with respect to conflict model predictions except insofar as they confirm large-scale imprinting effects on sleep.

At 11p15.5 are several genes that code for growth regulatory factors. *IGF2* is paternally expressed. Insulin may be paternally expressed. Beckwith-Widemann is an overgrowth syndrome involving duplication of the *IGF2* gene. Given that *IGF2* and *INS* are paternally expressed, and that they stimulate NREM, these data are not consistent with the conflict model, which aligns REM with patriline interests.

Serotonin, of course, is implicated in REM sleep regulation, and at least one 5HT receptor is imprinted. The 5HT2A receptor gene is maternally expressed. The Amici et al. (2004) study described above suggested that 5HT2A receptors in the PBL mediated aminergic inhibition of REM expression. Given that the 5HT2A receptor is maternally expressed, these data suggest that matriline genes act to inhibit REM, and thus these data are consistent with a conflict model wherein NREM expression is aligned with matriline genes, while REM is aligned with patriline genes.

In short, what little evidence exists suggests that selected aspects of expression of REM and NREM are regulated by separate sets of genes. Some of these regulatory genes may be imprinted with paternally derived alleles influencing REM expression more than NREM and maternally derived alleles influencing expression of NREM more than REM. But it has to be admitted that the evidence for this kind of a conflict model of REM and NREM expression is weak and only correlative. Nevertheless, the theory of evolutionary conflict with which we have been examining sleep phenomena throughout this book will at some point need to articulate with molecular aspects of sleep regulation. Although not yet a convincing link, the imprinting literature may be one such link.

CHAPTER 6

Theories of REM

Restorative Theory

The common sense explanation for the existence of sleep is that it restores us or "recharges our batteries." This explanation appears to account for major properties of NREM sleep, but it may not account for properties of REM. For example, periods of enforced waking lead to increased NREM sleep drive or sleepiness. This sleep need can be relieved by subsequent sleep, thus supporting the restorative theory for NREM sleep. Interestingly, the recovery sleep typically occurs first for NREM, and only after NREM is made up is REM made up. Sleep deprivation, in other words, produces compensatory increases in both NREM sleep time (specifically NREM delta activity) and REM sleep time during recovery sleep, but NREM is made up first. NREM delta activity has been shown to accumulate during normal periods of consolidated wakefulness, and it discharges or declines during subsequent NREM sleep. These changes in sleep drive are thought to reflect the accumulation of NREM sleep need during enforced waking and the homeostatic discharge of sleep need involving NREM delta wave or SWS during recovery. Apparently mammals need a certain amount of SWS to function properly.

The case of REM is more complicated. After decades of experimental work involving hundreds of REM sleep deprivation experiments (mostly in rats, cats, and humans), there is still no consensus on whether the compensatory REM rebound represents a form of sleep that must be made up (i.e., obligate sleep). Aside from the REM rebound effect, no significant psychologic or biologic effects are noted with REM deprivation—at least for short-term REM deprivation in humans. With prolonged (16 to 54 days) REM deprivation in rats, death will ensue (Kushida, Bergmann, & Rechtschaffen, 1989; Rechtschaffen & Bergmann, 2002). But it is questionable whether death is due to selective REM deprivation, since SWS deprivation results in death as well (in 23 to 66 days). In addition, it is difficult to separate the aversive/stressful effects of REM deprivation from effects of REM deprivation per se. It is very difficult to selectively deprive an animal of a given sleep type over a long period of time. Death in the prolonged SWS/REM deprivation studies is believed to be due to a significant decline in core body temperature (as much as 2°C), with compensatory attempts to increase temperature through increased energy expenditure. Another potential cause of death in rats after REM deprivation may be a systemic bacterial infection. On the other hand, administration of antibiotics to REM-deprived rats did not prevent death.

Problems With the "Restorative" Theory of Sleep

Many theorists of sleep function have argued that NREM restores physiologic functioning, while REM restores brain functioning. Certainly the subjective feeling of being refreshed after a good night's sleep supports these restorative theories, as do the findings of sleep rebound after sleep deprivation. In addition, the secretion of anabolic hormones (such as GH during NREM) supports the theory.

Despite the intuitive appeal of the restorative hypothesis for sleep, there are several problems with the theory. First, the amount of sleep that occurs during the rebound process is not always proportional to the amount of sleep lost during the deprivation period. If sleep need was homeostatically regulated, then the organism should adjust its sleep levels in such a way as to maintain relatively constant amounts of sleep over time. But if sleep loss is not recovered on a minute-for-minute basis, then the organism may not need a certain amount of sleep to homeostatically regulate some anabolic hormone or chemical. Perhaps sleep intensity, rather than sleep amount, is what really matters. But no one has yet produced unequivocal evidence for a measure of sleep intensity that is homeostatically regulated. NREM slow waves in the delta band have been investigated as the most likely candidate for an index of sleep intensity. They are in fact sensitive to sleep deprivation, and their presence in the EEG is correlated with subjective feelings of sleep need. Nevertheless, until the chemical is identified that is (theoretically) being restored via sleep (and delta waves) and shown to be homeostatically regulated, the restorative theory of NREM sleep will be missing its central and essential ingredient. On the other hand, there is every reason to believe that the missing ingredient will be identified eventually and then we will see whether it is indeed homeostatically regulated via sleep processes. Once this restorative chemical is identified, experiments will be needed to confirm that it actually does facilitate some restorative process in body or brain.

A second problem for the restorative theory of sleep is that many people do not feel restored after a night's sleep. Between one-third and one-half of the population complains of recurrent feelings of being unrested after a night's sleep. High-quality restorative sleep is actually quite rare. Surveys show that most people wake up feeling fatigued, groggy, sluggish, and disoriented. They struggle through the day feeling sleep deprived. They do not feel refreshed by their sleep.

Third, there is a rebound of delta sleep (slow-wave NREM sleep) after hibernation in hibernating animals. Hibernation, of course, is a low-energy state and thus should not need a process to restore energy or to repair tissue since little or no energy was consumed and little or no tissue was damaged during the hibernation period. Indeed, the standard explanation for hibernation is that it is a state designed to conserve energy.

Fourth, at least one form of sleep, REM, does not appear to replenish stores of metabolic energy—instead it dissipates significant amounts of energy. Neuroimaging studies of the REM state show that it reaches brain activation levels and brain glucose utilization levels exceeding those of the waking state.

Energy Conservation Theory

Given that sleep involves reduced levels of activity and body temperature, some investigators (Berger & Phillips, 1995; Walker & Berger, 1980a) have suggested that the function of sleep, and NREM sleep in particular, is to conserve energy. Once again, the subjective feeling of being low on energy when we become tired and feeling refreshed after a good night's sleep supports the conservation theory. In addition, comparative studies have revealed that bodily metabolic rates in small animals appear to correlate weakly with NREM sleep times such that the higher the metabolic rate in an animal, the longer the NREM sleep time.

If the conservation theory is correct, then the energetic gains that accrue from sleep must be greater than what can be achieved by simple daytime rest. Body temperature decreases by about 1 to 2 degrees during NREM sleep. At neutral ambient temperatures, this decrease in temperature can translate into a 10% decrease in metabolic rate. It is unclear whether this nighttime decrease in metabolic rate is better than what can be achieved via daytime rest.

Another problem with the conservation theory is that body temperature does not decrease during REM, and metabolic activity does not decrease during REM. Nor do metabolic rates correlate with REM times. If we recall that REM alternates with NREM throughout the night, then energetic savings would have to accrue selectively during the NREM periods. The energy savings must somehow be maintained across REM periods to result in any significant net reduction in metabolic rates across the night, or else whatever savings accrued in a given NREM period would be immediately dissipated in a subsequent REM period, resulting in no net gain for the animal.

While it therefore seems reasonable to suppose that NREM supports some form of regulatory function with respect to energy budgets, the role of REM in energy regulation is less clear. Bringing in the role of energy budgets with respect to reproductive functions may help to clarify the issue.

Energy Balance in Service to Reproductive Functions

There may be a connection between sleep and overall energy balance, as measured by change in metabolic rates and reproductive functions. The relationship between changes in energy balance and changes in reproductive behaviors may hold a clue to the functional role of sleep in conserving energy. It has long been recognized that fertility is inhibited or impaired when food intake is restricted or when energy expenditure is increased by enforced exercise. Women athletes, for example, may even experience a cessation in menstrual periods. Energy balance refers to the difference between energy intake and expenditure. When energy balance is perturbed in other animals (such as our close relatives, the nonhuman primates), reproductive functions are inhibited. To come into estrus, the female needs to be reasonably well fed. These effects have been demonstrated in several species. Morin's (1986) studies are representative. These studies showed that a fasting regimen decreased concentrations of plasma estradiol, inhibited the normal LH surge, enhanced the responsiveness of positive feedback of estradiol, and decreased activation of gonadotropin-releasing hormone (GnRH) immunoreactive cells in the mediobasal thalamus and preoptic area. The latter anatomic sites are known to be sleep regulatory centers.

Reproduction, in other words, is inhibited in service to maintaining energy balance. In both the well-fed and fasted conditions, reproductive function changes in systematic ways. In the well-fed or storage mode of metabolism (the case for most modern Westerners), glucose and amino acids pass from the intestine directly into the bloodstream and are delivered to end organs and the nervous system. The liver converts these nutrients to fuels (lactacte, pyruvate, and glucose) and into glycogen. Other tissues oxidize glucose and store the excess. Storage involves the conversion of fuel into fat via lipogenesis in white adipose tissue and in the liver. Brown adipose tissue (BAT) provides a special mechanism for fat storage in the developing organism and has a special relationship to sleep.

In humans, only infants evidence functional BAT. Brown adipose tissue functions in part to support facultative or nonshivering thermogenesis in response to cold exposure. This function is supported by a unique mitochondrial 32-k-kD protein, which uncouples oxidative phosphorylation in BAT mitochondria. BAT-mediated heat production is largely dependent on sympathetic stimulation. During cold exposure, the sympathetic innervation triggers the activation of BAT. Dewasmes, Loos, Delanaud, Dewasmes, and Geloen (2003) reported that activation of BAT in the adult rat increases SWS. Infants typically retain their body heat by huddling against siblings and their mother. If NREM activates another source of heat for the infant (namely BAT), then it would protect the mother against exploitation of her heat reserves.

Peripheral metabolism of nutrients is facilitated by the release of insulin from specialized beta cells of the pancreas. Insulin levels are known to vary systematically with sleep state, with high levels of insulin occurring in NREM relative to REM. During the day, insulin secretion is highest after meals, and it facilitates uptake of glucose. The brain is dependent on glucose for the production of adenosine triphosphate.

By contrast, in the fasting state (which many assume was a frequently experienced state of early human groups), blood glucose levels are maintained by the breakdown of glycogen into glucose. If fasting continues, lactate, pyruvate, and amino acids are diverted into formation of glucose by the process of gluconeogenesis in the liver. Pancreatic insulin and adipocyte leptin secretion fall to low levels, while pancreatic glucagons and adrenal glucocorticoid secretion rise. Not surprisingly, sleep is inhibited under these circumstances, at least until starvation sets in.

Inhibition of reproductive function by changes in energy balance may be mediated by events occurring in the hypothalmus. Low caloric intake relative to activity levels (negative energy balance) can decrease the pulse frequency of hypothalamic GnRH secretion. One possibility is that this decrease is mediated by or accompanied by reductions in SWS. Given that release of GnRH as well as GHRH and GH are all influenced by intensity of delta waves in SWS, reductions in release of these regulatory hormones may be related to reductions in SWS. Reduction in release of these hormones will inhibit sexual and reproductive functions. Thus, the regulation of energy budgets via sleep mechanisms may ultimately influence reproductive behaviors.

If NREM temperature and metabolic changes signal current energy balance (rather than conserving energy per se), then REM could use that information to modulate its effects on hormones implicated in reproduction. Thus, it may be that NREM's function with respect to energy budgets is not to conserve energy per se, but rather to signal changes in energy balance. NREM could use its ability to downregulate MR to signal current energy balance, and this signal is used by both REM and the waking brain to make adjustments in nutrient intake and so on. If the SWS-related downregulation of MR is too shallow or too deep, the signal will indicate a significant perturbation in energy balance. A number of sleep disorders involving changes in eating habits (Klein-Levin syndrome, Prader-Willi syndrome) as well as sleep changes in primary eating disorders such as anorexia nervosa are consistent with the idea that sleep, reproductive functions, and appetite are related.

Memory Consolidation

A number of sleep researchers have proposed that REM functions to consolidate various types of memories (Datta, Patterson, & Siwek, 1997; Dement, 1965; Smith, 1995). REM times, for example, increase after intense learning episodes, particularly after procedural types of learning tasks

(Peigneus, Laureys, Delbeuck, & Maquet, 2001). Smith (1996) has reported that consolidation of learning of Morris water maze tasks in rats can be blocked if the animal is deprived of REM during a critical time window, which typically occurs sometime (on the order of hours) after the learning trials. By comparison, Crick and Mitchison (1983) postulated a kind of reverse learning function of REM to rid relevant neural networks of unnecessary bits of information. Crick and Mitchison, however, did not consider the role of NREM.

Despite the focus on REM, sleep-associated consolidation of information gathered during the wake state appears to depend on hippocampal-cortical interactions that occur during both SWS and REM and involve some sort of replay during REM sleep of learned associations acquired while awake (Buzsaki, 1996; Plihal & Born, 1997; Smith, 1995; Wilson & McNaughton, 1994). Wilson and McNaughton (1994), for example, showed that hippocampal cells that are active when rats learn a new maze are also active during subsequent sleep. Using PET scanning techniques, similar effects (reactivation of brain sites activated during learning) have been reported in humans (Laureys et al., 2001). Stickgold, Scott, Fosse, and Hobson (2001) reported that learning a visual discrimination task was disrupted by selective deprivation of both REM and NREM. Similarly, Plihal and Born (1997) reported that learning of paired associates and mental rotation tasks but not procedural memory tasks is dependent on subsequent NREM (early sleep) rather than REM (late morning sleep) periods for their consolidation. Thus, while both sleep states appear to participate in learning and memory, their roles in consolidation of memories are postulated to be quite different. Other investigators (e.g., Datta, 1999) point to the PGO waves of REM sleep as crucial in the consolidation process.

While both sleep states probably participate in the formation and consolidation of memories, critics have pointed out that individuals with lesions to the brain stem and subsequent loss of REM can learn nevertheless. In addition, individuals with reductions in REM due to sleep apnea or to antidepressant medications can learn as well. The properties of both REM and NREM appear to be less than optimal for learning. The selective brain activation in REM and cortical depression in NREM argue against the view that these states were designed for learning. Similarly, it is difficult to see how the autonomic instabilities, sexual activation, or motor paralysis associated with REM facilitate memory. Nevertheless, the cumulative effects of converging lines of experimental evidence suggest to me that both REM and NREM participate in memory processing. This, however, does not necessarily speak to the evolutionary functions of sleep. The fact that brain plasticity does not cease when we sleep is not surprising. Neuronal networks can learn no matter what brain state they are in. Learning, after all, takes place during the awake state as well. Indeed, the awake state seems to be more efficient when it comes to learning all kinds of materials and tasks than is sleep. Thus, even if memory consolidation occurs in sleep, this does not tell us what the specific function of sleep may be. We do not say that the function of the waking state is learning simply because learning takes place during the waking state. On the other hand, information flow to and from the hippocampus during sleep apparently takes on unique properties during REM and NREM, and thus sleep's role in memory consolidation may indeed be special and selective.

Synaptic Stabilization

A number of investigators (e.g., Kavanau, 1996; Krueger, Obal, & Fang, 1999; Moruzzi, 1966) have suggested that both REM and NREM function to maintain and stabilize selected or local functional synapses that have either been overstimulated or insufficiently stimulated during waking activity. REM sleep is thought to specialize in stabilization of motor circuits in some of these theories. Krueger et al. (1999) suggest that sleep is initiated when a local group of cells release chemical factors such as nerve growth factor and selected cytokines that cause both sleepiness and strengthening of active synapses. Adenosine has been shown to build up in local cell groups in the basal forebrain, causing a local slowing of EEG potentials. Intensity of sleep within local regions of the forebrain is correlated with waking-related use of that area during intense cognitive tasks or training.

REM Functions to Promote Brain Development

After Roffwarg et al.'s (1966) initial suggestion concerning ontogenetic functions of REM, sleep researchers such as Mirmiran et al. (1983) and Vogel (1999) found that early (neonatal) suppression of REM resulted in later (adult) alterations in behavior or neurotransmitter activity or in reductions in cell and tissue volumes in certain regions of the cerebral cortex and medulla oblongata. Marks, Shaffrey, Oksenberg, Speciale, and Roffwarg (1995) found enhanced reduction of cell sizes in both lateral geniculate nuclei in monocularly occluded kittens after REM deprivation. The large amount of REM that occurs during the juvenile period also suggests a specific role for REM in brain development. Comparative studies found significant correlations between NREM-REM cycle length and brain weight among adults, even after body weight and metabolic rates were held constant. It is difficult to understand why, if REM's function is purely to promote brain development, it should persist into adulthood or have the properties it has both in the juvenile and in the adult. Nevertheless, there can be little doubt that REM in interaction with NREM is crucial for normal development of brain and behavior. What has yet to be identified is exactly what aspect of brain and behavior development REM is crucial for.

REM Functions in Interaction With NREM to Eliminate Parasitic Infection and Regulate Selected Immune System Functions

It is common knowledge that one becomes sleepy with the onset of infection, and this infection-related sleepiness occurs in nonhuman animals as well (Hart, 1990). Experimental work confirms that soon after infectious challenge, animals exhibit an increase in NREM durations and a decrease in REM (Kreuger & Fang, 2000). Conversely, sleep loss can render one more vulnerable to infection. After sleep deprivation, several immune system parameters change, including natural killer cell activity, interleukin-1, tumor necrosis factor, prostaglandins, nitric oxide, and adenosine. After prolonged (2 to 3 weeks) sleep deprivation, rats become septicemic (Rechtschaffen & Bergmann, 2001) and die. The relation between sleep states and parasite elimination has not been sufficiently studied but seems a very promising avenue for further research. I believe that many of the properties of NREM could in fact be accounted for by host-parasite interactions—a form, of course, of genetic conflict.

REM Modulates Expression of Innate or Inherited Behaviors

Jouvet (1962; 1999) observed that cats seemed to act out imaginary interactions with prey or with adversaries when lesions to their brain stems destroyed the motor inhibition normally associated with REM. Electrophysiologic recordings showed that these cats were nevertheless asleep, despite their vigorous motor activities. Jouvet believed he was seeing release of normally inhibited behaviors in these cats, and these behaviors seemed to be primary genetically programmed behaviors involving fear, flight, fighting, and sex. The role, if any, of NREM in the production of such behaviors is not clear.

REM Regulates Expressions of Emotions and/or Emotional Balance

Many studies involving deprivation of REM have resulted in enhanced motivational states and emotions. Thus, some investigators have suggested that REM functions to inhibit or to modulate emotional arousal and motivational striving. Vogel pointed out that REM deprivation improves depressive mood states in depressed patients (see recent review in Vogel, 1999). REM deprivation presumably alleviates depression by enhancing drives and other motivated behaviors (i.e., REM deprivation removes REM's tonic inhibitory effects on drives and emotions). Greenberg and Pearlman (1993) have pointed out that REM values vary with a person's stress levels and emotional history. Recent neuroimaging studies are consistent with the emotional regulation view of REM, as REM is associated with high activation levels in the limbic system and the amygdala. Meerlo, de Bruin, Strijkstra, and Daan (2001) have shown that social conflict in rats, particularly aggressive interactions, enhances NREM sleep, but had no effect on REM. On the other hand, sexual interactions were associated with mild inhibitory effects on REM. Finally, we have seen in chapter 4 that REM interacts with NREM over the course of a night, and these interactions are correlated with emotional changes in dream content.

The foregoing summaries of theories of REM do not exhaust existing accounts of REM function. I discuss several other such accounts in chapter 9 after I have reviewed the literature on dream phenomenology and content. In this chapter, I have summarized only those accounts that seek to articulate a function of REM that accommodates REM's interactions with NREM. Most other theories of REM ignore effects of NREM, thus making them less adequate than accounts summarized in the present chapter.

CHAPTER 7

Phenomenology of REM Dreams

This chapter and the next focus on properties of dreams associated with REM periods of sleep. While REM is the phase of sleep from which dream reports are most reliably elicited, dream reports can also be elicited from any other stage of sleep, including sleep onset and SWS. Dream reports from NREM stages of sleep tend to be shorter, less emotional, and less visually vivid than reports obtained from REM. Activation of REM, furthermore, does not necessarily eventuate in a dream or at least a dream report. Children who have abundant REM do not consistently report dreams until visuospatial and cognitive skills have matured enough to support reporting of visual narratives (Foulkes, 1982). Similarly, patients with lesions in the orbitofrontal cortex, basal forebrain, and near the occipitotemporoparietal junction sometimes report complete cessation of dreaming (Solms, 1997). In addition, Solms emphasized that disconnection of the ascending meso-limbic-cortical dopaminergic tracts from their termination sites in ventro-medial frontal lobes could also lead to the loss of dreaming. Given that this tract is associated with instinctual appetitive drive and motivational states, it seems reasonable to conclude that this dopaminergic system may participate in generation of some dreams. The loss of dreaming in these patients is not due simply to inability to recall dreams, as their basic memory and recall abilities are largely intact. REM physiology, as measured by sleep EEG, is normal in these individuals; thus REM is still operating.

Dissociation of REM and Dreaming Does Not Mean That REM Expression Excludes Dreaming

You can have activation of REM and no dreams, and you can have dreams without activation of REM (as in the case of NREM dreams). In short, REM is neither necessary nor sufficient to produce dreams (one needs a certain set of cognitive skills to produce dreams, although animals with

REM appear to have experiences that on the face of it suggest that they are experiencing mental content/mental simulations that appear to be dreams). On the other hand, REM is the brain state that most reliably produces what human beings have for centuries called dreams. Most spontaneously recalled dreams are dreams people remember upon awakening in the morning and, given that REM predominates in the later part of the night and early morning, these spontaneously recalled dreams are likely derived from REM. Thus, I assume in what follows that the majority of dreams reported as spontaneously recalled dreams by the persons from whom they were obtained are in fact REM dreams.

Cognition During Sleep

Despite the fact that there is little doubt that cognition occurs in all forms of sleep, many people still believe sleep is essentially a passive process in which the only thing of importance that occurs is rest. If rest were the sole object of sleep, it seems unlikely that Nature would have allowed cogitation to occur during sleep. Thinking requires energy and mental work. It is costly. Nor is the form of cognition that occurs in sleep simply random. Cognition during sleep is highly organized, with very unique and specific properties that require specialized brain circuits to be produced. Dreaming is metabolically and mentally costly. Why then should cognitive activity occur at all during sleep?

Traditionally, we think of cognition as serving very practical survival needs: it allows us to communicate with others, to think through plans of action, to reason about problems, and so on. All of these typical cognitive processes (communication, thinking, reasoning, and planning) seem to be designed to serve the waking state or to function during daytime events. We cannot, as far as we know, communicate with others during sleep (though the shared dreams of bed partners and close relatives, as well as significant hit rates in experiments with psi phenomena during dreams, etc., raise questions in this regard; see Van de Castle, 1994, for review). It is also not clear that thinking in the form of extended reasoning and planning about problems can occur at all during dream sleep. Recent findings from fMRI and PET studies of brain activation during REM sleep, for example, suggest that the thinking and reasoning part of the brain—the dorsolateral prefrontal cortex—is not fully activated during REM sleep.

Despite these findings, we know that some forms of cognition do in fact take place during sleep, including REM sleep. What types or forms of cognition are these? The answer might help us answer the question of why any form of cognition occurs at all during sleep and is vitally important for dream research. If we knew, for example, that planning-related cognitions around current concerns were the most frequently reported type of cognitive activity occurring in dreams, then we would be justified in exploring the possibility that the function of dreaming had something to do with planning or problem solving. Or if we found that no single type of cognitive activity predominated in dreams and instead dreaming images and cognitions were typically bizarre and random, then dreaming would probably have no important discernible cognitive functions. Finally, if mental states associated with dreaming enacted the same variety of cognitive phenomena as occurs in waking life, then we might conclude that dream cognition is basically no different from waking cognition, and that dreaming functions to satisfy the same constraints and the same goals as waking cognitions. To answer the question of what species of cognition we are dealing with when we deal with dreams, we need to catalog the list of formal mental features that characterize (REM) dreams.

Formal Properties of Dreams

What is the best way to study the formal features of dreams? Presumably, the same techniques used to study waking cognitive processes might be used to study cognitive systems that produce dreams. That is, one identifies the formal features of the dream and then conducts experiments to try to decompose the processes that support that formal feature. If, for example, we want to understand why the dream is often in the form of a mental simulation of an ongoing series of events, then we might take what is known of how mental models or simulations are produced during waking consciousness and see if the relevant principles apply to dream life. Similarly, if dreams often occur in the form of narratives or stories, then perhaps dream stories, like waking stories, are composed of a series of episodes that are in turn controlled by a specific grammar that imposes hierarchical structure on the order in which these episodes can occur within the dream. Such techniques have indeed been used successfully in study of dream processes and are reflected in the works of many dream researchers (see Foulkes, 1985, for example and review).

Basic Visual Features

Dreams are not chaotic assemblages of bizarre images but rather involve perceptually and thematically organized material in the form of images, themes, and simulations of the dreamer's lifeworld. Dreams can last as long as the longest REM episode (potentially 30–45 minutes). Visually, dreams exhibit greater clarity in the foreground of the dreamer's attention, while background details are vaguely represented. Although 20–30% of dreams are achromatic, most dreams are in color. Achromatic dreams may be due to lower levels of activation than is typical for REM in temporal and occipital association areas that support color processing.

Automaticity

Cognitive analyses of how dreams work assume that dreams are involuntary symbolic acts that utilize existing memory images to construct new images that more or less successfully simulate features of the dreamer's lifeworld. Whether we like it or not, dreams "happen" to us. We cannot shut them off. Given that sensory input is diminished relative to the waking state, dreams are more likely to access memories to produce the scenes we encounter in the dream than to create new images from current sensory experience. On the other hand, dreams are capable of producing brand-new images—images never before encountered by the dreamer (Dorus, Dorus, & Rechtschaffen, 1971). Dreams, although involuntary in one sense, are nevertheless characterized by a substantial level of creativity.

Dreams Are Not Confabulatory

The images occurring in dreams represent a combination of images drawn from memory traces and newly created images produced by the dream. Yet many of these memory traces are decontextualized memory fragments: images that are abstracted away from the context in which they originally occurred. These decontextualized images, along with new images created "on the fly" by the dream itself, are then packaged into a story or plot of varying complexity, with some dreams creating simple snapshots of an event and others involving long story lines with many subplots and changes along the way. It is as if the dream machinery, when fed decontextualized memory images, "confabulates" a story composed of both memory images and new images to explain the decontextualized images.

On the other hand, if the dream were a mere after-the-fact confabulation or rationalization for a series of decontextualized memory images, there would be no reason to expect consistent content across dreams. Confabulations, furthermore, do not require epic-length story structure to do the job. Short ad hoc explanations are the stock-in-trade of confabulatory responses during waking life and in clinical populations. Even if the cognitive system was bombarded with a relentless stream of decontextualized memory fragments, a confabulatory response would not produce the kind of intricate, thematically connected, self-involved narrative we call a dream.

Dream Creativity

Dreams, in short, are creative, productive, generative, and fecund. They are not mere reflections of waking consciousness, nor are they mere catalogues of floating memory fragments. They take specialized input (e.g., including that produced by selective brain activation associated with REM, memory fragments, day residues, fleeting visceral sensations, and other sources of content not yet characterized) and subject that input to specialized processing algorithms using selective neural processes, and then the dream machinery outputs a unique cognitive product that we call the dream.

Dreaming, in short, is a specialized cognitive process that produces a specialized product. It cannot be mere froth or epiphenomena of essentially random firing of brain stem neurons. The dream's specialized cognitive processes are further evidence for the idea that dreaming is functional. If the brain and cognitive system go through the trouble of creating specialized systems to produce a unique product, chances are that there is a reason for doing so.

Selective Processing Preferences of the Dream

In spontaneously recalled dreams, the visual sense predominates. It is rare to remember a smell or a taste from a dream. Many dreams contain unusual amounts of emotion, and dreams containing negative emotions are more typically recalled. Hobson points out that while dreams are in some sense hypermnesic, with greater access to memories while dreaming, dreams themselves are difficult to remember upon awakening. While we are dreaming, we also believe in the reality of what we are dreaming. Dreams compel belief, so dreaming must activate whatever cognitive system supports belief fixation. The fixation of belief during a dream is not mere uncritical acceptance of incongruous acts or events. While impairment in the critical sense may occur in dreams, suspension of a monitoring system would not produce the variety of belief phenomena we see expressed in dreams. Suspicion of the critical faculty may help to account for acceptance of bizarre and incongruous images and events (such as dream events that violate the laws of physics), but it cannot account for belief that the dream setting is real and that the individuals one interacts with in dreams are real and that the interactions matter. These are matters of emotional functioning that violate no laws of physics and that contain a logic of sentiment that is consistent with feeling's waking manifestations. On the other hand, it is often true that these emotional interactions occur within a dream plot that, from the point of view of the waking mind, is odd or puzzling or in some sense irrelevant to, or disproportionate to, the emotional interaction itself. One might, for example, be interacting with a friend in an emotionally important way, but the interaction will be occurring in an unfamiliar setting and in the context of an attempt to obtain some unusual goal or outcome.

Dreams as Simulations

A fundamental property of dreams is that they are mental simulations of the world and the dreamer's lifeworld. Dreams are actually mental images—they are not products of standard visual perception since the eyes are closed. Residual visuoperceptual procesess such as phosphenes within the closed eye might still operate, but these residua are impoverished relative to the richness of the content a typical dream expresses.

McNamara (2000) suggested that one such form of mental simulation in dreaming involved the processing of counterfactual simulations generated in response to an anomaly or negative event in a dream narrative. This idea was summarized in the following hypothesis: Cognitive operations in dreams function to identify a norm violation recorded in episodic and autobiographical memory and then to reinstate normality in memory by generating counterfactuals to the violation.

By "reinstating normality" in memory, I mean that the information content associated with the norm violation has to be integrated into the semantic networks of episodic and autobiographical memory. If the integration does not occur, then the person will perhaps be less able to interpret novel experiences and thus will be less able to effectively learn from them. Counterfactual processing may be crucial for this type of human learning (see chapters in Byrne, 1997; Roese, 1997; Roese & Olson, 1995).

In daily life, when we encounter an unhappy or frustrating event, we appraise the significance of the outcome by imagining alternatives or what might have happened if things had gone differently. We then cognitively generate simulations of imaginative scenarios that would allow or promote the alternative outcome. We do this typically by constructing a visual scenario of the events in question and then changing or mutating various causal antecedents of the outcome of the event. We next compare the simulations of what might have been to what actually happened in an attempt to restore the unwanted outcome to a more normative routine outcome. To the extent that the comparison process reveals that the counterfactual alternatives seem plausible or possible as compared to what actually happened, we feel tension, distress, or discomfort and are therefore motivated to try to right the situation or to make sense of the situation. By engaging in these counterfactual simulations, we may more easily learn how to avoid negative outcomes in the future, or we may learn how to strive more effectively for current unmet goals or desired outcomes. It is as if the counterfactual mechanism activates a motivational state in us such that we strive to "make right" what had gone wrong or "unmet" or what had almost happened. I suggest that we experience these counterfactually initiated motivational urges or states along with associated imaginative embodiments of these states, in some but not all dreams.

In some dreams, one can actually see the dreamer repeatedly generate a counterfactual scenario along with attempts to return to normal routines typically associated with the setting or situation depicted in the dream. This repeated generation of counterfactual alternatives to the dream theme or norm violation results in a story line or narrative format wherein the dreamer attempts to right or undo the abnormal situation. Take, for example, the following dream of a 25-year-old on the fourth night of a laboratory study of dreaming. The dream report is from Strauch and Meier (1996, p. 126), and occurred in the second phase of REM:

> I am in a major American city where there is a baptism of a rocket for a manned moon capsule. People have come from all over the world and expect

something sensational to happen. My sister and Suzanne and I have been invited. Everything took place at a harbor and there was some kind of breakdown at the start and the rocket took off ten or maybe a hundred meters beyond the ramp, and then simply fell back down. And we wondered what might have happened if it had toppled over—just plunged into the water or if it had lifted 200 meters into the air and maybe flipped over and then fallen into the water. If it had gone as high as one kilometer it might have fallen into the city and on top of a skyscraper. And then we fantasized whether the rocket might be propelled by the strength of a statesman—Giscard d'Estaing was there too—and thrown upwards like that, which would certainly have caused a debacle. And that was what happened. Several people representing all kinds of nations grabbed the rocket at its bottom, lifted it up and tried to propel it skyward. And the rocket did fly for about one hundred meters, twisted and returned toward the water and everything was tried to save it. And they succeeded once more in putting the rocket into orbit. Finally it did fall into the water. All this time we took photographs from all kinds of perspectives.

The dreamer starts by announcing the situation that will be subjected to counterfactual analysis: there was a breakdown in the takeoff pattern of a rocket about to undergo its maiden voyage. The norm violation in this case is the failed takeoff. The subject himself then (counterfactually) states, "And we wondered what might have happened if..." and the generation of counterfactual scenarios begins. As the attempt to undo the failed takeoff proceeds, more stringent, more desperate, and more bizarre scenarios are tried or at least imagined in order to undo the negative event. This progressive generation of counterfactual alternatives to an extranormal or unexpected event may be one source of bizarre imagery in dreams (e.g., Giscard d'Estaing propelling the rocket). After a number of scenarios are generated, the norm violation is "handled" or undone and counterfactual generation ceases: "they succeeded ... in putting the rocket into orbit." Now I realize this rather sketchy and facile analysis is much too open and ill-defined to be convincing. I mention it only to show the kinds of items a scoring of counterfactual content could target.

Play, Pretense, and Imagination in Dream Phenomenology

A number of investigators (Bulkeley, 1999; Cheyne, 2000; Humphrey, 2000; Piaget, 1962; Spinka, Newberry, & Bekoff, 2001) have suggested similarities between REM, dreams, and play. Both play and dreams involve a stance of "pretend" or simulations of actions, interactions of worlds, energetic displays of seemingly useless simulations for their own sake, creativity, strong emotions, and so forth. Thus, it seems reasonable to pursue the question of potential interrelations between play and dreaming.

Three types of play have traditionally been distinguished: locomotor, object, and social play. Locomotor play involves energetic displays of motor abilities and can occur in either a solitary or social arena; object play involves a focus on an object or objects that are manipulated in endless ways; and social play involves social interactions with a conspecific. Each of these three forms of play may have different causal bases, ontogenies, phylogenies, and functions, but may nevertheless occur together in a single bout of play. The consensus among biologists who study play appears to be that play is most common among mammals and birds, but that certain reptilian species such as crocodiles may exhibit play as well. This is because juvenile forms of play are not likely to occur unless extended parental care allows for the safety of a juvenile during play. Parental care may occur among crocodiles and certainly occurs in birds and mammals. This phylogenetic distribution of play fits well with what is known concerning the phylogenetic distribution of REM (see chapter 3). Thus, there are indeed many deep similarities between REM dreams and play. On the other hand, there are significant dissimilarities as well (see table 7.1).

While play is typically associated with pleasurable affect, dreams are not. While play involves a seeking after greater and greater forms of stimulation, dreams do not seem to seek increases in stimulation. On the contrary, dreams, many theorists suggest, may act as a safety valve to attenuate high levels of arousal. Displays of dominance, threat, and submission are relatively absent in play, while simulations of threat are frequent in dreams. Play utilizes special signaling procedures (e.g., the bow stance in canids) to convey to a conspecific that "this is pretend," not an attack, and so on. No such signals have yet been identified in dreams, though it must be admitted that dreams have not yet been analyzed for their signaling properties. Finally, play is most frequently observed among juveniles, while dreaming is a lifelong process, though REM expression is greater in juveniles than in adults.

It may be that some portion of dreams involve real instances of play, such as dreams that involve the production of verbal puns or funny situations. Thus, while dreams cannot be completely assimilated into the category of play, they nevertheless draw on cognitive systems whose roots are in play. While I can imagine dreams involving both locomotor and social forms of play, I doubt whether object forms of play are frequent in dreams. There is, in general, not a lot of manipulation of objects by the hands in dreams. On the other hand, many energetic motor sequences of various kinds (running, walking, flying, fighting, struggling, lovemaking, pushing, etc.) and a fair amount of social interaction occur in dreams.

Piaget (1962) was one of the first to link play and dreams, noting that both exhibit properties reminiscent of "preoperational" schemas of thought. Preoperational forms of cognition are characteristic of children before they reach adolescence. The dreamer therefore lacks the concepts or the abilities to perform cognitive operations of conservation and reversibility. On the

Table 7.1. Similarities and Dissimilarities Between REM Dreams and Play

Attribute of Play	Comment With Respect to REM Dreams
No obvious immediate function (play behaviors appear purposeless)	Dream features and content seem not to be ordered toward any special product or purpose.
Playful acts are sequentially variable	Dreams tend to display narrative and sequential structure with respect to content but order of themes may be variable.
Quick and energetically expensive	Brain activation studies suggest that REM and REM-related dreams are physiologically/energetically costly.
Motor sequences are exaggerated, incomplete, or awkward	Dream actions may sometimes be bizarre.
Most prevalent in juveniles	Dreams begin in childhood and then never cease.
Breakdown in social role relationships	Social roles are typically maintained in dreams but they may also be altered occasionally.
Special play signals (i.e., that tell a conspecific that this is play, not threat or attack)	It is not known whether dream features or content elements function as signals. Who would be the receiver of such signaling?
Mixing of behavior pattern from several contexts	Dream elements often composed of de-contextualized memory fragments.
Relative absence of threat and submission	Threat scenarios common in spontaneously recalled dreams.

(*Continued*)

Table 7.1. (continued)

Attribute of Play	Comment With Respect to REM Dreams
Relative absence of final consumatory acts	The self (dreamer) often struggles toward some goal and may or may not attain that goal.
Stimulation seeking	Dreams do not seem to seek stimulation.
Pleasurable affect	Most dreams are rated high in negative affect.

Excerpts from Table 7.1 published in Marc Bekoff and John A. Byers, eds. *Animal Play: Evolutionary, Comparative and Ecological Perspectives* (New York: Cambridge University Press, 1998). Reprinted with the permission of Cambridge Univerisity Press.

other hand, it seems to me that the dreaming mind assumes and understands principles of conservation and reversibility. Nevertheless, Piaget suggests that that is why dreams seem so odd to the adult consciousness. According to Piaget, it is as if each night we return to preoperational forms of cognition in our dreams and then, when we remember a dream, we try to translate this form of cognition into an adult language. Piaget emphasizes the role of the image in dreams as a first-draft form of imitation and of accommodation and adaptation to the external world. Once the child acquires the capacity to form images, these images begin to form a system of meanings and symbolic thought capable of representing some aspects of the child's world. Since imitative images develop in the context of the child's affective life, the system of meanings is bound up with the affective life. Affect-laden imitative imagery supports preoperational thought in the child and is never abandoned as the child develops and grows into the capacity to utilize operational and abstract forms of thought. The affect-laden system of imitative images also grows and can be used in various forms of activity, from dreams to play to art and imagination. Thus, dream thought should not be seen as regression away from more advanced forms of waking thought (though some of Piaget's writings seem to suggest just this); rather, dream thought is a living system supporting all of these extrarational, symbolic forms of cognition.

Humphrey (2000) noted that dreaming, like childhood play, allowed the dreamer to simulate participation in dramatic or dangerous situations in a safe context. Play, according to Humphrey, allows for practice in role-playing and empathy. Dreaming provides for education in simulating mental states of others via subjection of the dreamer to myriad emotional changes and social conflicts simulated in the dream.

Consistent with Humphrey's suggestion of the function of dreaming as practice in mind reading skills is a report of lack of dreaming in a patient with Asperger's syndrome (Godbout, Bergeron, Stip, & Mottron, 1998). Asperger's syndrome is considered to be related to autism. Like children with autism, children and adults with Asperger's syndrome evidence impaired social interactions, theory of mind deficits, restricted interests, and stereotyped behaviors. But unlike children with autism, children with Asperger's do not show any delay in acquisition of language or other cognitive skills. The case reported by Godbout et al. evidenced very low levels of SWS, reduced spindling and K-complex activity, with relatively normal REM indices. Despite three awakenings after onset of REM, the patient reported no dream recall. This case is remarkable, as it suggests one can have signs of REM but be without dreams. In addition, if the function of dreaming were to contribute to development of mind reading skills then we would expect poor social interactions in persons with impaired dreaming. If this case is any indication, it appears that dreaming per se is important for development of social skills—not just REM itself. Additionally, NREM SWS and stage 2 (including spindling and K-complexes) appear not to be crucial for maintenance of life, as this patient had abnormal NREM and probably had impaired NREM as a child as well. In any case, autistic children and presumably children with Asperger's as well do not evidence normal play behaviors—nor are sleep and dreaming functioning normally in these children. It may be that impaired dreaming contributes to these children's apparent inability to engage in normal play as well as to their later social deficits.

Proteanism

Miller (2000) and Driver and Humphries (1988) have called attention to "protean behavior" as an important quality of human behavior. Because proteanism in animal behavior has been related to play, intelligence, learning, and creativity, it may be related to dreams as well. Protean behavior is adaptively unpredictable behavior. A zebra, for example, emits protean or unpredictable behavior in its escape from a predator. If a zebra always chose a consistent escape route from a lion, the lion would be able to predict the zebra's trajectory, and the zebra would be eaten. The lowly housefly exhibits unpredictability in its escape flight pattern and so is notoriously difficult to swat. Rabbits have evolved the ability to zigzag in complex, unpredictable ways when they are chased. The flying fish can leap clear out of the ocean up to 400 meters in the sky before reentering the sea in an unpredictable location. Since zebras and other prey choose unpredictable escape routes and their predators attempt to adjust accordingly, it appears that proteanism may evolve from arms races between predator and prey, or between conspecifics with differing genetic interests. Animals whose brains produce only predictable behaviors will not survive such an arms race.

Driver and Humphries (1988) identified several types of protean behavior, including escape behaviors, death feigning, immobility, sexual display as a fertile conspecific, counterattack (pretending to be a predator), convulsions, startling screeches or vocalizations, piloerection (hair standing on end), penile erections, incontinence, rapid coloration changes, swellings, and "going beserk." The latter behavior may be added to seizure activity to maximize startle, confusion, and hesitation in a predator.

Predators use a similar array of devices to produce unpredictable behaviors in order to confuse their prey. Weasels and foxes, for example, perform a kind of "crazy dance" when approaching prey. Here is where play enters the picture: foxes will chase one another, wrestle one another, jump into the air, and roll wildly on the ground before attacking the prey. Play, then, enhances unpredictability. Often the prey watches these antics with a kind of mesmerized fascination, just as we do when watching the play of domesticated animals. Much protean behavior in mammals first emerges in the form of play. The single erratic escape display, in which the animal darts about in unpredictable patterns is a prominent feature of play in primates, including humans.

How, then, does the brain produce unpredictable behaviors? Something is known about brain mechanisms in seizures. Convulsive seizures probably involve a relaxation of inhibitory thresholds in cortical sites—particularly motor centers. Debilitating, chronic seizure activity, of course, is not adaptive but may represent a chronic disinhibition of brain centers around the seizure focus. What little is known about the neurobiology of proteanism in humans suggests that dopaminergic systems of the frontal lobes are crucial. For example, when asked to generate random sequences of numbers or letters, patients with Parkinson's disease are much less likely than healthy control subjects to be able to do so. Instead, they tend to produce nonrandom patterns of repeating sequences.

Does REM dreaming involve proteanism? It would be interesting to see if REM deprivation impaired the ability to produce random sequences of numbers. Although most REM dreams depict rather mundane everyday scenes and actions, some REM dreams seem to contain especially bizarre content, where the story line and imagery depict strange or unusual, even impossible scenes and the character's identities and features are uncertain and changeable, with frequent plot twists and plot surprises. These are dreams in which proteanism in the form of unpredictable content seems to obtain. Hobson and others have argued that such dreams present us with a ready-to-hand organic model of psychosis, delusion, and dementia. It is as if the brain goes into a chaotic protean state whenever REM dreams display unusual amounts of bizarre content.

On the other hand, even less spectacular, more mundane dreams display exceptional instances of creativity. REM deprivation certainly impairs creativity, which, on the face of it, likely draws on protean behavioral sources.

There are a number of accounts of people finding solutions to previously intractable problems during a dream. Finally, Stickgold, Scott, Rittenhouse, and Hobson (1998) reported that weakly related primes were more effective in facilitating word/nonword identification tasks than closely related primes after REM awakenings than after NREM awakenings, while the opposite was true for NREM, indicating perhaps that REM facilitates processing of more distant associates in a semantic network than does NREM. Creativity likely involves, at least in part, just such connecting of distant associates.

Despite the generative creativity in dreams and the occasional explosive production of an epic dream replete with bizarre imagery and intense affect, with inexplicable plot twists, most dream events are tightly constrained into the form of a story line or narrative.

Narrative

Narratives are composed of a plot or plots with goals and subgoals of a group of actors who strive to achieve these goals in the context of a setting and a plot. Typically, what drives the story line is conflict between the actors concerning their goals. Every story, furthermore, ends with some kind of resolution of the conflict. It may be that while waking cognition can certainly create a narrative, it appears to cost it some effort: storytelling is an effortful, attention-demanding cognitive process that requires keeping track of "who did what to whom and in what order." Dreams, by contrast, appear to create narratives effortlessly, with no monitoring mechanism to keep track of sequential ordering of narrative elements. Dreams nevertheless produce well-formed narratives, and the dream's natural cognitive product may be a narrative.

Foulkes and Schmidt (1983) attempted to quantify degree of temporal continuity or coherence in dream reports by examining which elements of dreams (characters, settings, activities, etc.) change from one temporal unit to another. They found that characters did not change arbitrarily with respect to their settings and that long dream reports tended to be more coherent than shorter reports or reports derived from sleep onset or NREM.

In order to investigate the question as to whether storylike organization is imposed on the content of a dream when a person recalls that dream, Cipolli and Poli (1992) collected (from 20 subjects) both night reports obtained immediately upon awakening from an EEG-defined period of REM sleep and corresponding morning reports. All of the reports were analyzed using a slightly modified version of a standard story grammar (Mandler and Johnson, 1977). The authors found that REM reports obtained immediately upon awakening and reports of the dream hours later during the morning did not differ significantly in terms of formal story grammar features. Number of units/episodes/transitions and themes were roughly the same. Cipolli, Bolzani, and Tuozzi (1998) later reported similar results with a different set of dream reports. These data indicate that the narrative structure of a dream emerges from the dream itself, is a product of the dream and not imposed upon it from waking consciousness.

REM dreams are better at creating narratives than are NREM dreams. Using a very detailed story grammar to score storylike structure in dream reports, Kuiken, Nielsen, Thomas, and McTaggart (1983) reported that REM dreams exhibited more storylike structure than did NREM reports. Nielsen et al. (2001) reported that more stage REM than stage 2 reports contained at least one story element and a greater proportion of instances of episodic progression, but only for late-night reports of high-frequency dream recallers.

The Narrative Self in Dreams

Narratives are particularly good vehicles for revealing character traits or dispositions of the actors depicted in the story: How does each actor respond when faced with a struggle or conflict? Narratives reveal character. Persons form their personal identities, in part, via construction of autobiographical narratives or life stories (Gallagher, 2003; Schectman, 1996). The self, as constructed by such autobiographical narratives, would not be fully unified or univocal but more a product of "incomplete summation and selective subtraction, imperfect memories and multiple reiterations" (Gallagher, 2003, p. 338), and thus could help to account for internal conflict, moral indecision, and self-deception at the heart of personal decision making in a life. Autobiographical memories are therefore central to the construction of a narrative self. These personal episodic memories, however, are a matter of inference and reconstruction of past events based on current available evidence and knowledge. This reconstructive work is done in service of the ego, and material inconsistent with current ego identity is disqualified or edited out of the system and awareness.

Mazzoni, Loftus, Seitz, and Lynn (1999) showed that "dream interpretation" could actually create false autobiographical memories in subjects who thought that dreams were useful for revealing new information. Mazzoni et al. simply had subjects attend a therapy session wherein the clinician interpreted one of the subject's dreams as suggesting that an early trauma (being attacked by a bully) had occurred to the subject, which the subject had forgotten. Even though these subjects had indicated previously on a life events questionnaire that they had never been attacked by a bully, after receiving the "dream interpretation," several subjects claimed that they had a specific "memory" of being attacked by a bully when they were children.

Clearly, autobiographical memory is quite malleable, and dreams and dream interpretation involve editing these autobiographical memories, presumably to assist in ongoing construction of a narrative self. We should not underestimate the extent to which people use dreams to reflect on their own behaviors and identities. Herman and Shows (1984) showed that college students (N = 295 subjects aged from 20s to 70s) recalled an average of 10 dreams per month. Dream recall declined steadily with age to an average of about 5 per month in the 70s group. Among participants, 42% indicated a preference for more recall and two thirds of the younger sample (20s) reported that they occasionally or frequently tried to interpret their dreams. Only about 30% of middle-aged subjects were interested in interpretation. Interest in interpretation, however, rose again in the 50s and 60s age groups.

Does REM sleep participate in this process of the construction of a narrative self? The dream research community associated with the psychoanalytic tradition might well answer in the affirmative and might well cite hundreds of studies that demonstrate changes in the sense of self that pattern with changes in the ways in which the self is presented in dream narratives. More recently, Fosse et al. (2003) examined the incorporation of life episodes (that presumably would become episodic memories) into dreams by asking a group of volunteers to write down all the dreams they could remember day by day over a 2-week period. Each day, the subjects were also asked to score their dreams for the incorporation of any of their waking experiences. The subjects also kept a log of daily experiences and concerns so that after the data collection period was completed, independent raters could look at the log with its record of daily experiences as well as any dreams recorded by participants and judge whether the dreams contained any evidence of processing of episodic memories. The investigators found that while 65% of dream reports contained some evidence of material from past experiences recorded in the logs, only about 1.4% of these past experiences met criteria to be narrative or episodic memories. Those criteria were the following: the past experience had to be associated with a waking event by the participants themselves, and it had to share with the real-life event the same location and at least two additional features involving the same characters, objects, actions, themes, or emotions. Finally, the reports in question had to be scored as episodic memories by the independent judges.

The results of this study are remarkable in several respects. First, it confirms that dreams do contain evidence of active memory processing. After all, 65% of dreams contained elements that were confidently identified as coming from the past waking experiences of the subject. One would think that these fragments of past experiences found in over two thirds of spontaneously recalled dreams would participate in consolidation of narrative memories. Basing themselves on the result that only 1.4% of the dreams contained clear episodic memories, the authors, however, concluded that REM dreams probably do not participate in consolidation of episodic memories. Instead they prefer a model of episodic memory consolidation based on Buzsaki's (1996) notion of a hippocampal-neocortical dialogue. Basing himself on electrophysiologic studies of hippocampal-cortical interactions, Buzsaki claims that during the waking state, information flows from the cortex into the hippocampus. The hippocampus then binds together different sensory-affective elements of an event into a protoepisodic memory. During slow-wave NREM sleep, these protomemories are consolidated into episodic memories and transferred to the cortex for storage. During REM sleep, hippocampal outflow to the cortex is blocked. Instead, the hippocampus receives information from cortical networks, thus preventing transfer of newly consolidated episodic memories to the cortex.

Whatever the merits of the current model of the hippocampal-neocortical dialogue in explaining processing and consolidation of episodic memories, at least Fosse et al. (2003) attempt to relate their findings to relevant neural models of memory. On the other hand, the data collected by Fosse et al. suggest that the raw material for processing of episodic memories clearly occurs in two thirds of REM dreams. It may be, as investigators have suggested in the past, that REM performs a kind of editing operation of memory records in service of construction of an "acceptable" self-narrative. Fosse et al. show that exact replicas (or replay) of previous experiences do not occur very frequently in REM. Instead, elements of previous experiences turn up as constituents of the dream narrative. One might then ask whether the memory elements identified as present in at least two thirds of dreams participate in any special way in the action of the dream narrative. Do they refer, for example, to dream characters or only to the background location? Do they define the goals of the dream-self or his or her feelings, and so on? What part do these memory fragments play in the dream narrative? While Fosse et al.'s results make it clear that the memory elements do not add up to a coherent episodic memory in any given dream, they may nevertheless make it possible to form ongoing autobiographical memory narratives by allowing for adjustments in one's autobiographical picture of the self insofar as it depends on episodic memories.

Metaphor

Many authors have suggested that many of the images in dreams function as metaphors. Metaphors, according to Lakoff (2001, p. 265), are "ways of understanding relatively abstract concepts in terms of those that are more concrete." Lakoff gives the example of the root metaphor "love is a journey" that then generates a number of derivative images: "Our relationship is at a dead end," "It's been a long bumpy road," "We're spinning our wheels," "We've lost our way," and so forth. It is easy to see how, if this root metaphor were activated in a dream, it could generate a number of corresponding images that could plausibly occur in a dream (being lost, car out of control, a bumpy ride, etc.). While investigators in the psychoanalytic tradition have studied the roles of metaphor in generation of dream imagery, I know of no recent studies that can give us basic information on metaphor in dreams. How frequently do metaphors occur in dreams? Do they structure the narrative? Are certain types of metaphor favored over others? Does use of metaphor in dreams change over time? Metaphor is not unique to dreams, but I suspect it is characteristic of dreams.

Self-Reflectiveness in Dreams

There seems to be a lapse in self-reflectiveness in dreams, and this lapse may be due to deactivation of the dorsolateral prefrontal cortex (as demonstrated by neuroimaging studies) and impaired attentional processing. On the other hand, some investigators have pointed out that these same neuroimaging studies show clear activation of other structures known to participate in high-level attentional processing. These sites include the hippocampus, orbitofrontal cortex, anterior cingulate, thalamus, selected sites in parietal lobes, and so on. These authors point out that the P300 evoked potential wave is intact during REM. The P300 is elicited in the waking state whenever high-level attentional processes are activated in response to unexpected events in the environment. Hippocampal theta waves are prominent in REM in many animals. In the waking state, hippocampal theta is involved in attentional processing of significant sensory information and thus may be playing a similar role in REM. Finally, LaBerge, Kahan, and Levitan (1995) and Kahan, LaBerge, Levitan, and Zimbardo (1997) directly compared levels of self-reflectiveness in dreams and in wake reports and found that they did not differ significantly. Thus, it may be that attentional skills and self-reflectiveness are not as impaired in dreams as Hobson, Pace-Schott, and Stickgold (2000b) and Freud have argued. Levels of attentional control and awareness appear to be appropriate to the drama unfolding in the dream narrative.

Suspension of Disbelief in Dreams

A certain level of "suspension of disbelief" is necessary if any "pretend" situation or emulatory narrative is to carry aesthetic or dramatic force. If, for example, a moviegoer were to constantly remind himself "this is only a movie, this is only a movie," he would never really experience the movie and certainly would never be moved by the movie's dramatic content. The same could be said, of course, for novels, pretend play in children, storytelling, painting, sculpture, and so forth. The suspension of disbelief is, in fact, necessary in order to experience the benefits of play, creativity, and the arts. Aesthetic experience depends on a shift away from a focus on the self and a relaxation of the insistence that the work before us is not "real." Suspension of disbelief is also necessary for all kinds of offline simulations that occur in the waking state. Counterfactual simulations could not be run unless one was willing to say, "suppose..." or "if only things had been different..." This ability to set aside the laws of everyday reality and Newtonian physics in order to build an alternate reality from which something is learned is clearly a fundamentally adaptive skill, a skill more complex and perhaps more advanced than self-reflectiveness or attentional control.

While it is certainly true that the suspension of disbelief in all of these waking-related simulations can be voluntarily reversed by the subject and that if queried the subject would instantly confess that the movie or the play or the counterfactual simulation was not real, the examples point to the fundamental importance of the capacity to suspend disbelief for everyday cognitive functioning and for intellectual and creative activity. Dreaming is the one form of offline simulation where the suspension of disbelief is not voluntarily entered into or voluntarily reversed (except in the special case of lucid dreaming). Thus, the running of offline simulations in the dream state cannot be easily derailed. Dream content, in other words, is an obligatory implementation of a series of offline simulations, typically of selected waking activities. Nevertheless, the suspension of disbelief in dreams is just that—and should not always be considered an instance of impairment in attentional control. The deactivation of the dorsolateral prefrontal cortex more likely acts to disinhibit sites in the anterior temporal lobe, the parietal lobes, and the limbic system than to modulate levels of self-reflectiveness in the dream.

On the other hand, there are a minority of dreams in which acceptance of bizarre events reaches delusional levels, and these dreams certainly mimic psychotic breaks with reality in the waking state. In such dreams (such as nightmares), the critical faculty is indeed impaired, but self-reflectiveness is enhanced. One might say that there is too much focus on the imagined threat to the self. Most dreams, however, are not exceptionally bizarre. The typical REM dream, on the contrary, depicts rather mundane social interactions. Before turning to a description of these typical dreams, it is worth mentioning how dream content is studied.

Mind Reading in Dreams

Many dreams involve the dreamer in interaction with at least one other being or person. To interact with another involves attributions or inferences about the other. Most fundamentally, we assume that the other person has a mind and possesses beliefs, desires, and goals just as we do. Therefore, dreaming must involve the attribution of intentionality toward other dream characters. To attribute intentionality to agents is to assume that they are motivated by beliefs, desires, intentions, hopes, fears, deceit, and so on.

The dreamer performs this kind of mentalizing in relation to other dream characters. This is a remarkable fact: the dream self is mind reading the "minds" of characters the dreamer himself has created! Given that the dreamer conjured up these characters from his own memory banks, it must be that the dreamer already "knows" what his created characters will think, believe, desire, and so on. The dreamer, here, is in much the same position as the author of a novel. He creates a character and watches how that character's subsequent actions and interactions with others unfold over time. Even when a dreamer dreams that he is being pursued by strangers or animals that intend to do him harm, he is attributing mind to those pursuers.

Given that some form of mind reading occurs in dreams, what does this fact entail about mechanisms of dreaming? Baron-Cohen (1997) has argued that mind reading involves the interaction of four separate cognitive systems. These are an intentionality detector (henceforth ID), an eye direction detector (EDD), a shared attention mechanism (SAM), and a theory of mind mechanism (ToMM). The ID is a perceptual device that interprets motion stimuli in terms of the primitive, volitional, mental states of goal and desire. According to Baron-Cohen, to see anything animate moving, all that is required to interpret its movement is the attribution of goal and desire. X is moving because its goal is to go over there or because it wants something. It would be interesting to investigate potential relationships between the rapid eye movements associated with REM sleep and the ID and the EDD, particularly the EDD for obvious reasons.

The EDD detects the presence and the direction of eyes or eyelike stimuli, and it infers that if another organism's eyes are directed at something, then that organism sees that thing. The EDD permits us to attribute perceptual states and therefore mind to other organisms. Interestingly, many autistics do not allow or maintain eye contact with another person. They find it extremely uncomfortable to meet the eyes of another.

These two mechanisms, the ID and the EDD, can construct dyadic representations such as Agent wants X, Agent has goal Y (in the case of ID); and Agent sees X, and Agent is looking at Y (in the case of EDD). From Baron-Cohen's point of view, they are not, however, sufficient to account for more complex representations such as Agent A sees that Agent B sees X. For such a representation, Baron-Cohen argues that we need an SAM.

The SAM builds triadic representations that specify the relations among an Agent, the Self, and a (third) Object, which can be another Agent. Such triadic relations would have the form of "Agent sees that I see X" or "You and I see that we are looking at the same object."

Baron-Cohen postulates one additional mechanism, ToMM. The ToMM specializes in detection of specific mental states such as pretending, thinking, knowing, and believing, in which agents are represented as having attitudes toward propositions. It is clear that "we" the dreamer in our dream attribute mind to other characters in our dreams and that therefore the dreaming mind uses ToMM. But what is remarkable is that we are attributing mind to a character that we created and that therefore in some sense must be part of ourselves. We, in essence, are therefore splitting off a piece of ourselves, attributing mind to that piece, and interacting with it as if it were another person. How does that splitting process occur? Why do dreams possess that capacity? Obviously, because simulations of social interactions would be impossible without that capacity.

Summary

Why do dreams have the formal properties that they do? If, for example, the functions of dreaming involve consolidation of memories, it seems odd that consolidation would yield a process that relies almost solely on the visual sense, narrative structure, enhanced emotion, suspended self-monitoring, and yet creativity in plot and images. One could tell a story that makes these features "not inconsistent" with memory consolidation, but the story would be strained and ad hoc. Similarly, if dreaming performs a mood-regulatory function, it seems odd that such a function would require narrative structure, enhanced emotion (why not diminished emotion?), and enhanced fixation of belief, or suspension of disbelief. If dreams reflect a wish-fulfillment function, why do they display narrative structure? Why not just straight scenes of fulfillment? Freud had to invent an elaborate theory of cognitive censorship to account for the manifest form of dreams.

In short, we find that the formal properties of dreams place constraints on theorizing about the dream: specifically, theoretical models of the dream must be consistent with formal cognitive properties of the dream, including narrative structure, creativity, fixation of belief, mind reading, hypermnesia within the dream and partial amnesia for the dream upon awakening, enhanced emotional levels for many dreams, enhanced visual (and to some extent auditory) impressions with diminished impressions from the other senses, and finally the involuntary nature of dreaming: we dream whether we want to or not.

The formal properties of dreams also make it clear that dreams (at least REM dreams) are a different species of cognition than that which occurs in the waking state. While many of the properties of dreams can also be identified in the waking state, they form a unified product when they coalesce in the dream state. While offline simulations do occur in the waking state, they are not obligatory and they do not typically involve intense emotion or scenes of social conflict. Daydreams, instead, are focused on wishes, goals, and plans. They also are more often episodic and fleeting impressions rather than organized narratives. Similarly, daytime counter-factuals focus solely on undoing a negative outcome: narratives and scenes of social conflict are not obligatory content themes for daytime counter-factuals.

Costly signaling theory may offer some insights into why dreams have the formal properties that they do. If REM and REM dreams were in the business of generating costly, hard-to-fake signals that would somehow inform daytime social interactions, then we would expect dreams to involve vivid simulations of daytime social interactions and that emotions would be prominent, as emotions are hard-to-fake signals (Frank, 1988). In addition, narratives involving negative emotions would be expected as they place the self in situations that handicap the self. According to Zahavi and other costly signaling theorists, handicaps are the most effective signals to produce in an exchange as they cannot be faked and they indicate that the bearer has good genes because he can survive and flourish despite the obvious handicap.

REM physiology and REM dreaming, in short, are designed to produce hard-to-fake costly signals, including physical and emotional handicaps. Production of such a signaling repertoire is crucial for social communication and interchange. REM deprivation, therefore, should impair social communication abilities, but I know of no such evidence yet available.

CHAPTER 8

Content of REM Dreams

What are dreams typically about? Do they mean anything beyond what they are obviously about? The reader should recall that in this book I am primarily concerned with REM and spontaneously recalled dreams, and thus all of these questions will need to be asked eventually about other dream types.

Many investigators believe that there are no real differences between REM dreams and all other dream types (in particular, NREM dreams). They argue that dreams can be elicited from virtually any point in the sleep cycle: at sleep onset, during stages 1 and 2, and even SWS of stages 3 and 4. My reading of the literature and exhaustive reviews of the literature on dreams and sleep stages by Hobson et al. (2000b) and by Nielsen et al. (2000), however, suggest that dreams associated with REM sleep periods are typically different in kind from dreams associated with any other sleep stage, even when length of dream reports from REM and NREM states are equated. REM dreams tend to be more storylike, more emotional, and more vivid visually than NREM dream types. Other REM dream characteristics are discussed below. The important point for my purposes is that, apart from very rare pathologic cases, no one disputes that REM-period awakenings are reliably associated with dream reports in most people. In fact, one is more likely to get a dream report after REM-period awakenings than after awakenings from any other point in the sleep cycle. This fact indicates that REM is the brain state that most reliably produces recallable dreams. REM dreams may therefore have a greater potential impact on waking life than other dream types that are more difficult to recall.

Isolation of the Dreaming Mind

To understand REM dream content, the reader should recall the very odd physiologic context in which dreams occur. First, sensory input into the dreaming brain is attenuated or entirely blocked. Second, motor output pathways are also entirely blocked (except, of course, for the respiratory muscles and part of the oculomotor system). Thus, the dreaming brain is set up to exclude significant amounts of incoming information and prevent significant amounts of outgoing information. Cognitive processing is therefore internally focused and whatever images are produced are internally generated. Of course, even when the subject is awake, images are in a strict sense internally generated, but the difference with the sleeping state is obvious: in the waking state, internally generated images are tied to incoming sensory information in a way that is not the case for images generated in the sleeping state. Incoming sensory information in the waking state can be used to adjust properties of whatever images are produced. This is not the case with the sleep state. Presumably, tacit knowledge and memory systems are used to adjust imagery in a dream.

REM Dreams as Simulations of Waking Life

REM dreams clearly have representational content in the sense that they are about something in the world. Indeed, they may exhibit content about two worlds: the waking real world and the dream world itself. Most likely, however, representational content in dreams is parasitic on previously acquired tacit knowledge and memories from waking life. Indeed, dreams are quite sophisticated simulations of waking life: so convincing are the emulatory powers of the dream that the dreamer most often does not realize that he or she is dreaming. On the other hand, dreams are not perfect simulations of waking life, as certain experiences of waking life are not represented in dreams as frequently as they should be (i.e., as frequently as the subject experiences them in waking life). For example, the sensations of taste, smell, and pain are only rarely experienced in dreams. In addition, reading, writing, and calculating are rarely reported in dreams, even in dreams of students, who presumably engage in these activities frequently.

Virtually all dreams, however, involve the self or the dreamer interacting with other characters, and this self is usually at the center of the action. Although there is debate as to whether the dream self should be described as a full-fledged agent, it is clear that the dreamer not only intends certain actions in dreams but that in many dreams this intention is actually a striving toward a goal, and this striving helps to create the narrative structure dreams typically employ. Although dreamers should be considered agents in the full sense of possessing intentional states and deploying plans to achieve those goals, the dreamer is nevertheless unable to critically reflect on the actions and interactions he or she undergoes in the dream. Most damning in this respect is the dreamer's inability to know that he is dreaming and the related noncritical acceptance of bizarre dream events as normal.

Methods of Studying Dream Content

All methods for study of dream content depend on the collection of samples of dreams. Dream reports can be collected in the sleep laboratory by awakening the volunteer whenever he or she enters the REM state. When lab-collected dreams are compared to spontaneously recalled dreams (e.g., in the home environment) only one difference consistently emerges: home dreams exhibit slightly greater amounts of aggression than dreams collected in the lab. This may indicate that subjects in the lab are censoring aspects of their dream content or that spontaneously recalled dreams are embellished to spice up the story. The true amount of aggression in the typical dream probably lies somewhere between the amounts reported in the lab and in those spontaneously recalled.

Outside of the lab, the most typical way in which dream researchers collect dream samples is to ask groups of subjects to recall their most recent dream and to write it down. Alternatively, subjects can be given a notebook, tape recorder, or dream diary to keep at their bedside so that they can record a week's worth (or longer) of dreams. Occassionally, persons may approach dream researchers with a gift: years of journals or dream diaries. Dream journals containing decades of dreams on a single subject are exceedingly valuable sources for the study of dreams, as they can help answer the question of how dream content changes across the life cycle and in relation to the subject's life events.

Obviously, for dream scientists to compare results of their analyses of dream content, they need standardized methods of scoring dream content. The Hall/Van de Castle system for scoring dream content (Domhoff, 1996; Hall & Van de Castle, 1966) is one such standardized system. The system has built-in techniques for controlling length effects via use of automated scoring of basic categories into percentages and ratios. In addition, it is the most comprehensive system yet available, encompassing many of the most common dream events, features, and elements. The quantitative scoring system consists of up to 16 empirical scales and a number of derived scales. The characters scale allows for classification of characters known to the dreamer (e.g., family members, friends, etc.) or unknown strangers, and these characters are classified as to gender, age, and so forth. Animals and imaginary figures are scored as well. Three major types of social interaction are scored: aggressive, friendly, and sexual, with other types possible as well. The character that initiated the interaction is identified as well as the target or recipient of the interaction. Subtypes of the interaction are scored as well. For example, aggressive interactions are scored as physical, verbal, and so on. Five different types of emotion are scored. The activities scales yield information on dreamer goals or strivings and whether success or misfortune is experienced. The settings scale refers to the location (familiar, unfamiliar, indoors, outdoors, etc.) of dream events. The objects scale is used to describe any tangible objects in the dream.

In a real service to the dream research community, Domhoff and Schneider have constructed a Web site (http://www.dreamresearch.net) that provides complete information on how to best make use of the Hall/Van de Castle system as well as an extensive archive of dreams. A spreadsheet program obtainable at the Web site, DreamSat, allows for automatic tabulation of dream content scores and automatic computation of derived scales and percentages. This spreadsheet program greatly increases the reliability of results obtained using the system. The program also produces Cohen's h statistic, which is an effect size for comparing differences in content relative to norms or other types of difference (e.g., REM-NREM differences).

While the Hall/Van de Castle system has been criticized as employing too narrow a range of categories (the emotions category, for example, is biased toward negative emotions), the system is nevertheless reliable and standardized. It should therefore be used as often as possible so that results are comparable across studies and labs. Winget and Kramer (1979) describe a number of other scoring systems along with studies on their reliability for scoring content not easily captured by the Hall/Van de Castle system.

Typical Dream Content

The typical REM dream contains between two and three characters in addition to the dreamer, and these characters typically interact with the dreamer. The dreamer is typically striving to attain or to accomplish some goal, and the other characters are either neutral or interfering with the dreamer's attempts to achieve that goal. The fact that two to four characters occur in an average dream suggests that dreams are social: that they depict social interactions. Social interactions do in fact frequently take place in dreams. For example, conversations between the dreamer and dream characters took place in two out of three dreams in the Strauch and Meier (1996) series. Interestingly, Strauch and Meier reported that they virtually never found a dream in which the dreamer was entirely alone. Instead, dreams typically involve the dreamer interacting with other persons or with other beings like animals. Dreams, in short, are often about social interactions, particularly social conflict, although friendly interactions also occur.

In one of their initial studies, Hall and Van de Castle (1966) selected five spontaneously recalled dreams, each from the dream diaries of 100 male and 100 female students (for a total of 1,000 dreams). The dreams of the students typically depicted nonbizarre, realistic life situations, with a mix of familiar and unfamiliar people interacting in everyday kinds of social events.

Reading, writing, and calculating were almost never represented (despite the frequency of these activities in the lives of college students). Later studies with the Hall/Van de Castle scoring system replicated these original results and extended them in significant ways.

A glance at the table of norms (see table 8.1) derived from the Hall/Van de Castle scoring procedures collected more recently largely agrees with the 1966 findings. Social conflict appears to be a common theme. The norms reveal that the percentage of dreams containing at least one instance of aggression is about 47% for males and 44% for females. Given that animals appear in less than 7% of all dreams (6% for males and 4% for females), many and perhaps most of the scenes involving aggression must be instances of social aggression (between persons). Dreamer-involved aggression (adjusted for number of all social interactions except sexual interactions) is present in 60% of male dreams and half (51%) of female dreams. The dreamer is an aggressor in 40% of male dreams and a third of all female dreams. More than half of all male dreams and 43% of female dreams involve a misfortune or a failure for the dreamer. One out of every three characters in male dreams and one out of every four characters in female dreams is involved in some kind of aggressive interaction. These high levels of social conflict, not surprisingly, are accompanied by high levels of negative emotions: 80% of dreams of both men and women contain negative emotions. In sum, it appears that at least half of all dreams involve aggressive social encounters.

It is worth pausing briefly here to note that these findings, concerning consistent themes of social aggression in dreams, decisively refute claims that dreams are chaotic or that dream plots are the result of the cortex or some other interpreter/confabulator attempting to impose order on chaotic neural impulses welling up from the brain stem. If dreams were the result of this kind of ad hoc, on-the-fly, interpretation of chaotic impulses, we would not see consistent themes of aggression. Instead, we would see mere reflections of current concerns in the dreamer's life.

The interpreter prediction is based on several implausible assumptions, if the "interpreter synthesis" story is to be taken at face value. One would have to assume that the interpreter synthesizer is not part of the dreaming mind—else it too would be subject to the barrage of random impulses welling up from the brain stem. Interpreter theorists surely do not hold that the interpretation is accomplished by the waking mind and then somehow magically imposed during the sleep state. But if the interpreter is not part of the waking mind, then it must be part of the dreaming mind. But here interpreter theorists seem to want us to accept some sort of executive, reflective, attentional control as part of the dream mechanism—the very capacity they deny to dreams in other contexts. If the dreaming mind, then, does indeed possess some evidence for attentional control in its capacity to impose order and an interpretation on chaotic impulses welling up from the brain stem

Table 8.1. A Comparison of the Male and Female Norms for the Hall/Van de Castle System

	Male Norms (%)	Female Norms (%)	Effect Size	p
Characters				
Male/female percent	67	48	+.39	.000**
Familiarity percent	45	58	−.26	.000**
Friends percent	31	37	−.12	.004**
Family percent	12	19	−.21	.000**
Animal percent	6	4	+.08	.037*
Social interaction percents				
Aggression/friendliness percent	59	51	+.15	.014*
Befriender percent	40	47	+.06	.517
Aggressor percent	40	33	+.14	.129
Victimization percent	60	67	−.14	.129
Physical aggression percent	50	34	+.33	.000**
Social interaction ratios				
Aggression/character index	.34	.24	+.24	.000**
Friendliness/character index	.21	.22	−.01	.852
Sexuality/character index	.06	.01	+.11	.000**
Self-concept percents				
Self-negativity percent	65	66	−.02	.617
Bodily misfortunes percent	29	35	−.12	.217
Negative emotions percent	80	80	+.00	.995
Dreamer-involved success percent	51	42	+.18	.213
Torso/anatomy percent	31	20	+.26	.002**
Other indicators				
Physical activities percent	60	52	−.38	.000**
Indoor setting percent	48	26	−.26	.000**
Familiar setting percent	62	79	−.38	.000**
Percent of dreams with at least one				
Aggression	47	44	+.05	.409
Friendliness	38	42	−.08	.197
Sexuality	12	4	+.31	.000**
Misfortune	36	33	+.06	.353
Good fortune	6	6	+.02	.787
Success	15	8	+.24	.000**
Failure	15	10	+.17	.007**
Striving	27	15	+.31	.000**

The p values are based on the formula for the significance of differences between two proportions. The effect size derives from Cohen's h. The h statistic is determined by the following formula: $h = \cos^{-1}(1 - 2P_1) - \cos^{-1}(1 - 2P_2)$ P_1 and P_2 are proportions between 0 and 1, the $\cos^{-1}$ operation returns a value in radians. * significant at the .05 level **significant at the .01 level.

Table 8.1 originally published as table 3.2 on page 73 of Domhoff, G.W. *The Scientific Study of Dreams* (Washington, DC: American Psychological Association, 2003). Copyright © 2003 by the American Psychological Association. Reprinted with permission.

REM generator, then where does this attentional control/interpreter dwell in the dreaming mind? During REM, most parts of the cortex are shut down. Perhaps interpreter theorists hold that the interpreter lies in the limbic system or in the amygdala or hypothalamus. But if so, then the interpreter's version of dream construction becomes indistinguishable from that of other theorists, who suggest that dreams are expressions of all brain sites activated and deactivated during REM. The interpreter position, however, only confuses matters because it suggests that dream images are constructed in reaction to these brain activations rather than as expressions of these activations.

The truth probably involves aspects of both points of view. It may be that the dream images can in turn modulate brain activation patterns as well. In sum, until further evidence is collected, we should assume that dream images emerge in reaction to and as expressions of brain activation states that in turn are partially a result of effects of previous dream images, and so on. Like any other brain/mind process, both bottom-up and top-down processes operate in the dream state.

In any case, dream images cannot be mere reflections of current concerns of the dreamer, as aggressive themes predominate. The remaining dream themes are split between dreams about the self and dreams involving friendly interactions and sexual encounters. Friendly encounters are slightly less common (38%) in dreams of males than in dreams of females (42%). Percentage of dreams with at least one instance of sexuality is higher in males than in females but still is quite uncommon (less than 10% of all dreams). About a third of the dreams of both men and women contain at least one misfortune. There is a very high level of "self-negativity" in dreams, where self-negativity is a composite measure of the degree to which the dreamer is the victim of an aggression or experiences a misfortune, and so forth. Settings of the action of dreams are familiar in about two thirds of dreams of males and about 80% of dreams of females.

Characters in Dreams
Females are more likely to dream of family members (19%) than are males (12%). Men dream more of other men than of women, and usually these other men are in aggressive interactions with the dreamer. This sex difference (women dream equally often of males and females, while men dream about aggressive encounters with other men) is consistent with theories of sexual selection and mating strategies in humans: males compete among themselves for access to females. Alternatively, females promote aggressive competition in order to identify males with good genes, that is, those who dominate other males in aggressive competition. Certainly, in many species of nonhuman primates, males who have demonstrated their dominance of other subordinate males do gain greater access to fertile females and thus increase their own reproductive success, but the picture is complex. In many primate

societies, females subvert the relationship with apparently dominant males to engage in copulations with other males. They use stealth and deceptive stratagems to do so. In any case, sex differences in human dream content may be partially related to effects of sexual selection and mating strategies.

In a study of 320 dream reports from 33 adults, Kahn, Stickgold, Pace-Schott, and Hobson (2000) reported that 48% of characters in dreams were known to the dreamer. The average report length was 237 words and contained an average of 3.7 characters. In the studies by Strauch and Meier (1996), familiar characters tended to be colleagues, coworkers, and friends from the dreamer's circle of acquaintances. To a lesser degree, parents and siblings were also represented in these dreams. In the Hall/Van de Castle norms, 12% of male dreams and 19% of female dreams contained family members. About a third of dreams (both male and females) contain friends of the dreamer.

Unfamiliar Characters in Dreams

According to the Hall/Van de Castle norms, about 50% of characters in dreams were familiar to the dreamer. This, of course, implies that 50% were strangers. In some dream series, up to 80% of characters are unknown to the dreamer. These facts may be an extremely important datum uncovered by these kinds of content analyses of dreams. Why is it that so many characters in dreams are strangers? Is it just due to chance? Is it a reflection of the number of strangers we meet each day? Noting that up to 80% of characters in dreams may be unknown to the dreamer, Kavanau (2002) suggested that they were epiphenomenal expressions of faulty or "incompetent" synaptic circuits. But this suggestion predicts that unknown characters would not show any particular patterns of expression. Incompetent circuitry, for example, would not be expected to clothe its unknown characters in male garb or that unknown characters would mostly function as threatening, aggressive personages in dreams, and so on. Indeed, one might instead predict, as Kavanau himself seems to, that incompetent circuitry would give rise to relatively undefined or vague characterizations and relationships. Yet empirical analyses of the properties and relationships of unknown characters in dreams reveals that they are most often male, threatening, and aggressive.

In an early study of over 1,000 thousand dreams, Hall (1963) reported (1) that strangers in dreams were most often male, (2) that aggressive encounters were more likely to occur in interaction with an unknown male than with an unknown female or a familiar male or female, and (3) that unknown males appeared more frequently in dreams of males than of females. Using the Hall/Van de Castle system, Domhoff (1996) looked at the role of "enemies" in dreams. Enemies were defined as those dream characters who typically interacted (greater than 60% of the cases) with the dreamer in an aggressive manner. Those enemies turned out to be male strangers and animals. Interactions with female strangers are predominantly friendly in the dreams of both males and females. Schredl (2000) reports that almost all murderers and soldiers in dreams are male. Domhoff (2003) has shown that when male strangers appear in a dream, the likelihood that physical aggression will occur in that dream far exceeds what would be expected on the basis of chance. In short, male strangers signal physical aggression. This is an extremely important result of research on dream content, as it suggests that a dream code is possible, as one feature of that code (unknown male adults) consistently signals danger. It, along with other findings described below, decisively refutes claims that dream content is random and meaningless.

Though Strauch and Meier (1996) do not comment directly on the role of strangers in dreams, they too reported that half of the characters they scored in their sample of dreams were unfamiliar to the dreamer. In fact, in about every third dream, the dreamer encountered only strangers. It would be quite interesting to see if these types of dreams (where the dreamer encountered only strangers) display any particularly unusual properties. Perhaps they exhibit very high levels of aggression or perhaps they are more bizarre or more dramatic. We simply do not know, as the question has never been investigated. Also it may be worth asking what such dreams portend for the dreamer. When a person reports dreams in which they encounter only strangers, does it predict any psychic or behavioral change in the dreamer?

Emotions in Dreams

When using the Hall/Van de Castle scoring rules, negative emotions appear in about 80% of dreams for both men and women. Scenarios involving dreamer-involved successes occur in only about half of male dreams and 40% of female dreams, and misfortunes occur in at least one third of all dreams. Strauch and Meier (1996) report similar findings in their studies of dreams collected from volunteers who provided content from REM and spontaneously recalled dreams. On the other hand, Strauch and Meier also reported that the most frequently cited emotion in dreams was joy. When Schredl and Doll (1998) asked their subjects to identify and rate the emotions in their own dreams, no excess of negative emotion (relative to ratings by independent raters) was found, thus suggesting that dreams are not biased with respect to negative emotions.

Are the dreamers in Schredl and Doll's study simply trying to make themselves look less negative, or are the independent raters overlooking instances of positive emotion in dreams? We have seen that aggressive social interactions are a common theme in dreams. It is possible that when the dreamer wins or dominates in such an encounter, he or she would rate the dream emotion as positive, whereas an independent rater would rate the dream negatively, as full of conflict, and so on. On the other hand, the Hall/Van de

Castle norms suggest that the dreamer is more often the victim in such encounters than the victor. Further studies are needed to clarify emotional content of typical dreams. My own feeling is that the weight of the evidence suggests that dreams more often involve negative than positive emotion. Dozens of studies across several laboratories using various methodologies (see reviews in Domhoff, 2003; Merritt et al., 1994; Revonsuo, 2000) consistently find an excess of negative emotions in dreams. Disorders of REM, particularly disorders involving disinhibition of REM, are also typically associated with frightening or very negative dream themes. At the very least, negatively toned dreams are more often remembered than are positively toned dreams, and this fact must contribute to the ways in which dreams function to affect waking mood and behavior.

Costly Signaling and Emotions

REM involves regular, periodic, and intense activation of the limbic system and the amygdala—the two major emotional centers of the brain. As the night progresses, activation patterns become more intense and likely color the person's mood for the day upon awakening. If the sleeper awakes and remembers an emotional dream, waking-related mood states are that much more likely to be influenced by REM. In short, REM is in a position to determine or at least influence a person's waking mood state. Kramer (1993) has summarized a large number of studies demonstrating sleep and dream effects of waking mood. There is little question that REM can influence waking emotional states. One might even suppose that long-term affective style can be modulated by or maintained by ongoing REM effects. Davidson and Irwin (1999) summarized an extensive body of work demonstrating consistent affective styles in otherwise normal individuals. Styles involving both positive and negative affect processing biases have been documented in both humans and nonhuman primates. In both cases, affective style is linked to selective activation (as demonstrated by EEG, PET, and fMRI neuroimaging studies) of right-sided (in the case of negative affective bias) or left-sided (positive affective style) prefrontal activation. It is conceivable that REM quality and duration could influence long-term temperament and affective style. In any case, it is clear that REM influences emotional functioning via its regulatory control over limbic system activation patterns and via dreams. Emotions are ubiquitous in dreams. This fact is particularly evident when you ask the dreamer to identify specific emotions that were associated with particular episodes in a dream.

If one of REM's specializations is emotional processing in support of daytime emotional expression, then REM itself should come under selective pressure to produce hard-to-fake emotional signals. As Frank (1988) has pointed out, most emotions are hard-to-fake signals (it is difficult to mimic an emotion effectively), and therefore they are extremely important behavioral signals that influence social interactions in daily waking life. People use information they gather from the ways in which a person "emotes" in various situations to gauge the honesty, trustworthiness, integrity, and behavioral competence of that person. Given the stock people put in the value of the information contained in a person's emotional repertoire, there is pressure to fine-tune one's emotional capacities as well as one's ability to read the emotions of others.

Given the role that REM sleep plays in its regular and periodic activation of the limbic system as well as its associated running of simulations of emotional interactions in dreams, REM itself must come under pressure to contribute to that fine-tuning and development of emotional signaling and reading abilities. To some extent, the brain activation patterns and the emotional signaling we experience in dreams can be analyzed as costly signals. If costly, they should to some extent function as handicaps. That may be one reason that negative emotion is more often portrayed in dreams than positive emotion.

Longitudinal Changes in Dream Content

Domhoff (2003) has pioneered use of the Hall/Van de Castle system to quantify dream content changes over time. In at least one case study, Domhoff was given access to the dream journals of "Barb Sanders," a woman in her late 50s. Sanders had kept records of her dreams covering the years from the 1970s to the late 1990s (although a few dreams extended back to the 1960s). In addition to being able to interview Barb Sanders herself, Domhoff was also able to interview four of Sanders's close female friends who had known her for many years. Thus, Domhoff was able to score the content of Sanders's dreams, and to study how that content changed over time and the extent to which that content reflected themes in Sanders's own life. Results showed that dream themes tracked emotional concerns of her life relatively faithfully. The themes most faithfully tracked appeared to be those concerning her social interactions, including those with her ex-husband, her ambiguous feelings toward her mother, her strong love for her favorite brother and her friends and children, a momentary romantic infatuation with a younger man, and so on. Potential indexes of character traits such as aggressiveness versus friendliness were remarkably stable in Sanders's dreams across decades, while the quality of social interactions with the significant people in her life changed over the years, with depictions of some relationships becoming more friendly and others more distant. It would be interesting to test whether the changes occurred first in dreams and then in the relationships themselves or if the dreams merely recorded what was occurring in the life of the dreamer.

Temporal Reference of Content

Freud thought that most dreams contained residues or images that could be traced back to an event occurring on the day previous to the dream.

Nielsen, Deslauriers, and Baylor (1991) have shown that a day's residues disappear after the first night's sleep, and then if they reappear they will do so about a week later (the "dream-lag effect"). Typically, emotionally significant images are the images that reappear after the lag. Does the lag effect represent the time it takes for the hippocampus to consolidate the image into long-term memory? If so, why does it reappear in a dream a week later? Presumably, consolidation can occur without conscious processing of memory images. Perhaps the lag effect reflects amygdaloid-hippocampal interactions and the selection of what emotional material will be allowed to influence future daytime functioning. Nielsen et al. contend that these dreams are rated as more memorable by subjects experiencing them.

Another temporal effect concerning REM dreams has to do with the temporal references of images contained in dreams obtained from different periods of the night. Foulkes (1962) reported that noncontemporaneous images (images dating back to the person's more distant past) were more likely to occur in REM than in NREM dreams. Offenkrantz and Rechtschaffen (1963) and Verdone (1965) reported a relation between date of memory images in dreams and time spent in sleep, such that as the night progressed the dreamer was more likely to report older personal memories.

These temporal effects associated with REM dreams should be of interest to researchers interested in the role of REM sleep and dreaming in memory, yet to my knowledge the effects have not been actively investigated.

REM-Related Disorders

As I want to use phenomenology of REM-related disorders to help reveal potential themes of REM dream content, I focus on symptoms that can plausibly be described as due to "too much" REM or to enhanced forms of "normal" REM physiology (or perhaps as disinhibited REM). Of course, attempting to infer normal functions of any physiologic process by observing the process in an abnormal state is potentially misleading. For example, if we observe "release" of the sucking reflex in adults after discrete lesions to the prefrontal cortex, we do not ascribe the function of sucking to the prefrontal cortex. At most, we can infer that the prefrontal cortex participated in a process of tonic inhibition of a neuronal network or circuit that encoded the sucking reflex. We could further infer that the circuit was probably located in a site that received inhibitory efferents from the prefrontal cortex. In addition, enhancing a circuit's function is different from activating that circuit and observing its typical functioning. Despite its limitations, however, the procedure of inferring normal functions from dysfunction has been used successfully in other domains (e.g., neuropsychology) and thus it may be useful here as long as we keep in mind its limitations. If we find, for example, that enhancement or loss of typical REM is associated with consistent patterns of change in dream content, then the claim that REM is designed to produce that kind of content is supported, though of course not demonstrated.

Nightmares

Nightmares are frightening dreams and most often occur during REM and during the early morning period between 4 and 7 a.m. They are typically accompanied by signs of sympathetic surge (increased heart rate and blood pressure, as well as respiratory changes), and they typically last between 5 and 30 minutes. The dominant emotion is terror, overwhelming in its intensity for most persons with repeat nightmares. Frequent themes include the dreamer involved in aggressive encounters, being chased or attacked by unknown threatening men or animals, enclosure in unpleasant surroundings, dread due to imminent violent assault by an unknown stranger, and so on. Violence by the dreamer against others is uncommon even when the dreamer is being physically attacked. Children between the ages of 4 and 8 report nightmares more frequently than any other age group, and nightmare frequency declines with age. Persons with psychiatric diagnoses report higher frequencies of nightmares than nonpsychiatric samples. Hartmann (1984, 1998) reported that chronic nightmare sufferers evidence "thin" boundaries in both the interpersonal sphere and in the cognitive sphere. These people evidenced artistic and creative interests but also tended to carry diagnoses of borderline personality disorder. One quarter of chronic nightmare sufferers have family members who have attempted or completed suicide (Hartmann, Russ, van der Kolk, Falke, & Oldfield, 1981). Mack (1970) reported that an unusually high percentage of REM is correlated with nightmare frequency and intensity.

Suicide

Though not usually considered a disorder of REM, REM percentages are increased in persons who plan, attempt, and complete suicide. In a review of the literature on sleep and suicide, Singareddy and Balon (2001) concluded that REM durations and REM density were increased in suicidal patients, but they could not rule out effects of depression on sleep in these patients. Sabo et al. (1991) compared EEG sleep measures of major depressives with and without a history of suicidal behavior. They found suicide attempters had longer sleep latency, lower sleep efficiency, and fewer late-night delta wave counts than normal controls. They also demonstrated that non-attempters, compared to attempters, had less REM time and activity in the second REM period, but more delta wave counts in the fourth non-REM period. Thus, if you are depressed, adding increased REM times and reducing SWS delta can push you into suicidal behavior. Increasing REM in the first half of the night is more likely to contribute to a reduction in NREM delta, apparently. Agargun et al. (1998) reported an association between repetitive nightmares and suicidal tendency in patients with major depression. Agargun and Cartwright (2003) found a significant negative correlation between suicidality scores and reduced REM latency, and a positive correlation between suicidality and increased REM percentage relative to REM indices in nonsuicidal controls. Interestingly, a reduction in "dreamlike quality" of the REM dream content reports between the first and second halves of the night was found to be associated with suicidal tendency.

REM Sleep Behavior Disorder

Patients with idiopathic REM sleep behavior disorder (RBD) typically complain of a history of vivid unpleasant dreams and excessive movements in sleep. They typically do not evidence a degenerative dementia until very late stages of the disease. The sleep-related movements in RBD may be violent enough to induce physical injury. There appears to be enactment of violent dream content and a concomitant failure of REM-related muscle atonia. When patients are asked to report dream content, they typically say that they dreamed that they were or their spouse was under attack by some strangers. Like Jouvet's (1999; Jouvet et al., 1964) pontine-lesioned cats, who were thought to exhibit oneiric behaviors that were normally under output inhibition, these patients are thought to suffer from a similar disinhibition of selective brain stem motor pattern generators. The disinhibition, in turn, is thought to be due to a pathologic process that affects pontine and some basal ganglia sites and other midline structures. Olson, Boeve, and Silber (2000) reported that 25.8% of their patients had histories of psychiatric disease or neurotic profiles, a figure somewhat lower than the 35% reported by Schenck and Mahowald (1990). According to Mahowald and Schenck (2000), the overall sleep architecture is typically intact, but most patients show increased SWS for their age. Schenk and Mahowald (2000) found that 28 of 65 patients they evaluated evidenced increased REM percentage (greater than 25% of total sleep time), while Tachibana and colleagues (1994) documented increases in REM density (or number of REM bursts or clusters) in their sample of RBD patients, despite grossly normal sleep architecture. In the Olson et al. study of 93 consecutive patients with RBD, 90 showed increased phasic activity in REM.

Narcolepsy

Narcolepsy is a disorder of excessive daytime sleepiness that typically is associated with cataplexy and other REM-related phenomena such as sleep paralysis, vivid dreams, and hypnagogic hallucinations. The cataplectic attack is usually triggered by intense emotion. Narcolepsy may be associated with expression of HLA-DR2, DQw6 DQB1-0602 and thus might be linked to HLA antigen and automimmune disease. The positional cloning of the canine narcolepsy gene (*canarc-1*) indicates that the disorder is related to exon-skipping mutations in the gene that encodes one of the G-protein-coupled receptors for the neuropeptide hypocretins (*Hcrtr2*). Excitatory hypocretin neurons project most heavily to the LC. Thus a lowering in hypocretins could decrease LC activity, thereby disinhibiting REM and producing narcolepsy, but the story is likely to be more complex as hypocretin neurons project diffusely throughout the forebrain, and narcoleptics evidence no hypocretin deficits in their cerebrospinal fluid. Sleep changes have been extensively documented in narcolepsy (see Guilleminault & Anagnos, 2000, for review) and remarkably parallel those found in depression (described below) with reduced REM latencies, increased REM percentage, increased REM densities, and sleep onset REM (SOREM). Dreams associated with REM sleep attacks are typically unpleasant or frightening. Often a strong emotion will trigger a sleep attack.

Depression

Depression is a major mood disorder involving unpleasant or dysphoric affect, inability to experience pleasure, weight changes (usually loss), psychomotor retardation, feelings of worthlessness, diminished ability to think or concentrate with intrusive, repetitive thoughts, and sleep disturbances. The sleep disturbances usually involve early morning awakenings, insomnia, nonrestorative sleep, and disturbing, unpleasant, and vivid dreams.

Barrett and Loeffler (1992) reported that dreams of depressed college women contained fewer characters, fewer strangers, and less anger than did dreams of nondepressed college women. It appears that social interactions, at least aggressive interactions, are reduced in dreams of depressed persons—at least in dreams of female depressives. Cartwright (1999) studied REM sleep and dreams of persons who were and were not depressed while undergoing divorce. Dreams of depressed people were vivid and evidenced increased "dream masochism" (the dreamer is deprived, attacked, excluded, or fails). A follow-up study showed that early-onset REM was correlated with the number of unpleasant dreams reported by depressed people. Hundreds of polysomnographic and other sleep studies have now been performed on patients with depression. Reviews can be found in Benca (2000). The primary sleep changes in depression include sleep fragmentation or reduced sleep continuity, reduced SWS, reduced REM sleep onset latency, increased REM density, prolongation of the first REM episode, and SOREM.

In summary (see table 8.2), all of the REM-related disorders involve a common set of symptoms that give us clues as to the functions of REM: there is an increase of levels of unpleasantness in dreams and increased self-attack (or masochism) in dreams. Evidence from many different laboratories and a variety of animal species indicates that the amygdala specializes in processing of fear, anxiety, and attention (see Davis & Whalen, 2001, for a review of animal studies). Electrical stimulation of the amygdala elicits a

Table 8.2. Polysomnographic Sleep Findings Indicating Enhanced REM in Target Disorders

	REM%	REM density	REM latency	Slow-wave sleep %	SOREM?
Nightmares	↑	↑	↓	-	yes
Depression	↑	↑	↓	↓	yes
Narcolepsy	↑	↑	↓	↓	yes
Suicide	↑	↑	↓	↓	yes
RBD	↑	↑	↓	?	?

Originally printed as Table 1 on page 127 in McNamara, P., Durso, R., & Auerbach, S. (2002). Dopaminergic Syndromes of Sleep, Mood and Mentations: Evidence from Parkinson's Disease and Related Disorders. *Sleep and Hypnosis 4(4)*, 119–131. Reprinted with permission of the authors and *Sleep and Hypnosis*.

pattern of behaviors that look like intense fear, aversion, and attention. Lesions of the amygdala block innate or conditioned fear and aversion as well as various measures of attention. N-methyl-D-aspartate receptors in the amygdala are important in the acquisition of learned fear responses. The peptide corticotropin-releasing hormone acts on the amygdala to orchestrate fear and aversive states within the organism.

All of the disorders reviewed above are also associated with serotoninergic and dopaminergic deficits. A lowering of the monoaminergic and catecholaminergic input to the amygdala will lead to heightened activation levels of the amygdala and thus the release of REM physiology along with signs of heightened amygdaloid functioning such as creation of a generalized aversive state and dreams of being under threat.

If these sets of co-ocurring sleep and clinical symptoms are confirmed to be due to amygdaloid and REM disinhbition, then REM suppression should effectively treat the symptoms, including the frontal dysfunction. Overnight REM deprivation, for example, should yield improvement on tests that measure depression. REM sleep deprivation is known to alleviate depression. Administration of antidepressants should also help, but degree of cognitive improvement may be blunted due to cognitive side effects of these drugs. Affect should improve with degree of REM percentage reduction. In short, when REM physiology is enhanced due to neuropsychiatric dysfunction, dream content is consistently reported as unpleasant. In addition, the self character (dreamer) undergoes significant distress, attack, harm, and so on.

If we can take the dreams associated with REM-related disorders as revealing basic trends in REM dream content (and they are remarkably consistent with the findings on normative content), then it appears that REM is specialized to produce dream scenarios that involve attacks on the self or place the self in socially shaming situations, or in situations involving negative emotions where the dreamer's goals and desires are blocked, and so on. In the language of costly signaling theory, dreams saddle the dreamer with handicaps.

CHAPTER 9

Theories of REM Dreams

What is the nature and function of the dream? Can we use what is known about the phenomenology and content of dreams to infer potential functions of dreams? Several hypotheses concerning the nature of dream cognition have been proposed. Many of these hypotheses are bound up with assumptions concerning the nature and function of REM sleep itself.

Early Hypotheses of REM Dreams

Snyder (1966) proposed that REM provided an arousal or preparatory phase to a brief awakening during the night that served a kind of sentinel or vigilance function for the animal who otherwise was vulnerable to predation while it slept. Hallucinated simulations of threat while the animal slept would also help prepare the animal for defense in case of attack. I mention Snyder's theory of REM as it has spawned many popular conceptions of the dream as a sort of "first warning system" that can somehow encode faint signals of impending threats or simulate threats that an animal is likely to encounter while it sleeps (see also discussion of the related work of Revonsuo later in this chapter). Snyder's theory seems to assume the point of view of prey. Aside from the fact that many predators have copious amounts of REM (including humans), Snyder's theory seems to assume that the all-important sleep state was NREM, and REM was there simply to protect the animal long enough that it could engage in NREM. Even if we set aside the fact that arousals from REM are not likely to create a state of consciousness adequate to meeting a mortal threat, all of the evidence reviewed in this book suggests that REM cannot be considered a mere adjunct to NREM, though the two are related. Rather, REM is likely to have functions that are both independent of, and actually oppose expression of, NREM (see previous chapters).

Many early dream theories based themselves on evidence derived from "Jouvet's cats." Jouvet et al. (1964) proposed that REM supplied the endogenous stimulation necessary for a resculpting or reprogramming of synaptic circuits that support epigenetic behavioral rules or strategies. Jouvet had placed lesions in the brain stems of cats that abolished the atonia usually associated with REM. When the cats' motor systems were no longer inhibited, they appeared to act out dreams when electrophysiologic signs of REM appeared. These acting-out episodes typically involved primary instinctual behaviors such as fear and rage postures as well as orienting reflexes and the like. Although Jouvet was always careful about extending these results to the case of human dreaming, many other investigators assumed that dreams reflected a process of reprogramming or repair of synaptic circuits involved in instinctual behavior.

Winson (1985), for example, argued that dreaming represents a form of offline processing of basic behavioral strategies important for survival. Winson assumed that these strategies are acquired during a critical period in early development. REM sleep, according to Winson, somehow allows access to survival-related strategies and updates these strategies by integrating them with recent past experience. Much of the evidence we reviewed in chapter 2 concerning REM expression across the life span is consistent with Winson's position. If REM sleep reactivates and updates basic and instinctual behavioral strategies, then these strategies might be reflected to a greater or lesser extent in REM dream content. The fact that patients with REM behavior disorder (and Jouvet's cats) appear to act out primitive defense and rage behaviors supports this idea. But controlled analyses of dream content suggest that much more than mere rehearsal of basic behavioral strategies is occurring during REM. It seems unlikely that such rehearsal would almost always yield dreams with negative emotional content or aggressive social interactions and so forth.

Cognitive Theories

I have reviewed theories concerning the role of dreaming in memory processing in other chapters. Here I focus on theories ascribing other nonmemory cognitive functions to dreams. Foulkes (1985) argued that dreams are "credible world analogs" or imaginative simulations of waking life that obey fundamental rules of waking cognition but that to a great extent lack reflective thought. Although he has argued that dreaming plays a role in the development of consciousness, he has also argued that dreams likely serve no adaptive function. Foulkes recommends that we focus more on the formal cognitive features of dreams rather than on dream content per se, as the formal features are more likely to be functional than are the content themes of dreams. On the face of it this seems like a reasonable recommendation, but it is not at all clear that mechanisms of production have functional content when the item or items produced by the mechanism do not. Most machines are produced in order to produce a product. It is the product that has functional relevance with respect to human needs rather than the machine per se. Obviously, both machine and product are important, but if forced to privilege one over the other, the product would likely yield more informational content as it would tell us why the machine was manufactured in the first place. Similarly, with respect to dreams, the mechanism we know produces at least one product, that is, the dream. It may be that it produces other products as well, but that prospect seems unlikely and in any case would return us to consideration of REM physiology per se rather than the dream. Thus, given that the mechanism is designed to produce the dream, it seems reasonable to investigate laws of dream content to understand why dreams are produced at all.

Foulkes proposed that dreaming involved a diffuse activation of mnemonic material and as such could serve no adaptive function. Yet, as Foulkes himself points out, dream content is not random. The dreamer is typically represented as playing a central role in the dream narrative, which typically involves a summation of selected past experiences personal to the dreamer. The past experiences inform the dream events—the dream is not a mere replay of these past experiences. Instead it is cognitively creative. Rechtschaffen (1978), on the other hand, emphasized the "single-mindedness" quality of the thought that occurs in dreams. Rechtschaffen claimed that we do not usually entertain two thoughts at once during a dream, and we usually naively and unreflectively accept whatever occurs in the dream action as real. It is not clear whether Rechtschaffen believed that the so-called single-mindedness quality of dreams pointed to any particular functional quality of dreams. Nor is it clear that dreams actually exhibit this quality of single-mindedness. I am not entirely sure that I understand what Rechtschaffen meant by this claim. If we assume that what Rechtschaffen meant was that the dream displayed a perseverative quality in terms of its thematic content, then he is clearly mistaken. Even if dreams were perseverative, would it tell us anything special concerning the nature of dream content? After all, many persons are described as perseverative and as having a "one-track mind" in daily life. We spend most of our lives in a relatively unconscious and automatized pursuit of a relatively narrowly defined set of objectives centered on satisfaction of appetites. This largely perseverative set of behaviors displayed during waking life, however, does not cancel out the occasions when human beings actually do rise to conscious choice and moral striving. So too in the case of dreams. Even if dreams occassionally display perseverative themes or resistance to entertaining two points of view at once, this does not mean that all dreams exhibit that quality.

Dreams, on the contrary, display immense creativity and the kinds of mentation that escape this narrow-minded focus on a single train of thought. Indeed, many commentators have accused dreams of being too unfocused and too willing to follow any train of thought that occurs to them. Dreams are said to be replete with too many themes and images to be considered as anything but fantastic. How can it be that dream cognition is both too narrow and too diffuse? On the whole, dreams are creative, and dreams are expert at simulating important social and emotional interactions and thus cannot be single-minded or perseverative.

More Recent Theories

I cannot review all of the extant theories of dreaming here, but I do wish to mention some of the theories that find some support from recent empirical studies. While all of the theories can claim some factual support, none of them in my view account for even the basic features of dream content. Nevertheless, they contain some truth and so deserve mention and investigation. Fiss (1993) argued that dreams can detect very faint signals (e.g., onset of illness) and depict these signals in concretized, metaphorical language that can potentially enter the awareness of the person having the dream. The information would be valuable, of course, if it accurately forecasted impending illness. Reviewing quantitative studies of dream content across a wide variety of populations, Domhoff (1996) showed that dream reports were typically fairly representative of waking thoughts and concerns of the dreamer formulated in terms of "unique picture stories or dramas" that we enter into at night. He raised the possibility that repetitive dreams may assist the dreamer in solving emotional problems and that metaphor in dreams may serve a similar problem-solving function. I return to Domhoff's more recent theories concerning dreams below. Rotenberg (1993) has argued that REM sleep and dreams restore high-level "search activity," where search activity appears to be similar to Winson's and Jouvet's references to instinctual behavioral strategies that enhance reproductive fitness (fight, flight, forage, etc.). Koukkou and Lehman (1993) suggest that the adult's sleep EEG is similar to the waking child's EEG and that sleep states, including dreams, recapitulate childhood states in a kind of nightly cycle of temporal regression and return. If I understand their argument correctly, Koukkou and Lehman argue that the function of the dream is to funnel old information into consciousness and to activate old emotional and cognitive-processing strategies in service to current needs. Access to these funds of old processing strategies is thought not to be available to the waking mind or brain. Globus (1993) argues that the dream allows for a kind of chaotic shake-up of the neural networks that support the cognitive systems activated during dreaming. This shake-up restores unbiased activation thresholds, and thus the entire cognitive system functions more efficiently. Hartmann (1996) has suggested that dreams are the product of spreading excitation between semantic nodes in a semantic network, except that the patterns of activation in dreams are guided by current emotional concerns and make meaning connections more broadly and more inclusively than does waking cognition. Hartmann suggested that certain dream images function to contextualize intense emotions. This latter capacity allows dreams to facilitate integration of traumatic or overwhelming emotions.

Emotional Processing Functions

Hartmann's position is similar to many contemporary views on functions of dreaming (Barrett & Loeffler, 1992; Greenberg & Pearlman, 1993; Koulack, 1993; Kramer, 1993) that emphasize potential emotional functions of dreams. All these investigators provide substantial evidence for adaptive emotional problem solving and processing in dreams. Kramer, for exmple, suggested that dreams function to contain a surge in emotional arousal associated with REM states; thus sleep is protected and the dreamer does not awaken. Kuiken and Sikora (1993) argue that impactful dreams reflect activations of components of the classical orienting response and that these emotionally intense, impactful dreams have lasting effects on mood states of waking experience. Except for these types of "big" impactful dreams, it is hard to see how other dream types, particularly ordinary dreams, can have an effect on waking experience if, as we know to be the case, most dreams are never recalled. On the other hand, if dreams do somehow promote emotionally related problem solving, then people who need to problem solve due to some current important emotional concern should recall more dreams than persons with fewer current emotional concerns. Up to now, however, it has appeared that people who are not good dream recallers did not differ in any significant way from people who were good dream recallers (Goodenough, 1991).

Recently, however, my colleagues and I (McNamara, Anderson, Clark, Zborowski, & Duffy, 2001) reinvestigated this issue. We demonstrated differential recall rates as a function of "attachment status." Attachment in this context denotes romantic emotional attachment to a significant other. Current attachment theory suggests that people generally fall into one of four attachment-related categories: (1) they are in a relationship and happy with the relationship (they are *securely* attached to their partner); (2) they are not in a relationship but want to be and are *preoccupied* with that goal; (3) they may or may not want to be in a relationship or may even be in a relationship but they are *dismissive* about the importance of the relationship to them; and (4) they are not in a relationship and do not want to be (*avoidant*). Now if dreaming somehow facilitates one's emotional goals and in particular facilitates pursuit of emotional attachment strategies, then dream recall should be relatively lower in the groups of people who are satisfied with their current status (secure, dismissive, and avoidant) and relatively higher among the group of persons who want to change their status (the preoccupied group), and that is exactly what we found (table 9.1).

Table 9.1. Dream Recall by Attachment Status

Attachment Status	Words/Dream Mean (Standard Deviation)	% Group Recall
Insecure	87.2 (40.1)	45.8 (4+ dreams per week)
Secure	91.5 (42.0)	28.5 (4+ dreams per week)
Preoccupied	66.2 (49.6)	81.8 (recalled at least 1 dream)
Dismissive	34.6 (63.4)	34.5 (recalled at least 1 dream)
Avoidant	30.3 (50.9)	45.8 (recalled at least 1 dream)
Secure	27.4 (53.3)	40.0 (recalled at least 1 dream)

Roughly 80% of preoccupied persons and about 35 to 40% of persons in the other three groups recalled at least one dream for purposes of the study. In general, the nonsecurely attached persons were much more likely to recall their dreams than securely attached persons. These results suggest that dreams that are recalled serve some emotional purpose: they facilitate the dreamer's attachment strategy.

History of the Theory of the Dream as Serving Emotional Expression

Freud should be credited with the first scientific attempt at elucidation of the role of emotional processing in the functions of dreaming. At the start of the 20th century, Freud (1900) suggested that dream cognitions are composed of memory fragments that are combined in such a way as to encode libidinal desires of the dreamer. Freud's model of dreaming has been masterfully reviewed by others more qualified than I (see, e.g., Van de Castle, 1994), so I do not review the entire model here. Modern work on dreams in the neural and cognitive sciences has largely been dismissive of Freudian and related psychoanalytic approaches to the meaning and function of dreams. This is unfortunate as the psychoanalytic tradition contains a wealth of information on how dreams process emotional information. On the other hand, circumspection is required, as this information was only rarely obtained under controlled conditions, and thus much of it is unusable. In any case, the entire tradition should not be dismissed out of hand before attempts are made to integrate its findings into modern dream sciences.

One of the coauthors (Hobson, 1988) of the often-cited activation-synthesis hypothesis of dream formation asserts that dreams, contrary to what Freud argued, have no disguised meaning at all. Rather, Hobson (at least in 1988) argued that dreams represent an attempt on the part of the cortex to "synthesize" or to interpret random activation patterns generated in subcortical centers. Dream content reflects these synthesizing efforts of the forebrain, and thus dream content directly represents the dreamer's drives, fears, and associations. A distorted version of Hobson's views on dreaming have been taken as the latest science on dreams by many scholars interested in dreams but who have not carefully studied dream formation. Thus, the view of dreams as meaningless epiphenomena of random brain firings (a misreading of Hobson's own view, I think) has gained wide currency in the rest of the sciences and in the humanities. Propagation of such a view of dreams has been hugely damaging to community support for research on dreams and thus has been hugely damaging to the cause of the scientific study of dreams.

Hobson derides the psychoanalytic theory of the dream as unscientific because (1) it is not empirically based and (2) it is not framed in such a way as to make it amenable to direct experimental test. Both claims are false. While many psychoanalytic assertions are circular and not amenable to experiment, many others are not. Hall (1963) subjected several claims of Freudian theory to scientific test in his studies of dream content and found some of them supported. While most of Freudian theory has to be discarded as disproven or nontestable, his basic insights concerning the emotional functions of dreams should be studied and incorporated into modern dream theory.

With regard to Freud's work, Crick and Mitchison (1986) have this to say: "There seems little point in dwelling on Freud's ideas since they hardly fit the biological data. Freudians have no unforced explanation for the large amount of REM in the unborn and the newly born and the occurrence of REM in so many different species of mammals and birds. To a modern neuroscientist Freud's theories, in spite of their appeal to the contemporary imagination, seem little better than the common belief in earlier times that dreams foretold the future, a belief which also held strong intuitive appeal" (p. 245). For Crick and Mitchison, dream content is essentially meaningless. REM sleep (and by extension dreams associated with REM) functions in order to reduce fantasy and the interaction of related ideas and concepts in memory. REM sleep, loosely speaking, is a form of reverse learning. During

REM, the cognitive system is purged of elements that might interfere with efficient functioning. It therefore might even be harmful to remember dreams. Setting aside the fact that Freud addressed the nature and function of the dream, not REM (REM had not even been discovered when Freud worked), Crick and Mitchison's claims concerning the meaninglessness of dreams simply reflect ignorance of the hundreds of dream content studies published in the past several decades. On the other hand, their ideas concerning REM function may have some merit and need to be tested along with other recent theories of REM.

For Foulkes (1985), the most prominent cognitive psychologist who has specialized in the study of dreams, "there is no more underlying meaning in dreaming than there are angels who might sit on the heads of pins" (p. 191). In his review of Freud's work, Foulkes (1978) argued for a distinction between Freud's topographic model (e.g., unconscious, preconscious, conscious) of the dream experience, which Foulkes believed was derived from the data-based free-association method, and the "economic" model of the dreaming mind, which constituted Freud's theory of the dream: "The wish-fulfillment hypothesis, the notion that repressed infantile sexual wishes instigate dreams, and the energetic characterizations of 'primary' and 'secondary' processes are not generated by, but are forced upon, the data in the free association matrix" (p. 86). Thus, Foulkes rejects the wish-fulfillment hypothesis and the associated ideas concerning the infantile and sexual character of the dream wish. But one can reject Freud's specific interpretations of dream content without rejecting his basic insight concerning emotional properties of dreams. Nor does it help to focus on solely on Freud's economic model of dreaming, as the mechanics of dreaming are in service to dream content.

Alongside this anti-Freudian "eliminativist" trend in modern cognitive neuroscience of dreaming, a second "revisionist" trend has developed, which finds some merit in Freud's theory of dreams but disputes some of his conclusions. Van de Castle (1994) finds dreams to be an abundant source of meanings for the dreamer but yet finds Freud's emphasis on the sexual nature of dreams to be excessive and even dogmatic: "Through his intense focus upon the neurotic, infantile, and sexual aspects of dreams, Freud gave dreams a bad name" (p. 139). Nor does Van de Castle agree that Freud's theory merits the name of science: "Although Freud constantly referred to his studies as 'scientific' he certainly did not follow the methods of quantification generally accepted as necessary to merit that label. He provided no ratings, rankings, percentage figures, tables, graphs, or statistics to document his claims" (p. 139).

Despite these largely negative assessments of Freud's work on dreams, there is (as demonstrated above) still some sympathy for the view that dreams have some kind of regulatory role to play in the emotional economy of the psyche. We have seen in previous chapters that there is considerable empirical support for this view of dreams. Strangely enough, the fact that dreaming has something to do with emotional processing has not been seriously addressed or integrated into the most current neurocognitive models of dreaming available. Instead, these models focus on narrowly construed cognitive functions of dreaming—if they allow that dreams have a function at all.

Current Neurocognitive Theories of the Dream

The activation-synthesis theory originally described by Hobson and McCarley (1977) and updated recently by Hobson et al. (2000b) as the activation-input source-neuromodulation model or AIM model of dreaming, represents some of the finest work accomplished in the study of sleep and dreams. The research team associated with Hobson has over the decades produced a huge and invaluable body of work concerning neurocognitive mechanisms of REM sleep and dreaming. The team's work represents a sustained attempt at identifying regulatory mechanisms of REM sleep and providing mechanistic accounts of dream processes and functions.

The original formulation of the activation-synthesis model identified the key regulatory neuronal populations for REM in the brain stem (the LDT/PPT nuclei in the brain stem, reviewed elsewhere in this volume). This model of REM regulatory events was also called the reciprocal-interaction model of REM expression. It was believed that an interplay between aminergic and cholinergic cellular interactions in these nuclei gave rise to ascending cholinergic tracts that facilitated activation of limbic sites involved in dreaming. Later, PGO waves were identified as important sources of ascending activation during REM. However, the role of limbic and sensorimotor sites of the forebrain was conceived as a kind of reactive attempt to produce a coherent experience from the barrage of otherwise chaotic impulses arising from brain stem REM-on cellular activation. The forebrain attempt to synthesize some sort of story out of the impulses generated by brain stem REM-on networks resulted in confabulatory generation of dream scenarios. Some of the writings of Hobson suggested that he believed that the greater the brain stem activation level, the poorer the forebrain synthesis. The inability of the forebrain to synthesize ordered imagery out of the impulses arising from the brain stem resulted in more bizarre dream content.

A model of dreaming that conceives dreams as mere confabulations or attempts to make the best (story) out of a bad situation (a collection of random impulses, etc.), of course, simply could not account for the orderliness of dream content. Given the overwhelming evidence for the orderliness of dream content (reviewed in previous chapters as well as in Domhoff, 1996, and Van de Castle, 1994), no reading of the activation-synthesis, which implies random content, is possible. In any case, the inability of the original model to account for normative dream content along with advances in our understanding of the neural correlates of REM sleep and dreaming, mostly from neuroimaging experiments, have forced Hobson et al. to abandon this old model and instead offer the AIM model.

As in the activation-synthesis model, the AIM model rests on an activation component, again centered in the brain stem, but now including thalamic and forebrain sites as well. Aminergic and cholinergic interactions in the LDT/PPT are retained as one factor in the regulation of REM expression. Unlike the original model, GABA-ergic, adenosinergic, and histaminergic influences are allowed to influence REM-on and REM-off networks. REM sleep generation is conceived as a process involving every level of the neuraxis, from the brain stem to the reticular activating system in the midbrain, to the hypothalamus and thalamus, basal forebrain, amygdala, limbic system, and cortex. Cortical activation (A in AIM), in addition to brain stem activation, is given great weight in the new model. Cortical activation allows for efficient access to significant amounts of stored information during dream synthesis. Dream construction depends on access to an internal (I) source of information, which is facilitated (or forced) by sensory blockade during REM. The shift of the brain from aminergic to cholinergic neuromodulation (M) reduces reliability of cortical circuits in dream construction, thus increasing the likelihood that dreams will contain bizarre elements.

Like many other dream researchers, Hobson, Pace-Schott, and Stickgold (2000a) have felt obliged to develop some account of waking conscious states in order to fully understand dream expression. Thus, their AIM model proposes that all possible experiential brain states can be described as a point in a three-dimensional state-space, with axes A (level of brain activation), I (input source; external vs. internal), and M (neurotransmitter modulatory balance). Brain states (e.g., REM, NREM, waking consciousness) are theorized to vary systematically and continuously along the three dimensions of brain activation level, input source, and cholinergic/aminergic neurotransmitter balance. These brain states can be thought of as inhabiting points in the space of a three-dimensional cube defined by these three axes, with REM situated at the high end of the activation axis, the low (internal) end of the input source, and the high end of the modulatory cholinergic (low end of the aminergic) axis. Waking consciousness shares REM's high activation level but switches to an external input source and to high aminergic modulation. Finally, NREM lies midway in the cube space, with intermediate values along all three axes.

All three parameters are conceived as continuous variables; thus the gradations in changes among major brain/mind states are theoretically limitless, according to the AIM model. It is an ingenious model and one that might illuminate our understandings of all three basic brain states (wake, REM, and NREM). But immediately one wonders how such states as hibernation might be captured in the model. Would it be classified as low activation, with internal inputs (if any) and no modulatory changes allowed once the animal was in the hibernating state? But then it would be hard to distinguish from NREM sleep using model parameters alone. Similarly, AIM attempts to account for lucid dream states (where the dreamer is aware that he or she is dreaming) by assuming high activation in the prefrontal cortex, normally a site deactivated in REM. REM behavior disorder (which involves loss of motor inhibition during REM) is accounted for by postulating a move toward waking values in the I parameter. Whatever the merits of the AIM model for developing new approaches to these atypical brain states, the model certainly elegantly accounts for key features of REM. Its elegance lies in its simplicity; yet this simplicity also raises problems for the model.

The activation component of the model, for example, has to somehow produce selective activation patterns in the forebrain and cortex rather than global activation levels. REM, after all, involves selective activation of limbic, amygdaloid, and parietal networks and relative deactivation of dorsolateral prefrontal cortex (DLPFC). Yet the AIM model only specifies global activation levels in its account of brain state changes. Hobson et al. appear to believe that bringing in the neuromodulatory influence (reduction of aminergic input/enhancement of cholinergic input) can account for selective deactivation of DLPFC. Perhaps the DLPFC is not deactivated during REM but only fails to be activated during REM. Perhaps activation is no different functionally from deactivation or inhibition. Yet inhibitory processes require an active expenditure of resources (e.g., release of inhibitory transmitters with synaptic activation at postsynaptic inhibitory sites on target neurons), while failure to activate requires only a refraining from release of transmitters. Even if we assume that DLPFC is simply not activated, then why is parietal cortex activated when DLPFC is not? They are both complex cortical networks responsible for executive and other high-level cognitive functions. What is more, parietal and DLPFC are densely interconnected via the superior longitudinal fasciculus and other tracts. One would expect an active inhibitory process to be at work on the DLPFC if it does not "light up," but parietal operculum does light up during REM.

More generally, it is unlikely that AIM can account for even basic aspects of dream phenomenology. The authors themselves acknowledge that the I (input/information source) parameter cannot account for dream features such as dream recall rates, bizarreness, and vivid imagery. Even, however, if you combine an internal source with high activation and a demodulated aminergic/cholinergic balance, you will not get typical dream phenomenology such as narrative structure, negative affect, presence of unknown characters, aggressive social interactions, and the like. What is needed is a theory of exactly how forebrain networks access the relevant memory networks and cognitive systems in order to construct a typical dream.

Nevertheless, AIM is an elegant and powerful model that provides a basic orienting system when considering physiologic dynamics of major brain/mind states as well as dissociations in these major states. It is remarkable how much can be explained given just these three parameters. It would be silly to ignore the model in future work. On the other hand, it would be a mistake to assume that the model accurately represents the "big picture" with respect to dream phenomenology and that all that was needed was to fill in the (cognitive) details of the model. Instead, we need a detailed cognitive account of just what informational sources are retrieved in the course of dreaming and how the cognitive system builds the various formal properties of a dream.

Antrobus (1987, 1991) attempted to provide just such a cognitive model—a model, furthermore, that was consistent with the neurology of dreaming. In his neural network simulations of dreaming, Antrobus assumed that the properties of both dream and waking mentation varied as a function of cortical activation and degree of external stimulation (indexed by sensory thresholds). What created the dream narrative was not so much the brain states NREM or REM but rather intracortical interactions of specialized cortical networks mediating relevant sensorimotor and cognitive functions along with incoming subcortical inputs that needed to be integrated into ongoing cortical processing. Dream bizarreness, in this model, is due to failure to adequately summate all of these competing inputs to ongoing dream construction.

The Antrobus model is strongly supported by its implementation in a neural network model of dreaming that accurately reproduces at least some features of dreaming. In addition, the model is supported by the fact that sleep mentation can occur at virtually any point in the sleep cycle (indeed, dreamlike states can and do occur during the waking state). There are problems, however, with the model's ability to capture specific properties of the dream state. Antrobus seems to believe that differences in the quality of sleep reports obtained from different sleep states are due to differences in the level of cortical activation rather than to any differences due to qualitative different physiologies associated with REM versus NREM. With higher activation levels, one gets more vivid and bizarre dreams typically associated with REM, while lower activation levels produce NREM dreams, and so on. Antrobus claims, furthermore, that the so-called qualitative differences among REM and NREM dream types vanish once length and other confounding variables are controlled. This claim seems to argue against Antrobus's prior claim that cortical activation levels matter for dream content. Either activation levels have an impact on dream content variables or they do not.

While no one disputes that sleep mentation can be elicited from any point in the sleep cycle, the fact is that the quality of reports obtained from different stages in the cycle varies substantially, and the statistical likelihood that one can obtain mentation reports after awakenings varies as a function of what sleep stage the sleeper is in. On average, dream recall rates for most subjects (not for all subjects) are generally higher after awakening from REM than any other stage. In addition, as Hobson et al. (2000a) and Nielsen (2000) have shown (after exhaustive reviews of the literature), qualitative differences in dream content are found for NREM versus REM reports, and these differences remain after adjustments for length of reports.

Now the fact that one can obtain qualitatively different kinds of reports from each stage of EEG sleep does not invalidate Antrobus's model of dream construction. It is entirely possible that some aspects of dream construction occur regardless of stage of sleep, while other aspects of dream content depend solely on brain activation patterns associated with stage of sleep. The investigator, in other words, does not have to choose between one-generator or two-generator models of dream production (Nielsen, 2000). Indeed, one reading of Antrobus's neural network simulation of dream construction as well as similar modeling enterprises (Globus, 1993) is that a dream is the product of many interacting subunits, each performing one or a few tasks crucial for dream construction. If one of the involved subunits is suppressed (e.g., pharmacologically or via brain lesion), one or more important features of dream construction will be missing and the end product will be anomalous.

Solms (1997, 2000) has systematically investigated the effects of brain lesions on dream expression. He submitted a questionnaire on recall of dreams to 332 patients with various types of cerebral lesions (and 29 non-lesioned controls). Reports of global cessation of dreaming were associated with lesions in the region of the inferior parietal lobes on either side or with lesions deep to the medial frontal region in the white matter tracts connecting the frontal lobes with both cortical and subcortical sites. Two hundred patients with lesions outside these areas reported no changes in their dreaming patterns. This set of lesions would presumably disconnect anterior frontal cortex from subcortical and limbic sites. Thus, the meso-frontal tracts likely play a role in the generation of dreaming. Many of these tracts are catecholaminergic, and Solms believes that the most important ones for dreaming are the dopaminergic tracts that predict reward-related incentives (the appetitive and expectancy circuits).

Though not sufficiently discussed by Solms, the set of lesions in the inferior parietal lobes may result in disconnection of anterior prefrontal cortex and posterior parietal lobes. In the waking state, frontal-parietal disconnections produce attentional dysfunction when lesions are in the parietal regions and "environmental dependency syndrome" or utilization behavior when lesions are in the anterior region. It is interesting that these sets of cortical lesions (either the frontal or the parietal) produce reports of cessation of dream recall, as these lesions are not typically associated in the waking state with poor episodic recall of visual or verbal materials. Thus the lack of dream recall is probably not due to memory defects. If we can assume that dreaming had in fact ceased in these patients, then Antrobus's claims concerning cortical generation of dreams are supported.

A third pattern of lesions was associated with enhanced dreaming or intrusion of dreaming into waking life. This set of lesions involved epileptic changes in the temporal lobes and lesions in the medial prefrontal cortex.

Solms also confirmed the existence of a syndrome of nonvisual dreaming (previously described by Doricchi & Violani, 1992; Greenberg & Farah, 1986). After their review of the extant literature, Greenberg and Farah concluded that dream generation was dependent on left-sided posterior sites. Solms assigns a potential symbolic abstract spatial capacity to these sites. Nonvisual dreaming was most often associated with bilateral medial occipital-temporal lesions—regions independently implicated in high-level visual processing streams. This syndrome, however, needs to be carefully disambiguated from the full or partial visual agnosias that typically accompany lesions to medial temporal lobes and occipital cortex.

Solms's model of dreaming postulates a crucial role for what he calls (following Panksepp partially) the appetitive, expectancy, and curiosity circuits associated with ascending mesolimbic-cortical dopaminergic circuits. These dopaminergic circuits project from basal ganglia and limbic sites to the mediobasal and prefrontal cortex. Independent evidence suggests that mesocortical catecholaminergic circuits are crucial for predicting reward and are therefore involved in motivational aspects of behavior. Solms claims that activation of these dopaminergic circuits instigates the dream formation process. Since Solms agrees with Freud that protection of sleep is one of the functions of dreaming, he provides a scheme for propagation and damping of activation levels away from anterior regions to posterior regions. REM-associated activation of anterior limbic sites is hypothesized to simultaneously prevent activation of motor cortex and to facilitate a process Solms calls back-propagation. In back-propagation, the activation levels in dopaminergic circuits are kept from prefrontal, supplementary motor and premotor areas and then rerouted posteriorly to sites in the inferior parietal lobes and occipital-temporal visual association areas. The sleeper then can safely experience a visual simulation (hallucination) that satisfies a wish and prevents awakening without becoming fully conscious or motorically active.

Although REM sleep can activate relevant dopaminergic circuits and thereby initiate the dream formation process, REM, according to Solms, is neither necessary nor sufficient for production of dreaming. Solms had 53 patients with brain stem lesions, 43 of whom nevertheless continued to experience dreams. Thus, REM generator processes in the brain stem could be impaired with preservation of dreaming. Solms points out that loss of dreaming can occur with preservation of REM and, conversely, REM can be significantly impaired but the patient may still experience dreaming. What needs to be determined in such cases is whether the residual dreaming after REM impairment is like typical REM dreams or more like NREM dreams. It is still possible that loss of REM dreaming (with preservation of NREM forms of dreaming) occurs when REM is impaired.

As to Solms's back-propagation hypothesis, one can only say that it is not needed to account for brain activation patterns during sleep and particularly during REM. Inhibition of motor output more likely acts to prevent injury rather than to preserve sleep, as individuals with REM behavior disorder or with sleepwalking disorder remain asleep even when motor inhibition fails. Nor are activation patterns confined to mesolimbic and posterior cortical sites during dreaming. Recent neuroimaging studies, for example, have demonstrated some activation of orbitofrontal cortex during REM. Finally, if preservation of sleep was the functional reason for dreaming and for rerouting of neural activation levels, it is odd that dreaming (according to Solms) involves activation of appetitive/approach circuits— circuits that normally impel one to act to obtain a reward. Similarly, it is odd that rerouting is to posterior cortical sites rather than, say, to thinking/ ruminative circuits in anterior regions or to planning circuits in the supplementary motor areas, and so on. The activation of posterior regions typically impels approach behaviors. Lhermitte (1986), for example, pointed out that when frontal areas are lesioned, the person comes under control of posterior parietal areas. Patients under control of parietal systems exhibit all kinds of compulsive and inappropriate approach behaviors, as in the case of utilization behavior. Examples include the patient compulsively utilizing anything with any salience that is put in front of him. Even if a hypodermic syringe is presented, he will pick it up and try to inject himself with it! So controlled by approach tendencies were these sorts of patients that Lhermitte called the syndrome environmental dependency syndrome.

If back-propagation truly occurs and functions to protect sleep, one would expect loss of dreaming to result in waking or at least poor sleep. While Solms claims that some of his patients do indeed report poor sleep, it is not clear that this is due to loss of dreaming per se or to their medical condition. I know of no evidence that suggests that patients with frontal leucotomies or with bilateral parietal lesions are rendered permanently awake. Indeed, Jus et al. (1973) demonstrated that REM occurred in leucotomized patients who nevertheless reported very few if any dreams.

One of the insights Solms's data gives us with respect to dreaming is that dream formation requires participation of large regions of the cortex, including the frontal lobes. This conclusion is supported by virtually all of the recent neuroimaging results as well. If global cessation of dreaming occurs when the orbitofrontal lobes are disconnected from subcortical sites, it suggests that the orbitofrontal lobes participate in dream formation. Yet it is not clear that Solms himself draws this conclusion. Instead, his back-propagation model seems to exclude the possibility that the orbitofrontal cortex participates in dreaming.

Domhoff (2003) draws on Solms's data, the recent set of findings gathered from neuroimaging studies, and his own extensive studies on dream content to propose a detailed neurocognitive model of dreaming. Like Hobson et al., Antrobus, and Solms, Domhoff suggests that dreaming depends on brain activation patterns, but the content of dreaming comes from access to the conceptual system of schemata and scripts housed in the cognitive system. This attention to cognitive detail and modern cognitive science theory is a real advance over previous neurocognitive models. Domhoff agrees with Hobson et al. in noting that REM provides the optimal substrate for dreaming and that the REM generator is likely the LDT/PPT cellular structures in the pons and that large-scale neural networks in the forebrain are required for shaping dream content. Among these dream-related networks are those regions identified by Solms in his clinical studies and by teams of investigators utilizing PET scan techniques. The convergence of these data indicate large-scale but selective neural networks responsible for dreaming including the brain stem generator, structures in the hypothalamus and thalamus, amygdala, limbic system, anterior cingulate, and cortical sites. These sets of neural structures constitute the neural substrate for dream activation and maintenance.

Domhoff draws on his extensive studies of dream content to note the following: Once adulthood is reached, little or no change in dream content occurs. In addition, patterns of basic elements of dream content vary little across cultures. These patterns include higher percentages of male characters in dreams of men versus women, higher aggression than friendliness percentages in dreams, and higher levels of negative than positive emotions in dreams of both men and women. Domhoff also adumbrates a "continuity principle" in dream content, noting that individuals' waking concerns and past emotional preoccupations are reflected in their dreams—there is a continuity between waking life and dream life, though dreams are not mere reflections of waking life. Again, this utilization of the actual facts concerning laws of dream content is a major advance over previous neurocognitive models of dreams.

Domhoff suggests a "repetition principle" in dreams, which concerns the tendency to repeat certain themes in dreams across time. He cites repetitive nightmares, recurrent dreams of childhood and adolescence, and repeated themes found in some dream series elicited from a single individual. Domhoff links this tendency to repeat content to activation of the amygydala's fear-vigilance system. This link makes sense, given that many repetitive dreams are unpleasant or are actual nightmares. On the other hand, repetition of nonfrightening themes may be related to active inhibition of the DLPFC during REM. Lesions to the DLPFC are associated with perseveration, and perseveration at the ideational level may play a role in some dreams.

The conceptual systems cited by Domhoff as important for formation of dream content include modules or systems involving the basic-level categories, spatial relations, and sensorimotor schemata. Basic-level conceptual categories can be characterized by a single concrete image and, combined with the spatial-directional sense (up/down) and sensorimotor schemata, they are drawn on to compose the dream. Dreaming, according to Domhoff, draws on memory schemata, general knowledge, and episodic memories to produce quasi-veridical simulations of the real world in dreams.

Domhoff's neurocognitive model of dreaming is powerful, as it combines detailed neural-cognitive correlations for dreaming's most consistent and fundamental features as well as the constants of dream content. Of all the major neurocognitive approaches to dreams, Domhoff takes the constants of dream content most seriously and therefore should be accounted the most successful to date in accounting for that content. While Domhoff points out that dreams, among other things, dramatize emotional preoccupations of the dreamer, he does not believe that dreaming per se has an adaptive function. He therefore parts company with the next theorist of dream content, the evolutionary theorist Revonsuo.

Revonsuo (2000) proposes that the function of dreaming is to simulate threatening events. Threat simulations are thought to allow for rehearsal of threat perception and thus to enhance threat avoidance. Revonsuo notes that dream content is not random but instead consistently overrepresents simulations of unpleasant or threatening events. In some cases, these simulations are repetitions of previous unpleasant dreams (Domhoff's repetition principle) such as a nightmare of being chased by a wild animal, and so on. Repeated simulations of such threatening events in the dreaming mind of an ancestral human are thought to confer a selective advantage on that individual relative to individuals not experiencing such simulations. The advantage might be a slightly faster response time when confronted with a threat or a slightly improved ability to detect an incipient attack, and so forth. Children, in particular, would benefit from such a threat simulation device, and studies of dreams of modern children show that wild threatening animals are overrepresented in their dreams. Nightmares and posttraumatic repetition dreams are thought to be instances of disinhibition of the threat simulation device. Dreams of modern hunter-gatherers also contain a fair number of unpleasant threatening events. Finally, most dreams are filled with negative emotions due to dreamer-experienced misfortune and/or aggression. The enemies in our dreams are typically male strangers. Male strangers and animals in the ancestral environment would have been a most dangerous threat faced by ancestral humans who lived in small, relatively isolated groups of hunter-gatherers.

Recent evidence from neuroimaging studies regarding brain activation during REM partially supports a threat simulation function for REM. The amygdala, in particular, is known to specialize in vigilance and fear behaviors. Real threats, when encountered in the environment, can enhance

REM, and when such threats are experienced by children, they can trigger abnormally early development of dreaming. Foulkes presented evidence that true dreaming involving a self in a dramatic scenario does not develop until age 7 to 8. Nightmares with remembered dream content can, however, occur in children younger than 7 if they experience trauma, as if the threat simulation mechanism kicks in as needed.

In my view, Revonsuo (2000) presents a compelling case for the operation of a threat simulation device in some dreams. I do not believe, however, that threat simulation accounts for all or even the majority of dreams. Revonsuo at some points in his argument appears to claim that all dreams can be assimilated to threat simulation, but that is unlikely in my view. There are too many dreams that are simply not about threats and/or not even unpleasant. An equally pressing necessity for ancestral humans had to do with interactions with other members of the group: how to find a mate, how to avoid conflict, how to build coalitions, and so forth. Dreams also simulate social interactions, and if simulating these interactions in dreams enhanced fitness outcomes for the individuals who experienced such dreams, natural selection would have supported development of such dreams, as seems to be the case. Nevertheless, Revonsuo has, in my view, performed a great service in identifying one of the important biologic functions of dreaming.

CHAPTER 10

Understanding REM

Some puzzling aspects of REM expression across the life span make sense in the light of evolutionary theories involving genetic conflict and costly signaling. REM sleep amounts are higher in juveniles than in adults in both mammals and birds, suggesting a role for REM in development of young. Obviously mammalian young, particularly altricial young, depend on care of a mother to survive. So do avian young. When a mother bird brings a worm back to her chicks, she finds herself faced with an array of apparently needy chicks, all of which vocalize loudly as if demanding the morsel for themselves. It is in her interest to identify the chick most likely to benefit from the meal (typically the hungriest). But it is in the interest of each chick to feign need in order to obtain the morsel. How does the mother discover true need in such a situation? Better, how does the mother identify her best bet: which chick is most likely to survive to reproductive maturity if given the morsel? Once again, costly signals can provide the mother with the requisite information. Loud begging is costly both in terms of the energy required to squawk loudly and in terms of attracting the attention of predators. Thus, only truly needy chicks will squawk loudly. For nonhungry chicks, the risk of predation will outweigh any potential gain from begging.

In human infants, a similar process may take place. The mother uses signaling displays of her offspring (e.g., crying, smiling, babbling, vocalizations, etc.) to help make investment decisions about offspring (Godfrey, 1995; Parker, Royle, & Hartley, 2002; Trivers, 1974). To reach their own investment optima (to maximize their fitness by bringing offspring to reproductive maturity), parents need accurate information on need of offspring in order to effectively allocate resources to young. There is thus an onus on offspring to accurately signal need and viability in order to receive a consistent level of parental investment. Given that mothers must use signaling displays of offspring to make decisions about care, the physiologic system in the infant that produces these signaling displays would come under strong selective pressures (i.e., those juveniles not producing strong displays would receive less investment and therefore not survive to maturity or not reproduce at maturity), and since the infant spends a large part of its life asleep during the critical first year of life when these maternal decisions are made, there would be pressure to produce effective signaling displays even in the sleep state.

The sleep state most likely to play this role is active sleep or REM. Juvenile REM physiology in many mammalian species (particularly altricial species), would have therefore evolved to specialize in facilitating production of signals that would elicit optimal care from the mother. As discussed in chapter 2, juvenile REM is associated with telltale physical signs that can be distinguished by visual inspection (e.g., muscle twitches, rapid eye movements under closed eyelids, etc.). Early bouts of crying are known to occur while the infant is in REM (i.e., is asleep; Wolff, 1987). Infant REM is not a passive state. The infant suckles, cries, coos, babbles, and smiles in REM. In addition, facial grimaces, grasping, clutching, head turning, and distal limb twitches can be observed while the infant is in REM. In contrast, NREM sleep is characterized by behavioral quiescence. Thus, mothers should be able to use REM-related signs and signaling to assess infant state and to help make decisions concerning investment of resources in particular offspring.

If REM-facilitated signaling displays in the infant are effective in manipulating maternal responding, then REM indices or expressions should be associated with formation of emotional ties (attachment) with the mother. I reviewed a large array of evidence in chapter 2 that supported the idea that infant REM is associated with formation of emotional attachment between mother and infant, which I will not repeat here. After the infantile years, REM steadily declines while NREM stabilizes, until we reach the transitional stage of puberty. Here, the release of gonadotropins becomes nocturnally entrained and the child undergoes the profound physiologic changes of puberty. During adolescence, SWS transiently declines while REM increases. In severe cases, this profile of relatively low SWS and high REM is associated with depression and self-harm. Dreams contain high levels of aggressive acts wherein the dreamer is the victim. In the adult years, REM and NREM expression stabilizes in the sense that their relative proportions of the total sleep amount remain roughly the same for the next few decades.

In chapter 3, I reviewed phylogenetic trends in REM expression. The model of REM that I have explored in this book, which claims that expression of REM has been influenced by evolutionary and genetic conflict, would predict that REM expression would vary with indices of genetic conflict across taxa. For example, altered REM-NREM dynamics (e.g., reduced REM) would be expected in species with reduced forms of genetic conflict (e.g., conflict over allocation of maternal resources in the context of paternity uncertainty). That expectation was confirmed.

In this text, I focused on the form of genetic conflict called genomic imprinting and thus argued that full polygraphic REM would be found in species that evidence genomic imprinting in addition to other forms of conflict. Developmental genomic imprinting is not found in most birds or reptiles, where the mother controls production of eggs. While there is clear parent-offspring conflict after hatchlings emerge from the egg, overall levels of conflict are reduced in egg-laying birds, reptiles, and monotremes up to the point of hatching because the egg ensures that a fixed amount of nutrient will be allocated to each offspring. As reviewed in chapter 2, the presence of REM-like sleep states in reptiles has yet to be convincingly demonstrated. Thus, the data from investigation of sleep states in reptiles is consistent with the conflict model of REM expression. Crocodiles may constitute a partial exception to that rule, but crocodiles apparently display some parental care and infant dependency, and thus some amount of parent-offspring conflict may occur in these species.

Birds do show some evidence of REM-like sleep states, but they are fleeting and do not evidence rebound effects after sleep deprivation. Imprinting does not occur in birds, but the search for imprinting effects among birds has not been extensive. Birds, in any case, do evidence intense forms of parent-offspring conflict, so the appearance of some REM-like sleep states is consistent with the conflict model.

The conflict model predicts reduced REM in monotremes (as they are egg-laying species) but abundant REM in marsupials given that viviparity (and with it, new opportunities for conflict) emerged in these animals. As reviewed in chapter 3, the evidence for REM in these species is equivocal. Siegel et al. (1996, 1998, 1999) found eutherian-like irregular reticular discharge patterns during SWS in the short-beaked echidna and rapid eye movements in the duck-billed platypus, despite no overt EEG signs of REM. While some have interpreted these data as suggesting abundant REM in the platypus, it must be emphasized that no unmixed or overt EEG signs of REM were recorded in this animal. Rather, consistent with predictions of the conflict model, full polygraphic REM is not seen in the monotremes. Instead, these new data suggest that monotremes exhibit a hybrid combination of both REM and NREM-like brain states and that this hybrid form of sleep represents the state from which distinct REM and NREM states emerge in marsupials and placental mammals.

The eutherian mammals gave rise about 130 million years ago to the two major classes of mammals: the marsupials and the placentals. The marsupials, such as the kangaroo and opossum, give birth to live and very immature young and carry them around in sacs or pouches until maturity. These reproductive relationships create the context for high parent-offspring conflict around growth schedules, resource transfer, and so on. In addition, imprinting effects are known to occur in these animals. Thus, consistent with predictions of the conflict model, REM percentages tend to be quite high in marsupials and mammals.

Genetic conflict is rife in placental mammals, and, in particular, patriline/ matriline genomic conflict obtains in species where paternity uncertainty is high (i.e., most mammalian species). Consistent with the conflict model of REM, full polygraphic REM is common in such species, and REM represents approximately 20% of the sleep of these animals, although there is wide variation. Conversely, the conflict model predicts reduction of REM indices in mammalian species where lifetime monogamy is the rule. To my knowledge, REM amounts have not yet been studied as a function of paternity uncertainty in mammals and thus as yet no data are available on this issue.

In apparent contradiction to the predictions of the conflict model, REM may be absent or reduced in at least three species of mammals. These are members of the cetacean suborder Odontoceti (the Amazonian dolphin, the bottlenose dolphin, and the common porpoise). Reduction of REM in these animals occurs in the context of so-called unihemispheric sleep, which is characteristic of several species of marine mammals (see chapter 3).

The conflict theory would predict monogamous mating strategies or reduction of paternity uncertainty in those marine mammals without full polygraphic REM. Available evidence supports the conflict model in this case: Reliable proxy measures of paternity uncertainty (testis size and sexual dimorphism) are reduced in at least two (the dolphins) of the three species evidencing absence of REM (Connor, Read, & Wrangham, 2000). The conflict model would predict that when measures of testis mass and sexual dimorphism increase in delphinids (indicating greater paternity uncertainty and therefore greater genetic conflict), so too will measures of REM. When these measures decrease, as they do in at least two of the species in question, REM characteristics will be reduced or absent. No data relevant to the issue of conflict and paternity uncertainty in the common porpoise could be found, but the conflict model predicts a reduction of conflict relative to other delphinids in this species as well.

In short, review of ontogenetic and phylogenetic trends in REM expression are broadly consistent with a model of REM that emphasizes the impact of genetic conflict on functional expression. What about the impact of conflict on dream expression?

Recall that I have argued in this book that REM specializes in production of costly signals. In the adult human, REM expression involves the whole suite of paradoxical traits described in chapter 1: intense limbic and amygdaloid brain activation levels, autonomic nervous system storms, cardiac and respiratory instabilities, vivid emotional dreams typically involving the dreamer in unpleasant actions and emotions, paralysis of the antigravity muscles, sexual activation, rapid eye movements and limb twitches, and so forth. I demonstrated in chapter 1 that these traits are associated with significant health risks, and we are therefore justified in calling them costly traits.

To date I know of no attempts, aside from Parmeggiani's (2000) descriptive analyses, to provide a theoretical account for this suite of maladaptive traits. Therefore I propose the following possibility: These traits are not by-products of some other more fundamental function of REM. Rather, REM is designed to produce these kinds of costly traits that are experienced as a handicap by the individual. REM's stock in trade is production of emotional signals, as these are hard-to-fake costly signals. The individual uses these signals in exactly the same way other animals use costly signals and handicaps: as signals in a communication game and as advertisements of one's genes as well as one's resources, willingness to cooperate, reliability, honesty, and so forth. In essence, the handicap sends the signal, "I am willing to sacrifice. I am not a free rider. You can believe and trust me."

REM-related production of emotional states and costly signals would influence dream content and the display of emotional signals the person emits the next day, whether or not the person remembered any dream that morning. Given the predominance of negative emotions in many dreams, it may be that the bias over time is in creating emotional handicaps, but these in turn allow the person to advertise honesty in communicative interchanges, and so the long-term results are better social interactions for the individual and thus increased fitness. It may seem odd to us that the way Mother Nature defeats free riders and achieves cooperative interchanges among her creatures is to have them develop and display handicaps, but this is apparently the case.

REM is certainly in a position to influence a person's waking mood state. REM involves regular, periodic, and intense activation of the limbic system and the amygdala—the two major emotional centers of the brain. As the night progresses, activation patterns become more intense and likely color the person's mood for the day upon awakening. If the sleeper awakes and remembers an emotional dream, waking-related mood states are that much more likely to be influenced by REM, but remembering a dream is not necessary.

In chapters 4 and 5, I reviewed the literature on REM-NREM interactions and suggested that these interactions were shaped in part by separate sets of genes in conflict with one another. These interactions, in turn, influence the amount and quality of the cognitive and emotional processing that occurs during sleep, with NREM specializing in initial processing stages (whether it be formatting to-be-remembered life episodes or highlighting to-be-worked-on emotional conflicts) and REM specializing in later stages of processing. As the night progresses, REM dream content becomes more vivid, emotional, memorable, and bizarre. Dreams that occur at this time in the morning are the ones we typically remember and the ones that likely influence our daily behaviors by subtly biasing the display of emotional signals we emit that day.

If we suppose that one function of these REM dreams is to produce the feeling states, memories, perceptual biases, intentional states, and behavioral goals that allow for display of costly signaling during the waking hours, then deprivation of REM dreaming would impair such displays. Given that the ultimate purpose of such displays is to facilitate cooperative social interactions, the person deprived of REM dreaming would eventually suffer in the quality of his or her social interactions. To the degree that REM itself is suppressed in a REM deprivation paradigm, the person would initially actually feel better than usual as he or she is no longer producing behavioral dispositions that are costly handicaps. This may be one reason why antidepressants that suppress REM help in elevating mood.

We saw in chapters 7 and 8 that a costly signaling approach to dream expression is broadly consistent with both the formal properties of dreams and with dream content. Typical dreams involve unpleasant emotions and scenes that place the dreamer in a victim role or under some handicap (naked, disoriented, without identification, unable to move, etc.). All of these properties of dreams, while obviously consistent with the costly signaling approach advocated here, are also somewhat consistent with Revonsuo's theory of dreaming as threat simulation (reviewed in chapter 9). Unlike the costly signaling theory, however, the threat simulation theory would have a more difficult time accounting for pleasant emotional states and dreams not involving attacks on the dreamer. The two theories suggest opposite functions for dreams: one to improve responding when under threat, and the other to handicap a person or to produce biased emotional responding when awake. To some extent, the two approaches predict opposite effects of dreams when an awake person faces a threat: according to threat simulation theory, that person would react a little faster if he had just experienced a dream wherein the dreamer was attacked or a victim of aggression, and so on. According to costly signaling theory, the person would be handicapped if he had just experienced such a dream. Whatever beneficial effects such a dream might confer on a person (in terms of reaction times, etc., in response to a real attack), they would potentially be canceled out by the real purpose of the dream: to produce a handicapped self or a biased set of emotional signals during the waking state.

One neglected area of research in dreams that costly signaling theory might impact is the cultural uses of dreams. We know that dreams and the sharing of dreams were a vitally important part of the lives and cultural practices of many premodern societies. The Jesuit missions to the North American Indian tribes in the 17th and 18th centuries describe in detail the centrality of the dream to these cultural groups. The Jesuit fathers claimed that the only true divinity that some of the tribes (particularly the Iroquois and Seneca) recognized was the dream. They marveled at what they considered to be the "utter folly" of the Indians who took their dreams so seriously that they would insist on acting out or following up on the dreams' messages the next day, no matter what the cost. The Jesuit fathers relate stories of a man dreaming about purchasing a dog from a tribe hundreds of miles away and then the next morning setting off to purchase that dog, despite the fact that the journey was perilous and in the dead of winter, or of tribes holding the dreams of elders as sacred and using the images produced in these dreams to design the tribe's clothes, dwellings, and tools. Most of the tribe's religious rituals were derived from dreams that their ancestors had had, and so forth. I am reminded of the story of the Indian boy called Black Elk. His response to the invasion of the whites is vividly described in the book *Black Elk Speaks* (Black Elk & Neihardt, 1932). Although modern scholarship has disputed some aspects of the following story, the gist of the story is consistent with other independent accounts of the role of dreams in Native American society. While an adolescent, Black Elk had a dream that entailed a series of dances and costumes and festivals involving his entire tribe. When he shared his dream with tribal members, the entire society ceased its regular ongoing life and spent weeks creating the costumes, dances, and events Black Elk had seen in his dream. They then spent another several weeks enacting the contents of the dream. From the modern point of view, this is a costly, extravagant waste on the part of the tribe—especially given the threat the tribe was facing from the whites.

We can surmise that if dreams were of such prime importance in the cultures of these premodern North American tribes, then they may have been equally or more important to the ancestors of anatomically modern humans. As is well known, anatomically modern humans have been around for a couple hundred thousand years and throughout that (relatively) long expanse of time, humans lived in tribal societies that likely practiced a hunter-gatherer lifestyle. It is reasonable to suppose dreams and dreaming were important to these peoples just as they seem to be to contemporary tribal cultures.

Why is the dream so important a cultural force among these tribal societies? The theory of costly signaling may help us understand why. If dreams are a source of costly, hard-to-fake signals, including emotional signals, and such signals are crucial in producing and maintaining the reliability and honesty of systems of communication among human beings, then the dream becomes a source of unity and cohesion for these tribal groups. In the case of Black Elk, for example, perhaps the point of the wasteful display was precisely to unite the tribe using costly signals to identify cooperative members as well as unreliable free riders in preparation for the coming struggle with the whites. The dream provided the constituent forms the costly signals would take for both individuals and the tribe itself. Premodern societies apparently often used the dreams (often lucid dreams) of shamans in much the same way. The dream's ability to produce forms for costly signals made it an extremely valuable cultural tool. The images in the dream provided the forms for healing ceremonies and religious ceremonies.

Consistent with this use of dreams (as sources for production of costly signals used in rituals and religious practices), several theorists (Iannacone, 1992; Irons, 1996, 2001; Sosis & Bressler, 2003) have argued that religious ritual and practices may function as an honest signal of commitment to the religious group, thus discouraging free riders and facilitating intragroup co-operation. It would be difficult for free riders to claim membership in the group (and thus obtain group benefits) if they could not adopt ritual require-ments and practices of the group (e.g., public attendance at ceremonies, tithing, food restrictions and fasting, restricted sexual and mating practices, daily prayer, beliefs in counterintuitive supernatural agents, etc.). The greater the requirement for public and private costly display of sacrifices, the more difficult it would be for free riders to fake commitment. Thus, religions func-tion to increase group cooperation and use costly signals to identify com-mitted members and exclude free riders.

If dreams are a source for the production of emotions and images that are costly, then the costly signal theory of the dream may help to account for the intuition that dreaming and religiosity are connected. Jung noted these deep connections but had no theory for them. He always claimed that he was simply pointing to facts, describing what he saw in the lives of his patients and in the literature on religiosity and dreams. Religion may call on the dream as a source for signals and images that are costly and that will work to establish cooperation in a local group of people and to punish potential free riders.

Costly signaling appears to be a common and powerful evolutionary strategy for development of systems of reliable and honest communication and therefore may not have been excluded from the realm of sleep biology. Both REM sleep and dreaming involve costly physiologic processes and signals. These sleep states may therefore both influence development of costly signals and be influenced by the pressure to evolve costly signaling.

If REM sleep and dreams are a primary source for the formation of hard-to-fake emotional and costly signals, then REM sleep and dreams are cru-cial to all forms of human communication that involve costly signals. REM sleep and dreams are therefore central to human behavior, well-being, and culture.

References

Affani, J. M., Cervino, C. O., & Marcos, H. J. A. (2001). Absence of penile erections during paradoxical sleep: Peculiar penile events during wakefulness and slow wave sleep in the armadillo. *Journal of Sleep Research, 10*, 219–228.

Agargun, M. Y., & Cartwright, R. (2003). REM sleep, dream variables and suicidality in depressed patients. *Psychiatry Research, 119*(1–2), 33–39.

Agargun, M. Y., Cilli, A. S., Kara, H., Tarhan, N., Kincir, F., & Oz, H. (1998). Repetitive frightening dreams and suicidal behavior in patients with major depression. *Comprehensive Psychiatry, 39*, 198–202.

Allison, T., & Cicchetti, D. V. (1976). Sleep in mammals: Ecological and constitutional correlates. *Science, 194*, 732–734.

Allison, T., Van Twyver, H., & Goff, W. R. (1972). Electrophysiological studies of the echidna, *Tachyglossus aculaelus*. 1. Waking and sleep. *Archives of Italian Biology, 110*, 145–184.

Amici, R., Sanford, L. D., Kearney, K., McInerney, B., Ross, R. J., Horner, R. L., et al. (2004). A serotonergic (5-HT2) receptor mechanism in the laterodorsal tegmental nucleus participates in regulating the pattern of rapid-eye-movement sleep occurrence in the rat. *Brain Res, 996*(1), 9–18.

Anderson, J. R. (1998). Sleep, sleeping sites, and sleep-related activities: Awakening to their significance. *American Journal of Primatology, 46*(1), 63–75.

Anokhin, A., Steinlein, O., Fischer, C., Mao, Y., Vogt, P., Schalt, E., et al. (1992). A genetic study of the human low-voltage electroencephalogram. *Human Genetics, 90*(1–2), 99–112.

Antrobus, J. S. (1987). Cortical hemisphere asymmetry and sleep mentation. *Psychological Review, 94*, 359–368.

Antrobus, J. S. (1991). Dreaming: Cognitive processes during cortical activation and high afferent thresholds. *Psychological Review, 98*, 96–121.

Argiolas, A., & Gessa, G. L. (1991). Central functions of oxytocin. *Neuroscience and Biobehavioral Reviews, 15*(2), 217–231.

Asplund, R., & Aberg, H. (1998). Sleep and cardiac symptoms amongst women aged 40–64 years. *Journal of Internal Medicine, 243*(3), 209–213.

Azmitia, E. C. (2001). Modern views on an ancient chemical: Serotonin effects on cell proliferation, maturation, and apoptosis. *Brain Research Bulletin, 56*, 413–424.

Bach, V., Telliez, F., & Libert, J.-P. (2002). The interaction between sleep and thermoregulation in adults and neonates. *Sleep Medicine Reviews, 6*(6), 481–492.

Bachevalier, J., Malkova, L., & Mishkin, M. (2001). Effects of selective neonatal temporal lobe lesions on socioemotional behavior in infant rhesus monkeys (*Macaca mulatta*). *Behavioral Neuroscience, 115*(3), 545–559.

Baron-Cohen, S. (1997). *Mindblindness: An essay on autism and theory of mind.* Cambridge, MA: MIT Press.

Barrett, D., & Loeffler, M. (1992). Comparison of dream content of depressed vs. nondepressed dreamers. *Psychological Reports, 70,* 403–406.

Bearder, S. K. (1987). Lorises, bushbabies, and tarsiers: Diverse societies in solitary foragers. In B. Smuts, D. Cheney, R. Seyfarth, R. Wrangham, & T. Struhsaker (Eds.), *Primate societies* (pp. 11–24). Chicago: University of Chicago Press.

Bechara, A., Damasio, H., Damasio, A. R., & Lee, G. P. (1999). Different contributions of the human amygdala and ventromedial prefrontal cortex to decision-making. *Journal of Neuroscience, 19*(13), 5473–5481.

Beebe, B., Gertsman, L., & Carson, B. (1982). Rhythmic communication in the mother-infant dyad. In M. Davis (Ed.), *Interaction rhythms: Periodicity in communicative behavior* (pp. 113–121). New York: Human Sciences Press.

Belsky, J., Fish, M., & Isabella, R. (1991). Continuity and discontinuity in infant negative and positive emotionality: Family antecedents and attachment consequences. *Developmental Psychology, 27,* 421–431.

Belsky, J., & Nezworski, T. (Eds.). (1988). *Clinical implications of attachment.* Hillsdale, NJ: Lawrence Erlbaum.

Belsky, J., Steinberg, L., & Draper, P. (1991). Childhood experience, interpersonal development, and reproductive strategy: An evolutionary theory of socialization. *Child Development, 62,* 647–670.

Benca, R. M. (2000). Mood disorders. In M. H. Kryger, T. Roth, & W. C. Dement (Eds.), *Principles and practice of sleep medicine* (3rd ed., pp. 1140–1148). Philadelphia: Saunders.

Benington, J. H., & Heller, H. C. (1994). Does the function of REM sleep concern non-REM sleep or waking? *Progress in Neurobiology, 44,* 433–449.

Benington, J. H., & Heller, H. C. (1995). Restoration of brain energy metabolism as the function of sleep. *Progress in Neurobiology, 45,* 347–360.

Benington, J. H., Woudenberg, C. M., & Heller, H. C. (1995). Apamin, a selective SK potassium channel blocker, suppresses REM sleep without a compensatory rebound. *Brain Research, 692,* 86–92.

Benoit, D., Zeanah, C. H., Boucher, C., & Minde, K. K. (1992). Sleep disorders in early childhood: Association with insecure maternal attachment. *Journal of the American Academy of Child and Adolescent Psychiatry, 31*(1), 86–93.

Berger, R. J. (1990). Relations between sleep durations, body weight and metabolic rate in mammals. *Animal Behaviour, 40,* 989–991.

Berger, R. J., & Phillips, N. H. (1995). Energy and sleep conservation. *Behavioural Brain Research, 69,* 65–73.

Bert, J., Balzamo, E., Chase, M., & Pegram, V. (1975). The sleep of the baboon, *Papio papio,* under natural conditions and in the laboratory. *Electroencephalography and Clinical Neurophysiology, 39,* 657–662.

Bert, J., Pegram, V., Rhodes, J. M., Balzano, E., & Naquet, R. (1970). A comparative sleep study of two Cercopithecinae. *Electroencephalography and Clinical Neurophysiology, 28*(1), 32–40.

Bischof, H. J. (1997). Song learning, filial imprinting and sexual imprinting: Three variations of a common theme? *Biomedical Reseach Tokyo, 18,* 133–146.

Black Elk, N., & Neihardt, J. G. (1932). *Black Elk speaks: Being the life story of a holy man of the Oglala Sioux.* Lincoln: University of Nebraska Press.

Bliwise, D. L. (2000). Normal aging. In M. H. Kryger, T. Roth, & W. C. Dement (Eds.), *Principles and practice of sleep medicine* (pp. 26–42). Philadelphia: Saunders.

Bole-Feysot, C., Goffin, V., Edery, M., Binart, N., & Kelly, P. (1998). Prolactin (PRL) and its receptor: Action, signal transduction pathways, and phenotypes observed in PRL receptor knockout mice. *Endocrine Reviews, 19,* 225–268.

Borbely, A. A., & Neuhaus, H. U. (1979). Sleep-deprivation: Effects on sleep and EEG in the rat. *Journal of Comparative Physiology, 128,* 37–46.

Borbely, A. A., & Tobler, I. (1989). Endogenous sleep promoting substances and sleep regulation. *Physiological Reviews, 69,* 605–670.

Brabbins, C. J., Dewey, M. E., Copeland, J. R. M., Davidson, I. A., McWilliam, C., Saunders, P., et al. (1993). Insomnia in the elderly: Prevalence, gender differences and relationships with morbidity and mortality. *International Journal of Geriatric Psychiatry, 8,* 473–480.

Bradbury, J., & Vehrencamp, S. (1998). *Principles of animal communication.* Sunderland, MA: Sinauer Associates.

Braun, A. R., Balkin, T. J., Wesenstein, N. J., Varga, M., Baldwin, P., Selbie, S., et al. (1997). Regional cerebral blood flow throughout the sleep-wake cycle. *Brain, 120,* 1173–1197.

Bronfenbrenner, U., & Crouter, A. (1982). Work and family through time and space. In S. Kamerman, & C. Hayes (Eds.), *Families that work* (pp. 39–83). Washington, DC: National Academy Press.

Brubaker, L. L. (1998). Note on the relevance of dreams for evolutionary psychology. *Psychology Reports, 82*(3, Pt 1), 1006.

Buhr, A., Bianchi, M. T., Baur, R., Courtet, P., Pignay, V., Boulenger, J. P., et al. (2002). Functional characterization of the new human GABA(A) receptor mutation beta3(R192H). *Human Genetics, 111*(2), 154–160.

Bulkeley, K. (1999). *Visions of the night.* Albany: State University of New York Press.

Burgess, R., & Draper, P. (1989). The explanation of family violence: The role of biological behavioral and cultural selection. In L., Ohlin, & M. Tonry (Eds.), *Family violence* (pp. 59–116). Chicago: University of Chicago Press.

Burghardt, G. M. (1998). The evolutionary origins of play revisited: Lessons from turtles. In M. Bekoff, & J. A. Byers (Eds.), *Animal play* (pp. 1–26). Cambridge: Cambridge University Press.

Burnham, M. M., Goodlin-Jones, B. L., Gaylor, E. E., & Anders, T. F. (2002). Nighttime sleep-wake patterns and self-soothing from birth to one year of age: A longitudinal intervention study. *Journal of Child Psychology and Psychiatry, 43*(6), 713–725.

Buzsaki, G. (1996). The hippocampo-neocortical dialogue. *Cerebral Cortex, 6*(2), 81–92.

Byrne, R. M. J. (1997). Cognitive processes in counterfactual thinking about what might have been. *Psychology of Learning and Motivation, 37*, 105–154.

Calvo, J. M., Badillo, S., Morales-Ramirez, M., & Palacios-Salas, P. (1987). The role of the temporal lobe amygdala in ponto-geniculo-occipital activity and sleep organization in cats. *Brain Research, 403*(1), 22–30.

Calvo, J. M., Simon-Arceo, K., & Fernandez-Mas, R. (1996). Prolonged enhancement of REM sleep produced by carbachol microinjection into the amygdala. *Neuroreport, 7*(2), 577–580.

Campbell, S. S., & Tobler, I. (1984). Animal sleep: A review of sleep duration across phylogeny. *Neuroscience and Biobehavioral Reviews, 8*, 269–300.

Carskadon, M., & Dement, W. C. (2000). Normal human sleep: An overview. In M. H. Kryger, T. Roth, & W. C. Dement (Eds.), *Principles and practice of sleep medicine* (3rd ed., pp. 15–25). Philadelphia: Saunders.

Cartwright, R. D. (1999). Dreaming in sleep disordered patients. In S. Chokroverty (Ed.), *Sleep disorders medicine: Basic science, technical considerations, and clinical aspects* (pp. 127–134). Boston: Butterworth-Heinemann.

Cavallero, C., Cicogna, P., & Bosinelli, M. (1988). Mnemonic activation in dream production. In W. P. Koella, F. Obal, H. Schulz, & P. Visser (Eds.), *Sleep '86* (pp. 91–94). Stuttgart: Gustav Fischer.

Chemelli, R. M., Willie, J. T., Sinton, C. M., Elmquist, J. K., Scammell, T., Lee, C., et al. (1999). Narcolepsy in orexin knockout mice: Molecular genetics of sleep regulation. *Cell, 98*(4), 437–451.

Cheyne, J. A. (2000). Play, dreams, and simulation. *Behavioral and Brain Sciences, 23*(6), 918–919.

Chisholm, J. S. (1993). Death, hope, and sex: Life-history theory and the development of reproductive strategies. *Current Anthropology, 34*, 1–24.

Chisholm, J. S. (1996). The evolutionary ecology of attachment organization. *Human Nature, 7*, 1–38.

Chisholm, J. S. (Ed.). (1999). *Death, hope and sex: Steps to an evolutionary ecology of mind and morality*. Cambridge: Cambridge University Press.

Cipolli, C., Bolzani, R., & Tuozzi, G. (1998). Story-like organization of dream experience in different periods of REM sleep. *Journal of Sleep Research, 7*, 13–19.

Cipolli, C., & Poli, D. (1992). Story structure in verbal reports of mental sleep experience in different periods of REM sleep. *Sleep, 15*, 133–142.

Clayton-Smith, J., & Laan, L. (2003). Angelman syndrome: A review of the clinical and genetic aspects. *Journal of Medical Genetics, 40*(2), 87–95.

Clutton-Brock, T. H. (Ed.). (1991). *The evolution of parental care*. Princeton, NJ: Princeton University Press.

Clutton-Brock, T. H., Albon, S. D., & Guiness, F. E. (1986). Great expectations: Dominance, breeding success and offspring sex ratios in red deer. *Animal Behaviour, 34*, 460–471.

Connor, R. C., Read, A. J., & Wrangham, R. (2000). Male reproductive strategies and social bonds. In H. Whitehead (Ed.), *Cetacean societies* (pp. 247–269). Chicago: University of Chicago Press.

Coons, S., & Guilleminault, C. (1984). Development of consolidated sleep and wakeful periods in relation to the day/night cycle in infancy. *Developmental Medicine and Child Neurology, 26*(2), 169–176.

Crick, F., & Mitchison, G. (1983). The function of dream sleep. *Nature, 304*, 111–114.

Crick, F., & Mitchison, G. (1986). REM sleep and neural nets. *Journal of Mind and Behavior, 7*, 229–250.

Curzi-Dascalova, L., & Callamel, M.-J. (2000). Neurophysiological basis of sleep development. In C. Lenfant (Ed.), *Sleep and breathing in children* (pp. 3–37). New York: Dekker.

Daenen, E., Wolterink, M., Gerrits, M., & Van Ree, J. (2002). Amygdala or ventral hippocampal lesions at two early stages of life differentially effect open field behavior later in life: An animal model of neurodevelopmental psychopathological disorders. *Behavioural Brain Research, 131*, 67–78.

Datta, S. (1999). PGO wave generation mechanism and functional significance. In S. Inoue (Ed.), *Rapid eye movement sleep* (pp. 91–106). New York: Dekker.

Datta, S., Patterson, E. H., & Siwek, D. F. (1997). Endogenous and exogenous nitric oxide in the pedunculopontine tegmentum induces sleep. *Synapse, 27*(1), 69–78.

Davenne, D., Fregnac, Y., Imbert, M., & Adrien, J. (1989). Lesion of the PGO pathways in the kitten. *Brain Research, 485*, 267–277.

Davidson, R. J., & Irwin, W. (1999). The functional neuroanatomy of emotion and affective style. *Trends in Cognitive Science, 3*(1), 11–21.

Davis, F. C., Frank, M. G., & Heller, H. C. (1999). Ontogeny of sleep and circadian rhythms. In F. W. Tureck, & P. Zee (Eds.), *Regulation of sleep and circadian rhythms* (pp. 19–79). New York: Dekker.

Davis, M., & Whalen, P. J. (2001). The amygdala: Vigilance and emotion. *Molecular Psychiatry, 6*, 13–34.

Dean, B. (2003). The cortical serotonin2A receptor and the pathology of schizophrenia: A likely accomplice. *Journal of Neurochemistry, 85*(1), 1–13.

Dement, W. C. (1965). Recent studies on the biological role of rapid eye movement sleep. *American Journal of Psychiatry, 122*, 404–408.

de Quervain, D. J., Henke, K., Aerni, A., Coluccia, D., Wollmer, M. A., Hock, C., et al. (2003). A functional genetic variation of the 5-HT2a receptor affects human memory. *Nature Neuroscience, 6*(11), 1141–1142.

Dew, M. A., Hoch, C. C., Buysse, D. J., Monk, T. H., Begley, A. E., Houck, P. R., et al. (2003). Healthy older adults' sleep predicts all-cause mortality at 4 to 19 years of follow-up. *Psychosomatic Medicine, 65*(1), 63–73.

Dewasmes, G., Loos, N., Delanaud, S., Dewasmes, D., & Geloen, A. (2003). Activation of brown adipose tissue thermogenesis increases slow wave sleep in rat. *Neuroscience Letter, 339*(3), 207–210.

Di Bitetti, M. S., Vidal, E. M., Baldovino, M. C., & Benesovsky, V. (2000). Sleeping site preferences in tufted capuchin monkeys (*Cebus apella nigritus*). *American Journal of Primatology, 50*(4), 257–274.

Domhoff, G. W. (1996). *Finding meaning in dreams: A quantitative approach.* New York: Plenum.

Domhoff, G. W. (2003). *The scientific study of dreams: Neural networks, cognitive development, and content analysis.* Washington, DC: American Psychological Association.

Domhoff, G. W., & Kamiya, J. (1964). Problems in dream content study with objective indicators: I. A comparison of home and laboratory dream reports. *Archives of General Psychiatry, 11*, 519–524.

Doricchi, F., & Violani, C. (1992). Dream recall in brain damaged patients: A contribution to the neuropsychology of dreaming through a review of the literature. In J. S. Antrobus, & M. Bertini (Eds.), *The neuropsychology of sleep and dreaming* (pp. 99–140). Hillsdale, NJ: Lawrence Erlbaum.

Dorus, E., Dorus, W., & Rechtschaffen, A. (1971). The incidence of novelty in dreams. *Archives of General Psychiatry, 25,* 364–368.

Douglas, N. J. (2000). Respiratory physiology: Control of ventilation. In W. C. Dement (Ed.), *Principles and practice of sleep medicine* (3rd ed., pp. 221–228). Philadelphia: Saunders.

Dreyfus-Brisac, C. (1975). Neurophysiological studies in human premature and full-term infants. *Biological Psychiatry, 10*(5), 485–496.

Driver, P. M., & Humphries, D. A. (1988). *Protean behavior: The biology of unpredictability.* Oxford: Clarendon Press.

Edwards, N., Blyton, C. M., Kesby, G. J., Wilcox, I., & Sullivan, C. E. (2000). Preeclampsia is associated with marked alterations in sleep architecture. *Sleep, 23*(5), 619–625.

Elgar, M. A., Pagel, M. D., & Harvey, P. H. (1988). Sleep in mammals. *Animal Behaviour, 36,* 1407–1419.

Elgar, M. A., Pagel, M. D., & Harvey, P. H. (1990). Sources of variation in mammalian sleep. *Animal Behaviour, 40,* 991–994.

Emde, R., & Koenig, K. (1969). Neonatal smiling and rapid eye movement states. *Journal of the American Academy of Child Psychiatry, 8,* 57–67.

Emery, R. (1988). *Marriage, divorce, and children's adjustment.* Beverly Hills, CA: Sage.

Ferraz, M. R., Ferraz, M. M., & Santos, R. (2001). How REM sleep deprivation and amantadine affects male rat sexual behavior. *Pharmacology, Biochemistry, and Behavior, 69*(3–4), 325–332.

Field, T. (1985). Attachment as psychobiological attunement: Being on the same wavelength. In M. Reite, & T. Field (Eds.), *The psychobiology of attachment and separation* (pp. 415–454). New York: Academic Press.

Fisher, C., Gross, J., & Zuch, J. (1965). Cycle of penile erection synchronous with dreaming (REM) sleep: Preliminary report. *Archives of General Psychiatry, 12,* 29–45.

Fiss, H. (1993). The "royal road" to the unconscious revisited: A signal detection model of dream function. In A. Moffit, M. Kramer, & A. R. Hoffman (Eds.), *The function of dreaming* (pp. 381–418). Albany: State University of New York Press.

Flanigan, W. F. (1973). Sleep and wakefulness in iguanid lizards, *Ctenosaura pectina. Brain, Behavior, and Evolution, 8,* 401–436.

Forsling, M. (1993). Neurohypophysial hormones and circadian rhythm. In A. M. W. North, & L. Share (Eds.), *The neurohypophysis: A window on brain function* (pp. 382–395). New York: New York Academy of Sciences.

Fosse, M. J., Fosse, R., Hobson, J. A., & Stickgold, R. (2003). Dreaming and episodic memory: A functional dissociation? *Journal of Cognitive Neuroscience, 15,* 1–9.

Foulkes, D. (1962). Dream reports from different stages of sleep. *Journal of Abnormal and Social Psychology, 65,* 14–25.

Foulkes, D. (1978). *A grammar of dreams.* New York: Basic Books.

Foulkes, D. (1982). *Children's dreams: Longitudinal studies.* New York: John Wiley.

Foulkes, D. (1985). *Dreaming: A cognitive-psychological analysis.* Hillsdale, NJ: Lawrence Erlbaum.

Foulkes, D., & Schmidt, M. (1983). Temporal sequence and unit composition in dream reports from different stages of sleep. *Sleep, 6*(3), 265–280.

Frank, M. G. (1999). Phylogeny and evolution of rapid eye movement (REM) sleep. In B. N. Mallick, & S. Inoue (Eds.), *Rapid eye movement sleep* (pp. 15–38). New Delhi, India: Narosa.

Frank, R. H. (1988). *Passions within reason: The strategic role of emotions.* New York: Norton.

Franken, P., Chollet, D., & Tafti, M. (2001). The homeostatic regulation of sleep need is under general control. *Journal of Neuroscience, 21,* 2610–2621.

French, T., & Fromme, E. (1964). *Dream interpretation: A new approach.* New York: Basic Books.

Freud, S. (1998). *The Interpretation of Dreams.* New York: Avon Books. (Original work published 1900).

Fruth, B., & Hohmann, G. (1993). Ecological and behavioral aspects of nest building in wild bonobos. *Ethology, 94,* 113–126.

Fruth, B., & McGrew, W. C. (1998). Resting and nesting in primates: Behavioral ecology of inactivity. *American Journal of Primatology, 46*(1), 3–5.

Gallagher, S. (2003). Self-narrative in schizophrenia. In T. Kircher, & A. David (Eds.), *The self in neuroscience and psychiatry* (pp. 336–360). Cambridge: Cambridge University Press.

Gardi, J., Obal, F., Jr., Fang, J., Zhang, J., & Krueger, J. M. (1999). Diurnal variations and sleep deprivation-induced changes in rat hypothalamic GHRH and somatostatin contents. *American Journal of Physiology, 277*(5 Pt. 2), R1339–1344.

Gardi, J., Szentirmai, E., Hajdu, I., Obal, F., Jr., & Krueger, J. M. (2001). The somatostatin analog, octreotide, causes accumulation of growth hormone-releasing hormone and depletion of angiotensin in the rat hypothalamus. *Neuroscience Letter, 315*(1–2), 37–40.

Genbacev, O., Zhou, Y., Ludlow, J. W., & Fisher, S. J. (1997). Regulation of human placental development by oxygen tension. *Science, 277*(5332), 1669–1672.

Giganti, F., & Toselli, M. (2002). The eyes of parents on infants awakening. In G. Ficca (Ed.), *Awakening and sleep-wake cycle across development* (pp. 171–186). Amsterdam: John Benjamins.

Giuditta, A., Ambrosini, M. V., Montagnese, P., Mandile, P., Cotugno, M., Grassi, Z. G., et al. (1995). The sequential hypothesis of the function of sleep. *Behavioural Brain Research, 69,* 157–166.

Globus, G. G. (1993). Connectionism and sleep. In A. Moffitt, M. Kramer, & R. Hoffmann (Eds.), *The functions of dreaming* (pp. 119–138). Albany: State University of New York Press.

Godbout, R., Bergeron, C., Stip, E., & Mottron, L. (1998). A laboratory study of sleep and dreaming in a case of Asperger's syndrome. *Dreaming, 8*(2), 75–88.

Godfray, H. (1995). Evolutionary theory of parent-offspring conflict. *Nature, 376,* 1133–1138.

Goodenough, D. R. (1991). Dream recall: History and current status of the field. In S. J. Ellman, & J. S. Antrobus (Eds.), *The mind in sleep: Psychology and psychophysiology* (2nd ed., pp. 143–171). New York: John Wiley.

Gottesmann, C. (2002). GABA mechanisms and sleep. *Neuroscience, 111*(2), 231–239.

Graber, J. A., Brooks-Gunn, J., & Warren, M. P. (1995). The antecedents of menarcheal age: Heredity, family environment, and stressful life events. *Child Development, 66*(2), 346–359.

Grafen, A. (1990). Biological signals as handicaps. *Journal of Theoretical Biology, 144*(4), 517–546.

Grant, V. J. (1998). *Maternal personality, evolution and the sex ratio.* New York: Routledge.

Greenberg, M., & Farah, M. J. (1986). The laterality of dreaming. *Brain and Cognition, 5*, 307–321.

Greenberg, R., & Pearlman, C. (1993). An integrated approach to dream theory: Contributions from sleep research and clinical practice. In A. Moffit, M. Kramer, & R. Hoffmann (Eds.), *The functions of dreaming* (pp. 363–380). Albany: State University of New York Press.

Guilleminault, C., & Anagnos, A. (2000). Narcolepsy. In M. H. Kryger, T. Roth, & W. C. Dement (Eds.), *Principles and practice of sleep medicine* (3rd ed., pp. 676–686). Philadelphia: Saunders.

Haig, D. (1993). Genetic conflicts in human pregnancy. *Quarterly Review of Biology, 68*(4), 495–532.

Haig, D. (2000). Genomic imprinting, sex-biased dispersal, and social behavior. *Annals of the New York Academy of Sciences, 907*, 149–163.

Haig, D. (2002). *Genomic imprinting and kinship.* Piscataway, NJ: Rutgers University Press.

Haig, D., & Westoby, M. (1988). Inclusive fitness, seed resources and maternal care. In L. L. Doust (Ed.), *Plant reproductive ecology* (pp. 60–79). New York: Oxford University Press.

Hajdu, I., Obal, F., Jr., Fang, J., Krueger, J. M., & Rollo, C. D. (2002). Sleep of transgenic mice producing excess rat growth hormone. *American Journal of Physiology: Regulatory, Integrative, and Comparative Physiology, 282*(1), R70–R76.

Hall, C. (1963). Strangers in dreams: An empirical confirmation of the oedipus complex. *Journal of Personality, 31*, 336–345.

Hall, C., & Van de Castle, R. (1966). *The content analysis of dreams.* New York: Appleton-Century-Crofts.

Hart, B. L. (1990). Behavioral adaptations to pathogens and parasites: Five strategies. *Neuroscience and Biobehavioral Reviews, 14*, 273–294.

Hartmann, E. (1984). *The nightmare.* New York: Basic Books.

Hartmann, E. (1996). Outline for a theory on the nature and function of dreaming. *Dreaming, 6*, 147–169.

Hartmann, E. (1998). *Dreams and nightmares: The new theory on the origin and meaning of dreams.* New York: Plenum.

Hartmann, E., Russ, D., van der Kolk, B., Falke, R., & Oldfield, M. (1981). A preliminary study of the personality of the nightmare sufferer: Relationship to schizophrenia and creativity? *American Journal of Psychiatry, 138*, 784–797.

Hartse, K. M. (1994). Sleep in insects and nonmammalian vertebrates. In M. H. Kryger, T. Roth, & W. C. Dement (Eds.), *Principles and practice of sleep medicine* (2nd ed., pp. 95–104). Philadelphia: Saunders.

Harvey, J. A. (2003). Role of the serotonin 5-HT(2A) receptor in learning. *Learning and Memory, 10*(5), 355–362.

Harvey, P. H., & Pagel, M. D. (1991). *The comparative method in evolutionary biology.* Oxford: Oxford University Press.

Herman, S., & Shows, W. D. (1984). How often do adults recall their dreams? *International Journal of Aging and Human Development, 18*(4), 243–255.

Hertz, G., Cataletto, M., Feinsilver, S. H., & Angulo, M. (1993). Sleep and breathing patterns in patients with Prader Willi syndrome (PWS): Effects of age and gender. *Sleep, 16*(4), 366–371.

Hicks, R. A., Bautista, J., & Phillips, N. (1991). REM sleep deprivation does not increase the sexual behaviors of male rats. *Perceptual and Motor Skills, 73*(1), 127–130.

Hobson, J. A. (1988). *The dreaming mind.* New York: Basic Books.

Hobson, J. A., & McCarley, R. (1977). The brain as a dream state generator: An activation-synthesis hypothesis of the dream process. *American Journal of Psychiatry, 134*, 1335–1348.

Hobson, J. A., & Pace-Schott, E. F. (2002). The cognitive neuroscience of sleep: Neuronal systems, consciousness and learning. *Nature Reviews, Neuroscience, 3*, 679–693.

Hobson, J. A., Pace-Schott, E. F, & Stickgold, R. (2000a). Consciousness: Its vicissitudes in waking and sleep. In M. Gazzaniga (Ed.), *The new cognitive neurosciences* (2nd ed., pp. 1341–1354). Cambridge, MA: MIT Press.

Hobson, J. A., Pace-Schott, E. F., & Stickgold, R. (2000b). Dreaming and the brain: Toward a cognitive neuroscience of conscious states. *Behavioral and Brain Sciences, 23*, 793–842; discussion 904–1121.

Hobson, J. A., Stickgold, R., & Pace-Schott, E. F. (1998). The neuropsychology of REM sleep dreaming. *Neuroreport, 9*(3), R1–R14.

Hofer, M. A. (1975). Studies on how early maternal separation produces behavioral change in young rats. *Psychosomatic Medicine, 37*(3), 245–264.

Hofer, M. A. (1984). Relationships as regulators: A psychobiologic perspective on bereavement. *Psychosomatic Medicine, 46*, 183–197.

Hofer, M. A. (1987). Shaping forces within early social relationships. In N. A. Krasnegor, E. M. Blass, M. A. Hofer, & W. P. Smotherman (Eds.), *Perinatal development: A psychobiological perspective* (pp. 251–274). New York: Academic Press.

Hofer, M. A., & Shair, H. (1982). Control of sleep-wake states in the infant rat by features of the mother-infant relationship. *Developmental Psychobiology, 15*(3), 229–243.

Hofle, N., Paus, T., Reutens, D., Fiset, P., Gotman, J., Evans, A. C., et al. (1997). Regional cerebral blood flow changes as a function of delta and spindle activity during slow wave sleep in humans. *Journal of Neuroscience, 17*, 4800–4808.

Horne, J. A. (2000). REM sleep--by default? *Neuroscience and Biobehavioral Reviews, 24*, 777–797.

Hrdy, S. B. (1999). *Mother nature.* New York: Pantheon.

Hublin, C., Kaprio, J., Partinen, M., & Koskenvu, M. (2001). Parasomnias: Co-occurrence and genetics. *Psychiatric Genetics, 11*(2), 65–70.

Humphrey, N. (2000). Dreaming as play. *Behavioral and Brain Sciences, 23*(6), 953.

Iannacone, L. R. (1992). Sacrifice and stigma: Reducing free-riding in cults, communes, and other collectives. *Journal of Political Economy, 100*, 271–291.

Inoue, S., Honda, K., Kimura, M., & Zhang, S.-Q. (1999). Endogenous sleep substances and REM sleep. In S. Inoue (Ed.), *Rapid eye movement sleep* (pp. 248–263). New York: Dekker.

Insel, T. R. (1992). Oxytocin and the neurobiology of attachment. *Behavioral and Brain Sciences, 15*, 515–516.

Insel, T. R., & Young, L. J. (2001). The neurobiology of attachment. *Nature Reviews: Neuroscience, 2*(2), 129–136.

Irons, W. (1996). Morality, religion and human evolution. In W. M. Richardson, & W. J. Wildman (Eds.), *Religion and science: History, methods, dialogue.* New York: Routledge.

Irons, W. (2001). Religion as a hard-to-fake sign of commitment. In R. M. Nesse (Ed.), *Evolution and the capacity for commitment* (pp. 292–309). New York: Russell Sage Foundation.

Jouvet, D., Vimont, P., Delorme, F., & Jouvet, M. (1964). [Study of selective deprivation of the paradoxal sleep phase in the cat]. *Comptes Rendus des Seances de la Societe de Biology et de ses Filiales, 158*, 756–759.

Jouvet, M. (1962). Recherches sur les structures nerveuses et le mecanismes respponsables des differantes phases du sommeil physiologique. *Archives of Italian Biology, 100*, 125–206.

Jouvet, M. (1999). *The paradox of sleep: The story of dreaming.* Cambridge, MA: MIT Press.

Juhasz, G., Emri, Z., Kekesi, K. A., Salfay, O., & Crunelli, V. (1994). Blockade of thalamic GABAB receptors decreases EEG synchronization. *Neuroscience Letter, 172*(1–2), 155–158.

Jus, A., Jus, K., Villeneuve, A., Pires, A., Lachance, R., Fortier, J., et al. (1973). Studies on dream recall in chronic schizophrenic patients after prefrontal lobotomy. *Biological Psychiatry, 6*, 275–293.

Kahan, T. L., LaBerge, S., Levitan, L., & Zimbardo, P. (1997). Similarities and differences between dreaming and waking cognition: An exploratory study. *Consciousness and Cognition, 6*, 132–147.

Kahn, D., Stickgold, R., Pace-Schott, E. F., & Hobson, J. A. (2000). Dreaming and waking consciousness: A character recognition study. *Journal of Sleep Research, 9*(4), 317–325.

Karacan, I. (1966). Erection cycle during sleep in relation to dream anxiety. *Archives of General Psychiatry, 15*, 183–189.

Karacan, I., Williams, R., Hursch, C., McCaulley, M., & Heine, M. W. (1969). Some implications of the sleep patterns of pregnancy for postpartum emotional disturbances. *British Journal of Psychiatry, 115*, 929–935.

Karmanova, I. G. (1982). *Evolution of sleep: Stages of the formation of the wakefulness-sleep cycle in vertebrates.* Basel: Karger.

Kato, M. V., Shimizu, T., Nagayoshi, M., Kaneko, A., Sasaki, M. S., & Ikawa, Y. (1996). Genomic imprinting of the human serotonin-receptor (HTR2) gene involved in development of retinoblastoma. *American Journal of Human Genetics, 59*, 1084–1090.

Kavanau, J. L. (1996). Memory, sleep, and dynamic stabilization of neural circuitry: Evolutionary perspectives. *Neuroscience and Biobehavioral Reviews, 20*(2), 289–311.

Kavanau, J. L. (2002). Dream contents and failing memories. *Archives of Italian Biology, 140*(2), 109–127.

Keverne, E. B., Martel, F. L., & Nevison, C. M. (1996). Primate brain evolution: Genetic and functional considerations. *Proceedings of the Royal Society of London (B: Biological Sciences), 263*, 689–696.

Kilduff, T. S., Krilowicz, B., Milsom, W. K., Trachsel, L., & Wang, L. C. (1993). Sleep and mammalian hibernation: Homologous adaptations and homologous processes? *Sleep, 16*(4), 372–386.

Kirov, R., & Moyanova, S. (1998). Age-dependent effect of ketanserin on the sleep-waking phases in rats. *International Journal of Neuroscience, 93*(3–4), 257–264.

Koukkou, M., & Lehmann, D. (1993). A model of dreaming and its functional significance: The state-shift hypothesis. In A. Moffitt, M. Kramer, & R. Hoffmann (Eds.), *The functions of dreaming* (pp. 51–118). Albany: State University of New York Press.

Koulack, D. (1993). Dreams and adaptation to contemporary stress. In A. Moffitt, M. Kramer, & R. Hoffmann (Eds.), *The functions of dreaming* (pp. 321–340). Albany: State University of New York Press.

Krackow, S. (1995). Potential mechanisms for sex ratio adjustment in mammals and birds. *Biological Review of the Cambridge Philosophical Society, 70*(2), 225–241.

Kraemer, G. (1992). A psychobiological theory of attachment. *Behavioral and Brain Sciences, 15*, 493–541.

Kramer, M. (1993). The selective mood regulatory function of dreaming: An update and revision. In A. Moffit, M. Kramer, & R. Hoffman (Eds.), *The functions of dreaming* (pp. 139–196). Albany: State University of New York Press.

Kreuger, J. M., & Fang, J. (2000). Host defense. In W. C. Dement (Ed.), *Principles and practice of sleep medicine* (3rd ed., pp. 255–265). Philadelphia: Saunders.

Kripke, D. F. (2003). Sleep and mortality. *Psychosomatic Medicine, 65*(1), 74.

Krippner, S., Posner, N. A., Pomerance, W., Barksdale, W., & Fischer, S. (1974). An investigation of dream content during pregnancy. *Journal of the American Society of Psychosomatic Dentistry and Medicine, 21*(4), 111–123.

Krueger, J. M., Majde, J. A., & Obal, F. (2003). Sleep in host defense. *Brain, Behavior, and Immunity, 17*(Suppl. 1), S41–S47.

Krueger, J. M., Obal, F., & Fang, J. (1999). Why we sleep: A theoretical view of sleep function. *Sleep Medicine Reviews, 3*(2), 119–129.

Kuiken, D., & Sikora, S. (1993). The impact of dreams on waking thoughts and feelings. In A. Moffitt, M. Kramer, & R. Hoffman (Eds.), *The functions of dreaming* (pp. 419–476). Albany: State University of New York Press.

Kuiken, D. L., Nielsen, T. A., Thomas, S., & McTaggart, D. (1983). Comparisons of the story structure of archetypal dreams, mundane dreams, and myths. *Sleep Research, 12*, 196.

Kushida, C. A., Bergmann, B. M., & Rechtschaffen, A. (1989). Sleep deprivation in the rat: IV. Paradoxical sleep deprivation. *Sleep, 12*, 22–30.

LaBerge, S. P., Kahan, T. L., & Levitan, L. (1995). Cognition in dreaming and waking. *Sleep Research, 24A*, 239.

Lai, Y.-Y., & Siegel, J. (1999). Muscle atonia in REM sleep. In S. Inoue (Ed.), *Rapid eye movement sleep* (pp. 69–90). New York: Dekker.

Lakoff, G. (2001). How metaphor structures dreams. The theory of conceptual metaphor applied to dream analysis. In K. Bulkeley (Ed.), *Dreams: A reader on religious, cultural and psychological dimensions of dreaming* (pp. 265–284). New York: Palgrave.

Landolt, H. P., Meier, V., Burgess, H. J., Finelli, L. A., Cattelin, F., Achermann, P., et al. (1999). Serotonin-2 receptors and human sleep: Effect of a selective antagonist on EEG power spectra. *Neuropsychopharmacology, 21*(3), 455–466.

Laposky, A. D., Homanics, G. E., Basile, A., & Mendelson, W. B. (2001). Deletion of the GABA(A) receptor beta 3 subunit eliminates the hypnotic actions of oleamide in mice. *Neuroreport, 12,* 4143–4147.

Laureys, S., Peigneux, P., Phillips, C., Fuchs, S., Degueldre, C., Aerts, J., et al. (2001). Experience-dependent changes in cerebral functioning connectivity during human rapid eye movement sleep. *Neuroscience, 105,* 521–525.

Lavie, P. (1990). Penile erections in a patient with nearly total absence of REM: A follow-up study. *Sleep, 13*(3), 276–278.

Ledoux, J. (Ed.). (1996). *The emotional brain.* New York: Simon and Schuster.

Ledoux, J. (2000). The amygdala and emotion: A view through fear. In J. P. Aggleton (Ed.), *The amygdala* (pp. 289–310). Oxford: Oxford University Press.

Lee, K. A. (1998). Alterations in sleep during pregnancy and postpartum: A review of 30 years of research. *Sleep Medicine Reviews, 2*(4), 231–242.

Lee, K. A., McEnany, G., & Zaffke, M. E. (2000). REM sleep and mood state in childbearing women: Sleepy or weepy? *Sleep, 23,* 877–885.

Lehtonen, J. (2002). Origins of dreaming. *American Journal of Psychiatry, 159*(3), 495.

Le Stunff, C., Fallin, D., & Bougneres, P. (2001). Paternal transmission of the very common class I INS VNTR alleles predisposes to childhood obesity. *Nature Genetics, 29*(1), 96–99.

Lhermitte, F. (1986). Human autonomy and the frontal lobes: Part II. Patient behavior in complex and social situations: The "environmental dependency syndrome." *Annals of Neurology, 19*(4), 335–343.

Lincoln, D. W., Hentzen, Q., Hin, T., Van del Schoot, P., Clarke, G., & Summerlee, A. J. S. (1980). Sleep: A prerequisite for replex milk ejection in the rat. *Experimental Brain Research, 38,* 151.

Lorenz, D. N. (1986). Alimentary sleep satiety in suckling rats. *Physiology and Behavior, 38,* 557–562.

Lorenz, D. N., Poppe, C. J., Quail, C., Seipel, K., Stordeur, S. A., & Johnson, E. (1998). Filling the gut activates paradoxical sleep in suckling rats. *Developmental Psychobiology, 32,* 1–12.

Lu, J., Bjorkum, A. A., Xu, M., Gaus, S. E., Shiromani, P. J., & Saper, C. B. (2002). Selective activation of the extended ventrolateral preoptic nucleus during rapid eye movement sleep. *Journal of Neuroscience, 22,* 4568–4576.

Lugaresi, E., Medori, R., Montagna, P., Baruzzi, A., Cortelli, P., Lugaresi, A., et al. (1986). Fatal familial insomnia and dysautonomia with selective degeneration of thalamic nuclei. *New England Journal of Medicine, 315,* 997–1003.

Lyamin, O. I. (1993). Sleep in the harp seal (*Pagophilus groenlandica*): Comparison of sleep on land and in water. *Journal of Sleep Research, 2*(3), 170–174.

Lyamin, O. I., Manger, P. R., Mukhametov, L. M., Siegel, J. M., & Shpak, O. V. (2000). Rest and activity states in a gray whale. *Journal of Sleep Research, 9*(3), 261–267.

Lyamin, O. I., Mukhametov, L. M., Chetyrbok, I. S., & Vassiliev, A. V. (1994). Sleep and wakefulness in southern sea lions (*Otari byronia*). *Journal of Sleep Research, 3*(Suppl. 1), 152.

Mack, J. E. (1970). *Nightmares and human conflict*. Boston: Little, Brown.

Mahowald, M. W., & Schenck, C. H. (2000). REM sleep parasomnias. In M. H. Kryger, T. Roth, & W. C. Dement (Eds.), *Principles and practice of sleep medicine* (3rd ed., pp. 724–741). Philadelphia: Saunders.

Malkova, L., Mishkin, M., Suomi, S. J., & Bachevalier, J. (1997). Socioemotional behavior in adult rhesus monkeys after early versus late lesions of the medial temporal lobe. *Annals of the New York Academy of Science, 807*, 538–540.

Mallick, B. N., Kaur, S., Jha, S. K., & Siegel, J. (1999). Possible role of GABA in the regulation of REM sleep with special reference to REM-off neurons. In B. N. Mallick, & S. Inoue (Eds.), *Rapid eye movement sleep* (pp. 152–166). New York: Dekker.

Mandler, J. M., & Johnson, N. S. (1977) Remembrance of things parsed: story structure and recall. *Cognitive Psychology, 9*, 111–151.

Maquet, P., & Franck, G. (1997). REM sleep and amygdala. *Molecular Psychiatry, 2*(3), 195–196.

Maquet, P., Peters, J.-M., Aerts, J., Delfiore, G., Degueldre, C., Luxen, A., et al. (1996). Functional neuroanatomy of human rapid-eye-movement sleep and dreaming. *Nature, 383*, 163–166.

Maquet, P., Peters, J.-M., Aerts, J., Delfiore, G., Degueldre, C., Luxen, A., et al. (1997). Functional neuroanatomy of human slow wave sleep. *Journal of Neuroscience, 17*, 2807–2812.

Maquet, P., & Phillips, C. (1999). Rapid eye movement sleep: Cerebral metabolism to functional brain mapping. In S. Inoue (Ed.), *Rapid eye movement sleep* (pp. 276–285). New York: Dekker.

Marks, G. A., Shaffrey, J. P., Oksenberg, A., Speciale, S. G., & Roffwarg, H. (1995). A functional role for REM sleep in brain maturation. *Behavioural Brain Research, 69*, 1–11.

Maunder, R. G., & Hunter, J. J. (2001). Attachment and psychosomatic medicine: Developmental contributions to stress and disease. *Psychosomatic Medicine, 63*, 556–567.

Mayer, G. (2003). Ritanserin improves sleep quality in narcolepsy. *Pharmacopsychiatry, 36*(4), 150–155.

Mazzoni, G. A. L., Loftus, E. F., Seitz, A., & Lynn, S. J. (1999). Changing beliefs and memories through dream interpretation. *Applied Cognitive Psychology, 13*, 125–144.

McCarley, R., & Hobson, J. A. (1975). Neuronal excitability modulation over the sleep cycle: A structural and mathematical model. *Science, 189*, 58–60.

McKenna, J. J., & Mosko, S. S. (1994). Sleep and arousal, synchrony and independence, among mothers and infants sleeping apart and together (same bed): An experiment in evolutionary medicine. *Acta Paediatrica, 397*(Suppl.), 94–102.

McKenna, J. J., Mosko, S., Dungy, C., & McAninch, J. (1990). Sleep and arousal patterns of co-sleeping human mother/infant pairs: A preliminary physiological study with implications for the study of sudden infant death syndrome (SIDS). *American Journal of Physical Anthropology, 83*, 331–347.

McKenna, J. J., Thoman, E. B., Anders, T. F., Sadeh, A., Schechtman, V. L., & Glotzbach, S. F. (1993). Infant-parent co-sleeping in an evolutionary perspective: Implications for understanding infant sleep development and the Sudden Infant Death Syndrome. *Sleep, 16*, 263–282.

McLoyd, V. C. (1990). The impact of economic hardship on black families and children: Psychological distress, parenting, and socioemotional development. *Child Development, 61*(2), 311–346.

McNamara, P. (2000). Counterfactual thought in dreams. *Dreaming, 10*(4), 237–246.

McNamara, P., Anderson, J., Clark, C., Zborowski, M., & Duffy, C. A. (2001). Impact of attachment styles on dream recall and dream content: A test of the attachment hypothesis of REM sleep. *Journal of Sleep Research, 10*, 117–127.

McNamara, P., Dowdall, J., & Auerbach, S. (2002). REM sleep, early experience, and the development of reproductive strategies. *Human Nature, 13*, 405–435.

Meddis, R. (1983). The evolution of sleep. In A. Mayes (Ed.), *Sleep mechanisms and functions* (pp. 57–106). London: Van Nostrand Reinhold.

Meerlo, P., de Bruin, E. A., Strijkstra, A. M., & Daan, S. (2001). A social conflict increases EEG slow-wave activity during subsequent sleep. *Physiology and Behavior, 73*(3), 331–335.

Meguro, M., Mitsuya, K., Sui, H., Shigenami, K., Kugoh, H., Nakao, M., et al. (1997). Evidence for uniparental, paternal expression of the human GABAA receptor subunit genes, using microcell-mediated chromosome transfer. *Human Molecular Genetics, 6*, 2127–2133.

Mendelson, W. B., Lantigua, R. A., Wyatt, R. J., Gillin, J. C., & Jacobs, L. S. (1981). Piperidine enhances sleep-related and insulin-induced growth hormone secretion: Further evidence for a cholinergic secretory mechanism. *Journal of Clinical Endocrinology and Metabolism, 52*, 409–415.

Merritt, J. M., Stickgold, R., Pace-Schott, E. F., Williams, J., & Hobson, J. A. (1994). Emotion profiles in the dreams of men and women. *Consciousness and Cognition, 3*, 46–60.

Miller, G. J. (2000). *The mating mind.* New York: Random House.

Ming-Chu, X., Morales, F. R., & Chase, M. H. (1999). Evidence that wakefulness and REM sleep are controlled by a GABAergic pontine mechanism. *Journal of Neurophysiology, 82*, 2015–2019.

Mirmiran, M. (1995). The function of fetal/neonatal rapid eye movement sleep. *Behavioural Brain Research, 69*(1–2), 13–22.

Mirmiran, M., Scholtens, J., van de Poll, N. E., Uylings, H. B., van der Gugten, J., & Boer, G. J. (1983). Effects of experimental suppression of active (REM) sleep during early development upon adult brain and behavior in the rat. *Brain Research, 283*, 277–286.

Monti, J. M., & Monti, D. (1999). Functional role of serotonin 5HT1 and 5HT2 receptors in the regulation of REM sleep. In S. Inoue (Ed.), *Rapid eye movement sleep* (pp. 142–152). New York: Dekker.

Morin, L. P. (1986). Environment and hamster reproduction: Responses to phase-specific starvation during estrous cycle. *American Journal of Physiology, 251*, R663–R669.

Morrison, A. R. (1979). Brainstem regulation of behavior during sleep and wakefulness. In J. M. Sprague, & A. W. Epstein (Eds.), *Progress in psychobiology and physiological psychology* (pp. 91–131). New York: Academic Press.

Morrison, A. R., Sanford, L. D., & Ross, R. J. (1999). Initiation of rapid eye movement: Beyond the brainstem. In S. Inoue (Ed.), *Rapid eye movement sleep* (pp. 51–68). New York: Dekker.

Moruzzi, G. (1966). The functional significance of sleep with particular regard to the brain mechanisms underlying consciousness. In J. C. Eccles (Ed.), *Brain mechanisms and conscious experience* (pp. 437–439). New York: Springer-Verlag.

Mueller, E., Locatelli, V., & Cocchi, D. (1999). Neuroendocrine control of growth hormone secretion. *Physiological Reviews, 79*(2), 511–607.

Mukhametov, L. M. (1984). Sleep in marine mammals. *Experimental Brain Research, 8*(Suppl.), 227–238.

Mukhametov, L. M., Supin, A. Y., & Polyakova, I. G. (1977). Interhemispheric asymmetry of the electroencephalographic sleep patterns in dolphins. *Brain Research, 134*, 581–584.

Nathanielsz, P. W. (1996). *Life before birth: The challenges of fetal development.* New York: W. H. Freeman.

Nedergaard, J., & Cannon, B. (1990). Mammalian hibernation. *Philososphical Transactions of the Royal Society of London (B, Biological Sciences), 326*(1237), 669–685.

Nicholls, R. D. (2000). The impact of genomic imprinting for neurobehavioral and developmental disorders. *Journal of Clinical Investigations, 105*(4), 413–418.

Nicol, S. C., Andersen, N. A., Phillips, N. H., & Berger, R. J. (2000). The echidna manifests typical characteristics of rapid eye movement sleep. *Neuroscience Letter, 283*(1), 49–52.

Nielsen, T. A. (2000). A review of mentation in REM and NREM sleep: "Covert" REM sleep as a possible reconciliation of two opposing models. *Behavioral and Brain Sciences, 23*(6), 851–866; discussion 904–1121.

Nielsen, T. A., Deslauriers, D., & Baylor, G. W. (1991). Emotions in dream and waking event reports. *Dreaming, 1*, 287–300.

Nielsen, T. A., Kuiken, D., Hoffman, R., & Moffitt, A. (2001). REM and NREM sleep mentation differences: A question of story structure? *Sleep and Hypnosis, 3*(1), 9–17.

Nielsen, T. A., Laberge, L., Paquet, J., Tremblay, R. E., Vitaro, F., & Montplaisir, J. (2000). Development of disturbing dreams during adolescence and their relation to anxiety symptoms. *Sleep, 23*(6), 727–736.

Nishino, S. (2003). The hypocretin/orexin system in health and disease. *Biological Psychiatry, 54*(2), 87–95.

Nobili, L., Baglietto, M. G., De Carli, F., Savoini, M., Schiavi, G., Zanotto, E., et al. (1999). A quantified analysis of sleep electroencephalography in anorectic adolescents. *Biological Psychiatry, 45*(6), 771–775.

Nofzinger, E. A., Mintun, M. A., Wiseman, M. B., Kupfer, D. J., & Moore, R. Y. (1997). Forebrain activation in REM sleep: An FDG PET study. *Brain Research, 770*, 192–201.

Noser, R., Gygax, L., & Tobler, I. (2003). Sleep behavior and social rank in gelada baboons [Abstract]. *Sleep, 26*(Abstr. Suppl.), A432.

Nunn, C. L., & Barton, R. A. (2000). Allometric slopes and independent contrasts: A comparative study of Kleiber's law in primate ranging patterns. *American Naturalist, 156,* 519–533.

Nunn, C. L., & Barton, R. A. (2001). Comparative methods for studying primate adaptation and allometry. *Evolutionary Anthropology, 10,* 81–98.

Obal, F., Jr., & Krueger, J. M. (2003). Biochemical regulation of non-rapid-eye-movement sleep. *Frontiers in Bioscience, 8,* 520–550.

Offenkrantz, W., & Rechtschaffen, A. (1963). Clinical studies of sequential dreams. I. A patient in psychotherapy. *Archives of General Psychiatry, 8,* 497–508.

Oksenberg, A., Shaffery, J. P., Marks, G. A., Speciale, S. G., Mihailoff, G., & Roffwarg, H. P. (1996). Rapid eye movement sleep deprivation in kittens amplifies LGN cell-size disparity induced by monocular deprivation. *Brain Research: Developmental Brain Research, 97,* 51–61.

Olson, E. J., Boeve, B. F., & Silber, M. H. (2000). Rapid eye movement sleep behaviour disorder: Demographic, clinical and laboratory findings in 93 cases. *Brain, 123,* 331–339.

Orem, J., & Barnes, C. D. (Eds.). (1980). *Physiology in sleep.* New York: Academic Press.

Pace-Schott, E. F., & Hobson, J. A. (2002). The neurobiology of sleep: Genetics, cellular physiology and subcortical networks. *Nature Review: Neuroscience, 3,* 591–605.

Parker, G., Royle, N., & Hartley, I. (2002). Intrafamilial conflict and parental investment: A synthesis. *Philosophical Transactions of the Royal Society of London, B, 357,* 295–307.

Parmeggiani, P. L. (2000). Physiological regulation in sleep. In W. C. Dement (Ed.), *Principles and practice of sleep medicine* (2nd ed., pp. 169–178). Philadelphia: Saunders.

Partridge, L., & Hurst, L. D. (1998). Sex and conflict. *Science, 281,* 2003–2008.

Peigneus, P., Laureys, S., Delbeuck, X., & Maquet, P. (2001). Sleeping brain, learning brain: The role of sleep for memory systems. *Neuroreport, 12,* A111–A124.

Peters, R. W., Zoble, R. G., & Brooks, M. M. (2002). Onset of acute myocardial infarction during sleep. *Clinical Cardiology, 25*(5), 237–241.

Petre-Quadens, O., DeBrsy, A. M., Devos, J., & Sfaello, Z. (1967). Sleep in pregnancy: Evidence of foetal-sleep characteristics. *Journal of the Neurological Sciences, 4,* 600–605.

Piaget, J. (1962). *Play, dreams, and imitation in childhood.* New York: W. W. Norton.

Plihal, W., & Born, J. (1997). Effects of early and late nocturnal sleep on declarative and procedural memory. *Journal of Cognitive Neursocience, 9,* 534–547.

Polychronakos, C., & Kukuvitis, A. (2002). Parental genomic imprinting in endocrinopathies. *European Journal of Endocrinology, 147,* 561–569.

Pomiankowski, A. (1999). Intragenomic conflict. In L. Keller (Ed.), *Levels of selection in evolution* (pp. 121–152). Princeton, NJ: Princeton University Press.

Pompeiano, O., Pompeiano, M., & Corvaja, N. (1995). Effects of sleep deprivation on the postnatal development of visual-deprived cells in the cat's lateral geniculate nucleus. *Archives of Italian Biology, 134*(1), 121–140.

Porkka-Heiskanen, T., Strecker, R. E., & McCarley, R. W. (2000). Brain site-specificity of extracellular adenosine concentration changes during sleep deprivation and spontaneous sleep: An in vivo microdialysis study. *Neuroscience, 99*(3), 507–517.

Provini, F., Plazzi, G., Montagna, P., & Lugaresi, E. (2000). The wide clinical spectrum of nocturnal frontal lobe epilepsy. *Sleep Medicine Reviews, 4*(4), 375–386.

Ramakrishnan, U., & Coss, R. G. (2001). A comparison of the sleeping behavior of three sympatric primates: A preliminary report. *Folia Primatologia (Basel), 72*(1), 51–53.

Rattenborg, N. C., & Amlaner, C. J. (2002). Phylogeny of sleep. In T. L. Lee-Chiong, M. J. Sateia, & M. A. Carskadon (Eds.), *Sleep medicine* (pp. 7–22). Philadelphia: Hanley and Belfus.

Rattenborg, N. C., Amlaner, C. J., & Lima, S. L. (2000). Behavioral, neurophysiological and evolutionary perspectives on unihemispheric sleep. *Neuroscience and Biobehavioral Reviews, 24*, 817–842.

Rechtschaffen, A. (1978). The single-mindedness and isolation of dreams. *Sleep, 1*, 97–109.

Rechtschaffen, A., & Bergmann, B. M. (2001). Letter (in response to Everson and Toth). *American Journal of Physiology, 280*, R602–R603.

Rechtschaffen, A., & Bergmann, B. M. (2002). Sleep deprivation in the rat: An update of the 1989 paper. *Sleep, 25*(1), 18–24.

Reite, M., & Capitanio, J. (1985). On the nature of social separation and social attachment. In M. Reite, & T. Field (Eds.), *The psychobiology of attachment and separation* (pp. 223–255). New York: Academic Press.

Reite, M., Kaemingk, K., & Boccia, M. L. (1989). Maternal separation in bonnet monkey infants: Altered attachment and social support. *Child Development, 60*, 473–480.

Reite, M., Kaufman, I. C., Pauley, J. D., & Stynes, A. J. (1974). Depression in infant monkeys: Physiological correlates. *Psychosomatic Medicine, 36*, 363–367.

Reite, M., & Short, R. (1978). Nocturnal sleep in separated monkey infants. *Archives of General Psychiatry, 35*, 1247–1253.

Reite, M., Short, R., & Seiler, C. (1978). Physiological correlates of maternal separation in surrogate-reared infants: A study in altered attachment bonds. *Developmental Psychobiology, 11*(5), 427–435.

Reite, M., Short, R., Seiler, C., & Pauley, J. D. (1981). Attachment, loss, and depression. *Journal of Child Psychology and Psychiatry, 22*(2), 141–169.

Reite, M., Stynes, A. J., Vaughn, L., Pauley, J. D., & Short, R. A. (1976). Sleep in infant monkeys: Normal values and behavioral correlates. *Physiology and Behavior, 16*(3), 245–251.

Reppert, S. M., Duncan, M. J., & Weaver, D. R. (1987). Maternal influences on the developing circadian system. In N. A. Krasnegor, E. M. Blass, M. A. Hofer, & W. P. Smotherman (Eds.), *Perinatal development: A psychobiological perspective* (pp. 343–356). New York: Academic Press.

Revonsuo, A. (2000). The reinterpretation of dreams: An evolutionary hypothesis of the function of dreaming. *Behavioral and Brain Sciences, 23*, 877–901; discussion 904–1121.

Ridgway, S. H., Harrison, R. J., & Joyce, P. L. (1975). Sleep and cardiac rhythm in the gray seal. *Science, 187*, 553–555.

Rodriguez, S., Gaunt, T. R., O'Dell, S. D., Chen, X. H., Gu, D., Hawe, E., et al. (2004). Haplotypic analyses of the IGF2-INS-TH gene cluster in relation to cardiovascular risk traits. *Human Molecular Genetics.* (in press)

Roese, N. J. (1997). Counterfactual thinking. *Psychological Bulletin, 121*(1), 133–148.
Roese, N. J., & Olson, J. M. (1995). *What might have been: The social psychology of counterfactual thinking.* Mahwah, NJ: Lawrence Erlbaum.
Roffwarg, H., Muzio, J., & Dement, W. C. (1966). Ontogenetic development of the human sleep-dream cycle. *Science, N.Y., 152*, 604–618.
Rosenblum, L. A., & Moltz, H. (Eds.). (1983). *Symbiosis in parent-offspring interactions.* New York: Plenum.
Rotenberg, V. S. (1993). REM sleep and dreams as mechanisms of the recovery of search activity. In A. Moffitt, M. Kramer, & R. Hoffmann (Eds.), *The functions of dreaming* (pp. 261–292). Albany: State University of New York Press.
Rozycka, A., Skorupska, E., Kostyrko, A., & Trzeciak, W. H. (2003). Evidence for S284L mutation of the CHRNA4 in a white family with autosomal dominant nocturnal frontal lobe epilepsy. *Epilepsia, 44*, 1113–1117.
Russell, J. A., Bachorowski, J. A., & Fernandez-Dols, J. M. (2003). Facial and vocal expressions of emotion. *Annual Review of Psychology, 54*, 329–349.
Sabo, E., Reynolds, C. F., 3rd, Kupfer, D. J., & Berman, S. R. (1991). Sleep, depression, and suicide. *Psychiatry Research, 36*(3), 265–277.
Sadeh, A., Dark, I., & Vohr, B. R. (1996). Newborns' sleep-wake patterns: The role of maternal, delivery and infant factors. *Early Human Development, 44*(2), 113–126.
Sagi, A., van Ijzendoorn, M. H., Aviezer, O., Donnell, F., & Mayseless, O. (1994). Sleeping out of home in a Kibbutz communal arrangement: It makes a difference for infant-mother attachment. *Child Development, 65*(4), 992–1004.
Sah, P., Faber, E. S. L., Lopez de Armentia, M., & Power, J. (2003). The amygdaloid complex: Anatomy and physiology. *Psychological Review, 83*, 803–834.
Saint-Mleux, B., Eggermann, E., Bisetti, A., Bayer, L., Machard, D., Jones, B. E., et al. (2004). Nicotinic enhancement of the noradrenergic inhibition of sleep-promoting neurons in the ventrolateral preoptic area. *Journal of Neuroscience, 24*(1), 63–67.
Salzarulo, P., & Ficca, G. (Eds.). (2002). *Awakening and sleep cycle across development.* Amsterdam: John Benjamins.
Schectman, M. (1996). *The constitution of selves.* Ithaca, NY: Cornell University Press.
Scheffer, I. E., Bhatia, K. P., Lopes-Cendes, I., Fish, D. R., Marsden, C. D., Andermann, E., et al. (1995). Autosomal dominant nocturnal frontal lobe epilepsy a distinctive clinical disorder. *Brain, 118*, 61–73.
Schenck, C. H., & Mahowald, M. W. (1990). Polysomnographic, neurologic, psychiatric, and clinical outcome report on 70 consecutive cases with REM sleep disorder (RBD): Sustained clonazepam efficacy in 89.5% of 57 treated patients. *Cleveland Journal of Medicine, 57*(Suppl.), s9–s23.
Scher, A. (2001). Attachment and sleep: A study of night waking in 12-month-old infants. *Developmental Psychobiology, 38*(4), 274–285.
Scher, A., Tirosh, E., Rubin, L., Sadeh, A., & Lavie, P. (1995). Sleep patterns of infants and young children in Israel. *International Journal of Behavioral Development, 4*, 701–711.
Schins, A., Honig, A., Crijns, H., Baur, L., & Hamulyak, K. (2003). Increased coronary events in depressed cardiovascular patients: 5-HT2A receptor as missing link? *Psychosomatic Medicine, 65*(5), 729–737.

Schmidt, M. H. (2000). Sleep related penile erections. In W. C. Dement (Ed.), *Principles and practice of sleep medicine* (3rd ed., pp. 305–318). Philadelphia: Saunders.

Schredl, M. (2000). Dream research: Integration of physiological and psychological models. *Behavioral and Brain Sciences, 23*, 1001–1003.

Schredl, M., & Doll, E. (1998). Emotions in diary dreams. *Consciousness and Cognition, 7*, 634–646.

Schweiger, M. S. (1972). Sleep disturbance in pregnancy. A subjective study. *American Journal of Obstetrics and Gynecology, 114*(7), 879–882.

Sei, H., & Morita, Y. (1999). Why does arterial blood pressure rise actively during REM sleep? *Journal of Medical Investigations, 46*(1–2), 11–17.

Sejnowski, T. J., & Destexhe, A. (2000). Why do we sleep? *Brain Research, 886*(1–2), 208–223.

Shaw, P. J., Tononi, G., Greenspan, R. J., & Robinson, D. F. (2002). Stress response genes protect against lethal effects of sleep deprivation in Drosophila. *Nature, 417*(6886), 287–291.

Siegel, J. M., Manger, P. R., Nienhuis, R., Fahringer, H. M., & Pettigrew, J. D. (1996). The echidna *Tachyglossus aculeatus* combines REM and non-REM aspects in a single sleep state: Implications for the evolution of sleep. *Journal of Neuroscience, 16*, 3500–3506.

Siegel, J. M., Manger, P. R., Nienhuis, R., Fahringer, H. M., & Pettigrew, J. D. (1998). Monotremes and the evolution of rapid eye movement sleep. *Philosophical Transactions of the Royal Society of London (B: Biological Sciences), 353*, 1147–1157.

Siegel, J. M., Manger, P. R., Nienhuis, R., Fahringer, H. M., Shalita, T., & Pettigrew, J. D. (1999). Sleep in the platypus. *Neuroscience, 91*(1), 391–400.

Siegel, M., & Varley, R. (2002). Neural systems involved in "theory of mind." *Nature Reviews: Neuroscience, 3*, 463–471.

Simpson, J. A. (2000). Attachment theory in modern evolutionary perspective. In J. Cassidy, & P. R. Shaver (Eds.), *Handbook of attachment theory research and clinical applications* (pp. 115–140). New York: Guilford.

Singareddy, R. K., & Balon, R. (2001). Sleep and suicide in psychiatric patients. *Annals of Clinical Psychiatry, 13*(2), 93–101.

Smith, C. (1995). Sleep states and memory processes. *Behavioural Brain Research, 69*(1–2), 137–145.

Smith, C. (1996). Sleep states, memory processes and synaptic plasticity. *Behavioural Brain Research, 78*, 49–56.

Smith, E., Udry, J., & Morris, N. (1985). Pubertal development and friends: A biosocial explanation of adolescent sexual behavior. *Journal of Health and Social Behavior, 26*, 183–192.

Snyder, F. (1966). Toward an evolutionary theory of dreaming. *American Journal of Psychiatry, 123*, 121–136.

Snyder, F. (1974). Sleep-waking patterns of hydracoidea. *Sleep Research, 3*, 87.

Snyder, F., Bugbee, N., & Douthitt, T. C. (1972). Telemetric studies of 24-hour sleep-waking patterns in some primitive mammals. *Psychophysiology, 9*, 122.

Solms, M. (1997). *The neuropsychology of dreams.* Mahwah, NJ: Lawrence Erlbaum.

Solms, M. (2000). Dreaming and REM sleep are controlled by different brain mechanisms. *Behavioral and Brain Sciences, 23*, 843–850; discussion 904–1121.

Solodkin, M., Cardona, A., & Corsi-Cabrera, M. (1985). Paradoxical sleep augmentation after imprinting in the domestic chick. *Physiology and Behavior, 35,* 343–348.

Sosis, R., & Bressler, E. (2003). Cooperation and commune longevity: A test of the costly signaling theory of religion. *Cross-Cultural Research, 37,* 211–239.

Spinka, M., Newberry, R. C., & Bekoff, M. (2001). Mammalian play: Training for the unexpected. *Quarterly Review of Biology, 76*(2), 141–168.

Stearns, S. (1992). *The evolution of life histories.* New York: Oxford University Press.

Steiger, A. (2003). Sleep and endocrinology. *Journal of Internal Medicine, 254,* 13–22.

Steinlein, O., Smigrodzki, R., Lindstrom, J., Anand, R., Kohler, M., Tocharoentanaphol, C., et al. (1994). Refinement of the localization of the gene for neuronal nicotinic acetylcholine receptor alpha 4 subunit (CHRNA4) to human chromosome 20q13.2-q13.3. *Genomics, 22*(2), 493–495.

Steklis, H., & Kling, A. (1985). Neurobiology of affiliative behavior in nonhuman primates. In T. Field (Ed.), *The psychobiology of attachment and separation* (pp. 93–135). New York: Academic Press.

Steriade, M., & McCarley, R. (1990). *Brainstem control of wakefulness and sleep.* New York: Plenum.

Stern, D. N. (1985). *The interpersonal world of the infant.* New York: Basic Books.

Stickgold, R., Scott, L., Fosse, R., & Hobson, J. A. (2001). Brain-mind states: I. Longitudinal field study of wake-sleep factors influencing mentation report length. *Sleep, 24*(2), 171–179.

Stickgold, R., Scott, L., Rittenhouse, C., & Hobson, J. A. (1998). Sleep induced changes in associative memory. *Journal of Cognitive Neuroscience, 11,* 182–193.

Strauch, I., & Meier, B. (1996). *In search of dreams: Results of experimental dream research.* Albany: State University of New York Press.

Surbey, M. (1990). Family composition, stress, and human menarche. In F. Berkovitch, & T. Ziegler (Eds.), *The socioendocrinology of primate reproduction* (pp. 71–97). New York: Alan R. Liss.

Sutor, B., & Zolles, G. (2001). Neuronal nicotinic acetylcholine receptors and autosomal dominant nocturnal frontal lobe epilepsy: A critical review. *Pflugers Archiv, 442,* 642–651.

Szymusiak, R., Alam, M. N., Steininger, T. L., & McGinty, D. (1998). Sleep-waking discharge patterns of ventrolateral preoptic/anterior hypothalamic neurons in rats. *Brain Research, 803,* 178–188.

Tachibana, N., Howard, R. S., Hirsch, N. P., Miller, D. H., Moseley, I. F., & Fish, D. (1994). Sleep problems in multiple sclerosis. *European Neurology, 34*(6), 320–323.

Tafti, M., & Franken, P. (2002). Invited review: Genetic dissection of sleep. *Journal of Applied Physiology, 92,* 1339–1347.

Taheri, S., & Mignot, E. (2002). The genetics of sleep disorders. *Lancet Neurology, 1*(4), 242–250.

Tannenbaum, G. S., & Ling, N. (1984). The interrelationship of growth hormone releasing factor and somatostatin in generation of the ultradian rhythm of GH secretion. *Endocrinology, 115,* 1952–1957.

Toppila, J., Alanko, L., Asikainen, M., Tobler, I., Stenberg, D., & Porkka-Heiskanen, T. (1997). Sleep deprivation increases somatostatin and growth hormone-releasing hormone messenger RNA in the rat hypothalamus. *Journal of Sleep Research, 6*(3), 171–178.

Toppila, J., Asikainen, M., Alanko, L., Turek, F. W., Stenberg, D., & Porkka-Heiskanen, T. (1996). The effect of REM sleep deprivation on somatostatin and growth hormone-releasing hormone gene expression in the rat hypothalamus. *Journal of Sleep Research, 5*(2)115–122.

Trivers, R. L. (1974). Parent offspring conflict. *American Zoologist, 14*, 249–264.

Trivers, R. L., & Willard, D. E. (1973). Natural selection of parental ability to vary the sex ratio of offspring. *Science, 179*(68), 90–92.

Trosman, H., Rechtschaffen, A., Offenkrantz, W., & Wolpert, E. (1960). Studies in psychophysiology of dreams: IV. Relations among dreams in sequence. *Archives of General Psychiatry, 3*, 602–607.

Tycko, B., & Morison, I. M. (2002). Physiological functions of imprinted genes. *Journal of Cellular Physiology, 192*, 245–258.

Van Cauter, E., Plat, L., & Copinschi, G. (1998). Interrelations between sleep and the somatotropic axis. *Sleep, 21*, 553–566.

Van Cauter, E., & Speigel, K. (1999). Circadian and sleep control of hormonal secretions. In F. Turek, & P. Zee (Eds.), *Regulation of sleep and circadian rhythms* (pp. 397–421). New York: Dekker.

Van de Castle, R. (1970). Temporal patterns of dreams. In E. Hartmann (Ed.), *Sleep and dreaming* (pp. 171–181). Boston: Little, Brown.

Van de Castle, R. (1994). *Our dreaming mind.* New York: Ballantine.

Vazquez-Palacios, G., Bonilla-Jaime, H., Retana-Marquez, S., & Velazquez-Moctezuma, J. (2002). Copulatory activity increases slow-wave sleep in the male rat. *Journal of Sleep Research, 11*(3), 237–245.

Vela-Bueno, A., Kales, A., Soldatos, C. R., Dobladez-Blanco, B., Campos-Castello, J., Espino-Hurtado, P., et al. (1984). Sleep in the Prader-Willi syndrome: Clinical and polygraphic findings. *Archives of Neurology, 41*(3), 294–296.

Velasquez-Moctezuma, J., Salazar, E. D., & Retana-Marquez, S. (1996). Effects of short- and long-term sleep deprivation on sexual behavior in male rats. *Physiology and Behavior, 59*, 277–281.

Veldhuis, J. D. (2003). A tripeptidyl ensemble perspective of interactive control of growth hormone secretion. *Hormone Research, 60*(Suppl. 1), 86–101.

Verdone, P. (1965). Temporal reference of manifest dream content. *Perceptual and Motor Skills, 20*(Suppl.), 1253–1268.

Verona, R. I., Mann, M. R., & Bartolomei, M. S. (2003). Genomic imprinting: Intricacies of epigenetic regulation in clusters. *Annual Review of Cell and Developmental Biology, 19*, 237–259.

Vgontzas, A. N., Kales, A., Seip, J., Mascari, M. J., Bixler, E. O., Myers, D. C., et al. (1996). Relationship of sleep abnormalities to patient genotypes in Prader-Willi syndrome. *American Journal of Medical Genetics, 67*, 478–482.

Vogel, G., & Hagler, M. (1996). Effects of neonatally administered iprindole on adult behaviors of rats. *Pharmacology, Biochemistry, and Behavior, 55*(1), 157–161.

Vogel, G. W. (1999). REM sleep deprivation and behavioral changes. In S. Inoue (Ed.), *Rapid eye movement sleep* (pp. 355–366). New York: Dekker.

Vogel, G. W., Feng, P., & Kinney, G. G. (2000). Ontogeny of REM sleep in rats: Possible implications for endogenous depression. *Physiology and Behavior, 68*, 453–461.

Voloscin, L. M., & Tramezzani, L. H. (1979). Milk ejection reflex linked to slow wave sleep in nursing rats. *Endocrinology, 105*, 1202–1207.

Vuillon-Cacciuttolo, G., Balzamo, E., Petter, J. J., & Bert, J. (1976). [Wakefulness-sleep cycle studied by telemetry in a lemurian (*Lemur macaco fulvus*)]. *Revue d'Electroencephalographie et de Neurophysiologie Clinique, 6*(1), 34–36.

Wagner, U., Gais, S., & Born, J. (2001). Emotional memory formation is enhanced across sleep intervals with high amounts of rapid eye movement sleep. *Learning and Memory, 8*(2), 112–119.

Walker, J. M., & Berger, R. J. (1980a). The ontogenesis of sleep states, thermogenesis, and thermoregulation in the Virginia opossum. *Developmental Psychobiology, 13*(5), 443–454.

Walker, J. M., & Berger, R. J. (1980b). Sleep as an adaptation for energy conservation functionally related to hibernation and shallow torpor. *Progress in Brain Research, 53*, 255–278.

Weksberg, R., Smith, A. C., Squire, J., & Sadowski, P. (2003). Beckwith-Wiedemann syndrome demonstrates a role for epigenetic control of normal development. *Human Molecular Genetics, 12*(Spec. No. 1), R61–R68.

Whalen, P. J., Shin, L. M., Somerville, L. H., McLean, A. A., & Kim, H. (2002). Functional neuroimaging studies of the amygdala in depression. *Seminars in Clinical Neuropsychiatry, 7*(4), 234–242.

Wilson, M. A., & McNaughton, B. L. (1994). Reactivation of hippocampal ensemble memories during sleep. *Science, 265*, 676–679.

Winget, C., & Kramer, M. (1979). *Dimensions of the dream*. Gainesville: University of Florida Press.

Winson, J. (1985). *Brain and psyche*. New York: Doubleday.

Wolff, P. (1987). *The development of behavioral states and the expression of emotions in early infancy: New proposals for investigation*. Chicago: University of Chicago Press.

Wu, F. C., Butler, G. E., Kelnar, C. J., Huhtaniemi, I., & Veldhuis, J. D. (1996). Ontogeny of pulsatile gonadotropin releasing hormone secretion from midchildhood, through puberty, to adulthood in the human male: A study using deconvolution analysis and an ultrasensitive immunofluorometric assay. *Journal of Clinical Endocrinology and Metabolism, 81*, 1798–1805.

Zaborszky, L., & Duque, A. (2003). Sleep-wake mechanisms and basal forebrain circuitry. *Frontiers in Bioscience, 8*, 1146–1169.

Zahavi, A. (1975). Mate selection: A selection for a handicap. *Journal of Theoretical Biology, 53*, 205–213.

Zepelin, H. (1980). REM sleep and the altricial-precocial dimension. *Sleep Research, 9*, 114.

Zepelin, H. (1989). Mammalian sleep. In M. H. Kryger, T. Roth, & W. C. Dement (Eds.), *Principles and practice of sleep medicine* (1st ed., pp. 30–48). Philadelphia: Saunders.

Zepelin, H. (1994). Mammalian sleep. In W. C. Dement (Ed.), *Principles and practice of sleep medicine* (2nd ed., pp. 30–48). Philadelphia: Saunders.

Zepelin, H. (2000). Mammalian sleep. In W. C. Dement (Ed.), *Principles and practices of sleep medicine* (3rd ed., pp. 82–92). Philadelphia: Saunders.

Zepelin, H., & Rechtschaffen, A. (1974). Mammalian sleep, longevity and energy metabolism. *Brain and Behavioural Evolution, 10*, 425–470.

Zhdanova, I. V., Wurtman, R. J., & Wagstaff, J. (1999). Effects of a low dose of melatonin on sleep in children with Angelman syndrome. *Journal of Pediatric Endocrinology and Metabolism, 12*(1), 57–67.

Index

About the Author

PATRICK MCNAMARA is Assistant Professor of Neurology at Boston University School of Medicine and the Veterans Affairs New England Health Care System.